Elizabeth Bowen

Elizabeth Bowen

Theory, Thought and Things

Edited by Jessica Gildersleeve and
Patricia Juliana Smith

Edinburgh University Press is one of the leading university presses in the UK. We publish academic books and journals in our selected subject areas across the humanities and social sciences, combining cutting-edge scholarship with high editorial and production values to produce academic works of lasting importance. For more information visit our website: edinburghuniversitypress.com

© editorial matter and organisation Jessica Gildersleeve and Patricia Juliana Smith, 2019, 2021
© the chapters their several authors, 2019, 2021

Edinburgh University Press Ltd
The Tun – Holyrood Road
12(2f) Jackson's Entry
Edinburgh EH8 8PJ

First published in hardback by Edinburgh University Press 2019

Typeset in 11/13 Adobe Sabon by
IDSUK (DataConnection) Ltd

A CIP record for this book is available from the British Library

ISBN 978 1 4744 5864 1 (hardback)
ISBN 978 1 4744 5865 8 (paperback)
ISBN 978 1 4744 5866 5 (webready PDF)
ISBN 978 1 4744 5867 2 (epub)

The right of Jessica Gildersleeve and Patricia Juliana Smith to be identified as the Editor of this work has been asserted in accordance with the Copyright, Designs and Patents Act 1988, and the Copyright and Related Rights Regulations 2003 (SI No. 2498).

Contents

Acknowledgements — vii

Introduction: Thinking in/about Bowen — 1
Jessica Gildersleeve and Patricia Juliana Smith

1. How to Be Yourself – But Not Eccentric: Clothes, Style and Self in Bowen's Short Fiction — 9
Aimee Gasston

2. Elizabeth Bowen: Surrealist — 28
Keri Walsh

3. Elizabeth Bowen and the Pleasure of the Text — 48
Jessica Gildersleeve

4. Obnoxiousness and Elizabeth Bowen's Queer Adolescents — 62
renée c. hoogland

5. Tender Ties: Elizabeth Bowen and Habit — 79
Ulrika Maude

6. 'One is Somehow Suspended': Elizabeth Bowen, Katherine Mansfield and the Spaces in Between — 96
Emma Short

7. 'How Much of Nothing There Was': Trying (Not) to Understand Elizabeth Bowen — 113
Damian Tarnopolsky

8. Bowen's Recesses: From Realism to Inter-Objectivity — 127
Laurie Johnson

9. 'Some Really Raging Peculiarity': Female Fetishism *The Little Girls* — 145
Patricia Juliana Smith

10 Housekeeping and the Fiction of Subjectivity
    in *Eva Trout*   165
    Jasmin Kelaita
11 Elizabeth Bowen on the Telephone   182
    Andrew Bennett

Notes on Contributors   199
Index   202

Acknowledgements

The editors express their thanks to the contributors to this volume for their belief in the project and their passion for Elizabeth Bowen.

Introduction: Thinking in/about Bowen

Jessica Gildersleeve and Patricia Juliana Smith

Elizabeth Bowen's first short story, 'Breakfast' (1923), begins with a thought: '"Behold, I die daily," thought Mr Rossiter, entering the breakfast-room.'[1] It is a story primarily structured by thought: Mr Rossiter says very little, and the reader is privy to his reflections on the odious people with whom he must daily share his morning meal. The emphasis on consciousness and subjectivity is a typically modernist move, as is the story's sense of a 'life in death', its allusion, perhaps, to the end of the second canto of T. S. Eliot's 'The Waste Land' (1922), and the hopelessness of its conclusion, in which '[a]ll his days and nights were loops, curving out from breakfast time, curving back to it again. Inexorably the loops grew smaller, the breakfasts longer; looming more and more over his nights, eating more and more out of his days' ('B', p. 20).[2] Yet as one moves further into her *oeuvre*, thought becomes more complex, less transparent – less, we might paradoxically say, easily modernist.

Bowen's work has never been simple to categorise. From experiments in language and identity to innovations in the novel, the short story and life narratives, Bowen's work between 1923 and her death in 1973 straddles, informs and defies the existing definitions and categories of modernist and postmodernist literature which dominate twentieth-century writing. This makes her extremely difficult to position in literary history and as such, her work has often fallen between those cracks, or been overlooked in comparison to the major figures of High Modernism, such as Eliot, Virginia Woolf or James Joyce, even while her readability has meant that she has always been more popular than, say, Rosamond Lehmann or Elizabeth Taylor. The very presence of 'Bowen studies', then, is a strange critical genre, at once marginalised and affirmed. This is the paradoxical state Bowen currently occupies as an almost-but-not-quite canonical author. Historically, the notion of Bowen as a 'middlebrow' writer rather than the innovative intellectual author that she is has resulted in her being regarded as someone who wrote fiction about women having affairs in 'Big Houses' and concerned primarily with the affective qualities of middle-class women's heightened sensibilities. This, in turn, has led to a degree of critical neglect: much of the relatively small existing body of older Bowen criticism is informed, consciously or otherwise, by this limited and overly simplistic perception. In recent years, Bowen's works have received critical attention that looks beyond such previous attitudes, and with recent events, including conferences and special journal issues devoted to her legacy, the founding of the Elizabeth Bowen Society and its related journal, the *Elizabeth Bowen Review*, and an ever-growing critical interest in her *oeuvre*, she has been more widely recognised as a highly sophisticated and original thinker, as complex as her older modernist contemporaries. Even so, there is still much work to be done to correct the middlebrow stigma that has for so long clung to her reputation.

Therefore, this collection aims to develop wider discussion of Bowen's contribution to and place in twentieth-century literature and theory through a re-evaluation of the ways in which her work, in its refusal of categorisation, can be seen as textually, politically and theoretically 'new' by focusing on her engagements with processes of theory and thought, and the frequent attachment of these to 'things'. This takes the form, for example, of an interest in narrative techniques which explore the psyche, models of the ways in which characters interact and influence themselves, each other and the world around them through thought, as well as Bowen's engagement with and anticipation of theories of narrative and culture. Although recent research on Bowen has begun to move away from a perception of her as an author concerned only with conservative themes, 'Big House' settings, and middle-class, drawing-room romance, no work has yet been conducted on precisely the ways in which Bowen's sophisticated texts have, for example, disrupted and developed the work of the modernist avant-garde, anticipated postmodern self-consciousness, challenged the constructs of the literary critic, or influenced literary theory. *Elizabeth Bowen: Theory, Thought and Things* marks a response to this in its argument for the importance of Bowen's work in our understanding of twentieth-century British and Irish literature by articulating some of the many ways in which she revolutionised writing during this time. This collection thus presents new scholarship on Bowen's inventiveness and uniqueness of style and fresh readings of her place in twentieth-century literature and history in order to rejuvenate and develop scholarship regarding an author who resists generic categorisation.

This collection addresses Bowen's work in terms of an intervention in and an extension of the extant criticism. It seeks to provide new avenues for research in Bowen studies in ways that are concerned primarily with Bowen's perception of writing and narrative, and which seek to understand her wide-ranging positions in literary history and contemporary cultural movements and phenomena. In its close examination of Bowen's work and its representation of contemporary research in the field, this study recognises Bowen's innovation, experimentation and impact on her contemporaries and literary descendants as a way to situate her connections and her place(s) in twentieth-century literary history. Heather Laird has recognised these multiple places or identities (Anglo-Irish Bowen, modernist Bowen, postmodernist Bowen, Irish Gothic Bowen, bisexual Bowen, Bowen the woman writer, Bowen the wartime writer . . .) as a fragmentation in existing scholarship.[3] However, the essays collected in *Elizabeth Bowen: Theory, Thought and Things* propose that Bowen should be viewed as occupying and interrogating multiple places and roles in literary history. Indeed, renée c. hoogland has argued that it is precisely Bowen's 'refusal to be classified in terms of established generic and/or stylistic categories' that marks her out as 'a truly radical, innovative, and critically practicing feminist'.[4] Thus, in this collection, and in a kind of dialogue with each other, the contributors consider Bowen in a professional rather than an ideological sense, tracking Bowen's various reputations as, for example, a theorist (Gildersleeve), artist (Walsh) and stylist (Gasston), positioning her as a writer intimately engaged with the literary and social world around her. In particular, the collection works to understand Bowen's position as a modern intellectual, a thinker, and in this way contributing to our understanding of twentieth-century literature in ways as profound as any of her contemporaries.

With reference to Bowen's favoured tripartite narrative structure, the essays collected here operate under the subtitle 'Theory, Thought and Things' and the interconnected nature of these themes in Bowen's work means that they coalesce throughout all of the essays. Although it is true that an interest in thought – on thinking, on intellect, on being liberated or constrained by one's own thoughts or the thoughts of another – is common to existing studies of Bowen, it has not yet been the subject of extended analysis. For Maud Ellmann, Bowen's attitude to thought is a key means of distinguishing her work from Woolf's:

> In Woolf, consciousness exists in opposition to the object; in Bowen, consciousness escapes into the object, leaving human beings as vacant as the landscapes that threaten to devour them. While Woolf uses fiction to flesh out her ideas, which could be translated into other idioms, Bowen *thinks in fiction*: her ideas are inseparable from her objects, settings, plots, and characters, and from the oddities of her unnerving syntax. This means that Bowen is a greater novelist than Woolf, though Woolf is arguably a finer prose-poet.[5]

Ellmann's point also suggests the ways in which, in Bowen, to think about thought is also to think about things and to think about theory. The chapters by Aimee Gasston, Keri Walsh and Jessica Gildersleeve address Bowen's conceptualisation of theory as a critical context in precisely this sense. While Walsh argues for Bowen's influence by Surrealist artists and thus for a consideration of her as a kind of art historian or theorist, Gildersleeve explores Bowen as a literary theorist, through the lens of Roland Barthes' work on the pleasure of the text. Here, thought is theorised. Gasston takes up these points as a question of style, both in and as a function of Bowen's writing. To be oneself, she argues, is 'an ethical imperative' in Bowen's narratives, and a determination of both characters, their 'things' and the fiction which brings them to life. In theorising the function of the short story, Gasston shows how Bowen's characters think beyond their individual narratives. In each case presented in this first section, Bowen's self-reflexivity about her writing and its theoretical significance is underscored. If Bowen is a greater novelist than Woolf, as Ellmann has it, perhaps it is for such reasons: Bowen, these chapters argue, thinks in theory rather than in genre.

For Andrew Bennett and Nicholas Royle, Bowen's narratives insist that 'there is no possibility of escape from the catatonia of others' conceptions and constructions, no escape from the interior quietness which is being thought ... In Bowen, there is nothing outside the text of the other.'[6] In Bowen's fiction, they argue, people are not 'characters' so much as they are 'thought', highlighting their very fictionality, the fact that 'people in novels are constructed by language, by thoughts, by reading.'[7] Neil Corcoran agrees, noting that Bowen's stories are made up stories 'which people tell about themselves to one another, or even, more poignantly sometimes, which they tell about themselves to themselves, in order to maintain identities in peril'.[8]

Thus, in *The House in Paris* (1935), Leopold engages in 'thought-reading'; in *The Hotel* (1927), Sydney feels that she does not exist unless she is thought of by her idol, Mrs Kerr; in *The Last September* (1929), Lois resists being thought of or defined by others; in *To the North* (1932), Cecilia finds it so difficult to imagine a world without herself, a world in which she is not thought of by others, that she keeps piles of letters on her desk to be mailed after her death.

Thinking, then, is critical to Bowen's conceptualisation of both what she calls 'so-called real life' and fiction.⁹ It is one of the ways in which she might most clearly be defined as a modernist writer: the preference for the cerebral over the affective is central to much modernist writing. Indeed, as Eliot famously and acerbically argued in 'Tradition and the Individual Talent' (1919), '[p]oetry is not a turning loose of emotion, but an escape from emotion: it is not the expression of personality, but an escape from personality. But, of course, only those who have personality and emotions know what it means to want to escape from these things.'¹⁰ But this is not thought for the mere sake of performance: rather, thought in Bowen is more prominently aligned with her articulation of literary theory before that term even came into existence. Her own repeated self-reflexiveness about writing and its processes, in particular, testify to her interest in articulating a theory not just about her own writing, but about literature more generally. It is for this reason, then, that Ellmann sees part of the uncanny power of Bowen's writing to lie in the way in which it 'constantly outsmarts the interpretative methods brought to bear on it': 'Her fiction interprets its interpreters, shaking our assumptions, undermining our defences, and penetrating deep into the haunted chambers of the mind.'¹¹ Thus even as Bowen is considered within those boundaries of genre or identity, none of which ever seem to wholly apply to or explain her work, her writing persistently challenges those conceptualisations.¹² What this means is that, as Allan E. Austin puts it, even as 'Bowen's characters confront dislocation and mutability . . . as everyday conditions of life,' so too this collection considers Bowen's narratives as a whole in these terms.¹³ In a sustained reflection on Bowen's engagement with theory and thought and the ways in which these influence and are influenced by 'things', this collection seeks to trace the significance of the ways in which these function as questions of both form and content in her work and in her reception.

With reference to the collection's focus on 'Thought' in Bowen's work, renée c. hoogland (perhaps the most theory-driven of all Bowen's critics) takes up the question of affective thought as it applies to what she calls Bowen's 'queer adolescents' and to the 'queerness' or innovations of her writing itself. These characters are frequently identified as liminal or in-between and in this way are suggested to be static or frozen, but hoogland shows how their process of becoming means that they operate as figures of hope, and the text itself offers up an ethical openness. In Emma Short and Damian Tarnopolsky's chapters, thought is taken up as an issue of communication both within Bowen's own narratives and in terms of her engagement with her contemporaries. Thus, Short takes up an exploration of Katherine Mansfield's influence on Bowen's work. For Short, that liminality which is so critical to hoogland's discussion is a feature of both Mansfield and Bowen's writing, and marks out their work as sites of transition, innovation and independence, particularly for their female characters. Like Gasston in the previous section, Tarnopolsky is interested in questions of Bowen's narrative style, and considers the repetition of 'something' and 'nothing' in her work not as an issue of objects, but of the difficulty in making sense of the object of her writing. Her mannered style is shown to be an ethical demand on the reader, an engagement with the subject, the object and often their absence. Ulrika Maude extends that analysis, suggesting that it is in their relations to objects, their thinking about objects, that Bowen's characters form the habits that constitute their lives. In each reading, therefore, it is only in thinking through and with objects and the world that characters can think themselves.

Finally, the later parts of the collection pays close attention to the 'things' which have emerged in the first two parts: the strange, thought-filled objects which fill her novels and stories and which act so powerfully upon her impressionable characters. Questions of identity are a particular focus for Kelaita, who argues that for Bowen and for her contemporary Jean Rhys it is in the home and its objects that the self is constituted. Indeed, she asserts, '[t]o be a subject, in Bowen's world, one must have a home.' That objects impact upon one's state of belonging is also critical to the chapters by Andrew Bennett, Patricia Juliana Smith and Laurie Johnson. Bennett argues that telephones, a critical symbol of modernity, both connect and divide people from one another (in almost every novel, the telephone is associated with a moment of epiphany); Smith shows how belongings and unlikely objects are fetishised and invested with personal meaning; and Johnson considers how in Bowen's wartime writing objects become more real than people themselves. It is ultimately, this collection demonstrates, in those intersections between theory, thought and things that personal identity is constituted, and through which Bowen's work also defies the identifying characteristics of genre itself.

No collection of essays can possibly provide a comprehensive study of all the topics yet to be explored in addressing Bowen's multifaceted and abundant body of work. The performative, topography and place, religion, suffering, war and terror, tactile poetics, non-human animals, the environment, Bowen's engagement with philosophy and her relationships (both professional and personal) with other authors are only a few of the issues awaiting to be addressed. It is hoped that the present volume is one more step in the development of a nuanced critical reputation for Bowen. By opening the door to such conversations, we invite future readers to continue to explore the richness and depth of Elizabeth Bowen's intellect and humanity.

Notes

1. Elizabeth Bowen, 'Breakfast' (1923), in *The Collected Stories of Elizabeth Bowen*, ed. Angus Wilson (London: Vintage, 1999), pp. 15–20 (p. 15). Hereafter cited parenthetically as 'B'.
2. The lines, from 'A Game of Chess' in 'The Waste Land', are repeated as a kind of 'last call': 'HURRY UP PLEASE IT'S TIME' (T. S. Eliot, *Selected Poems* (London: Faber & Faber, 1954), lines 141, 152, 165, 168, 169).
3. Heather Laird, 'The "Placing" and Politics of Bowen in Contemporary Irish Literary and Cultural Criticism', in *Elizabeth Bowen*, ed. Eibhear Walshe (Dublin: Irish Academic Press, 2009), pp. 193–207 (p. 193). See also Julie Anne Stevens, 'Bowen: The Critical Response', in Walshe, *Elizabeth Bowen*, pp. 179–92 (p. 179); and Phyllis Lassner, *Elizabeth Bowen: A Study of the Short Fiction* (New York: Twayne, 1991), p. 157.
4. renée c. hoogland, *Elizabeth Bowen: A Reputation in Writing* (New York: New York University Press, 1994), p. 20.
5. Maud Ellmann, *Elizabeth Bowen: The Shadow Across the Page* (Edinburgh: Edinburgh University Press, 2003), p. 7 (original emphasis).
6. Andrew Bennett and Nicholas Royle, *Elizabeth Bowen and the Dissolution of the Novel* (Basingstoke: Palgrave, 1995), p. 9.
7. Ibid. p. xvii, p. 3.
8. Neil Corcoran, *Elizabeth Bowen: The Enforced Return* (Oxford: Clarendon, 2004), pp. 169–79.
9. Elizabeth Bowen, 'Out of a Book' (1946), in *The Mulberry Tree: Writings of Elizabeth Bowen*, ed. Hermione Lee (London: Harcourt Brace Jovanovich, 1986), pp. 48–53 (p. 49).

10. T. S. Eliot, 'Tradition and the Individual Talent' (1919), *The Egoist*, 4.4 (September and December 1919), 54–5, 72–3 (p. 73). Available from <https://www.bl.uk/collection-items/tradition-and-individual-talent-by-t-s-eliot>.
11. Ellmann, *The Shadow Across the Page*, pp. 4–5. See also Susan Osborn, who argues that 'there is something in Bowen's fiction that unsettles . . . an unregulated quality . . . which points to a presumably cast off and more indeterminate heterogeneity of the real that is both difficult to approach and to analyse and that challenges the reader's efforts to control the interpretive field' ('Introduction', in *Elizabeth Bowen: New Critical Perspectives*, ed. Susan Osborn (Cork: Cork University Press, 2009), pp. 1–12 (p. 3)).
12. 'Bowen's work offers unfamiliar ways by which we might reconceptualise the relationship between realism and modernism, the ambiguities of identity, and the obscuring effects of many familiar critical assumptions, including those pertaining to canonicity, notions of genre, and the representation of gender, sexuality, class, nationhood and ethnicity in literature' (Osborn, 'Introduction', p. 7).
13. Allan E. Austin, *Elizabeth Bowen* (New York: Twayne, 1971), p. 18.

Chapter 1

How to Be Yourself – But Not Eccentric: Clothes, Style and Self in Bowen's Short Fiction

Aimee Gasston

> Slight risks of oddness – do they matter so much? Even those who smile at them, they may well delight.[1]

The modern short story and fashion, as we have come to understand each, shared a contemporary genesis at the end of the nineteenth century.[2] While new, ready-to-wear clothing became democratically accessible, the evolution of print and magazine culture brought short fiction into the everyday life of a swelling public sphere. Both arts were facilitated by industrial as well as creative advancement, reliant on a mechanised industry curiously at odds with their fluid forms. Each was invigorated and restricted by their youth: 'at once impetuous and halting', they nonetheless had the capacity to be 'very affectable'.[3]

In this chapter, I will consider these complementary art forms, both so important to Elizabeth Bowen, to explore the meaning of the individual style which informed her 'careful shaping of materials'.[4] Her 'slow meticulous style' was mastered in the oblique, narrow gaze of the 'elaborate self-contained' short story form, in which 'language is engrossed to match' and balanced with visual detail, weight, texture and shading.[5] Allan E. Austin has noted that in her 'personal life', Bowen 'displayed an exemplary style and vivacity', and that these characteristics also 'mark her fiction'.[6] It is this interdependence of the personal and the literary that I explore here, in opposition to Eudora Welty's belief that '[w]riting did not take for Elizabeth Bowen the direction or the form of "self-expression".'[7] If Bowen always displayed an 'enthrallment in the act of writing itself', this fascination with the matter of style relied on rather than precluded personal expression and ontological exploration.[8] If '[w]hat we are is, most of all, what we have to give', we should repay Bowen's extravagant generosity with the attention it deserves.[9]

A style reviled

As Jean Baudrillard has asserted, '[f]ashion exists only within the framework of modernity, that is to say, in a schema of rupture, progress and innovation.'[10] Risk is implicit to change; if 'every short story is an experiment' then we should expect the outcomes to be diverse.[11] Bowen's rich collection of stories encompasses a full gamut of geographies and subjects, encompassing hotels, bungalows, castles, ships, ghosts, murders, war, personal violence and lust, and is testament to Bowen's belief that while the novel was wedded to more orthodox terrain, the story could (and should) capture what is 'crazy about humanity'.[12] Playful, challenging and colourful, the rich array of stories Bowen crafted can be viewed as a portfolio as lively and inventive as that of Elsa Schiaparelli, whose self-referential designs exulted in their own materiality and earned their creator a reputation as a major innovator, experimenter and iconoclast of the twentieth century.[13]

Yet Bowen's inventiveness has rarely been conceived of in this spirit. Writing in an era when, as she saw it, '[f]ashions – in art, in physical appearance, in love, in decoration, in manners – sprang up with frenetic rapidity', it is all the more peculiar that the perceived unconventionality of Bowen's literary style remains something to be considered an obscure idiosyncrasy rather than a celebrated innovation – as an obstacle rather than a bridge to meaning and wider resonance.[14] As Phyllis Lassner has observed, the 'critical dilemma has always been one of situating and stabilising Bowen's oeuvre and style in literary history and theory.'[15] As such, her identity is one of 'a trouble-maker', though there is no consensus as to whether this identity is purposefully orchestrated – it often seems to represent some (typically uncategorised) literary failure rather than a more penetrating and deliberate ethics of production.[16] Even admirers speak of Bowen's style in terms of its strangeness, its otherness and resistance to interpretation. In an otherwise complimentary article in *The Observer* in 1935, A. G. Macdonell described it as 'like a giraffe in a drawing-room' because 'you could not overlook its presence but you would find it hard to account for.'[17]

Yet is style something that can or should be accounted for? It seems likely that Bowen expected that it should; she saw it as the duty of writers to 'impose a reasonableness of [their] own' and balance the poetic with the rational.[18] With specific reference to the short story, in a lecture she delivered on 'The Poetic Element in Fiction' (1950), Bowen called for a sympathetic reception to an art that was still young and attempting to express the new:

> ... if in our experimentation we bungle or fail, if our language offends and seems incomprehensible, the allowance for the attempt, the hope of capturing, not for ourselves but for art and comprehension, a new position, a new forward post for the story must be allowed for.[19]

It is difficult to know how far Bowen's statement is borne from an awareness of the way in which her own literary style would be received, but despite the expansive determiner 'our', it speaks forcefully as a personal appeal. Dick Hebdige has observed the way in which style provokes a 'double response', as it is 'alternately celebrated (in the fashion page) and ridiculed or reviled (in those articles which define subcultures as social problems)'.[20] If we think of literary criticism in such terms, Bowen's experimental style has most often been considered as a 'problem' of one sort or another; the subculture she created in the space of her unique literary style has not, despite reinvigorated academic interest, been successfully incorporated into the canonical avant-garde.

There is an almost bourgeois undercurrent of disapproval for Bowen's unique style which she might have got away with had she been less daring and more worried about the basic etiquette of prose-making, the literary equivalent of the manners she would satirise in those texts. Victoria Glendinning describes how as a girl Bowen would wear 'rather dotty, flamboyant, often home-made clothes' and, as an adult, 'retained ... a penchant for overdressing on occasion'.[21] Throughout much critical commentary there runs a conservative distaste for Bowen's prose, as if it too is overdressed, not quite suited to the occasion. As has been observed elsewhere, if, as a reader, you are not 'with' Bowen, it is easy to be shaken by what can seem like proofing errors – for example, in 'The Needlecase' (1934) the contents of a sewing box are 'routed through' and, in a delightfully carnivalesque but otherwise unexplained statement, in 'Emergency in the Gothic Wing' (1954) we are told that Anastasia comes down to dinner 'dressed like a snake'.[22] Bowen's exploration of signs and the surfaces to which they adhere and from which they slip is especially evident in her literary use of clothing. If, as Baudrillard asserts, '[f]ashion is one of the more inexplicable phenomena' due to its 'compulsion to innovate signs, its apparently arbitrary and perpetual production of meaning – a kind of meaning drive', Bowen's style is often confused with what it seeks to portray, conceived of as arbitrary and inexplicable.[23]

Criticisms of Bowen's style are almost always related to its indefatigable presence; early detractors remarked upon Bowen's 'distracting detail', her 'decorative elaboration' as well as her 'pointless verbal excess'.[24] The 'problem' spoken of here is clearly material – what Maud Ellmann refers to as a 'material intrusiveness'.[25] There is a resistance in Bowen's prose to the felicities of narrative convention, disrupting the reader's desire for a propulsion of plot which is not interfered with by the brute materiality of its style or contents. This outrage seems to be fuelled not only by philological but philosophical concerns – Bowen's prose is too unsettlingly *contingent* in both form and content, capable of not only describing but invoking an ontological insecurity. The reader can feel let down by a writer whose concerns are not strictly teleological, whose pleasure in language and the detail of the external world is felt to be 'excessive' because it is not understood (and perhaps cannot be in a rationalist sense). Like the interfering hat brims from under which Bowen's characters are perpetually peering, the intrusion of a too-fabric prose that revels in the curious detail of everyday life seems to obscure critical perception.

Like fashion, Bowen's prose exhibits a 'theatrical sociality [which] delights in itself'; in this way the text becomes a 'sort of festival and an increasing excess of communication' which is in danger of being deemed unwarranted by those it does not captivate.[26] The following paragraph from 'The Contessina' (1924) demonstrates well the 'peculiar deliciousness' of Bowen's intricate prose when it is enjoying itself, her ability to 'caress every detail' and 'make every word work'.[27] It counterpoises a knowingly specialist register with a naive freshness of expression that conveys the ambivalence of the character of the Contessina herself:

> 'This is very nice,' said Mr Barlow, looking at the Contessina. She had on a dress of heliotrope organdie, with a fichu folded across the bosom with that best discretion for the display of pretty curves. Her skin was very dark against the heliotrope, as fresh as a young petal,

as brown as old, old ivory. Her white Tuscan hat enhanced this peculiar deliciousness, and the little loops of hair corrugated against the curves of her cheeks looked almost blue. Her puffed sleeves were very short, and there was a dimple on each elbow.[28]

The effusion of detail here can be difficult to keep up with: layers of colour, shape and texture jostle against each other and pull the composition in different directions. It creates a powerful effect, but Bowen does little to control the riot. This is just one example of what Hermione Lee would describe as Bowen's 'supremely stylish' treatment of 'chaotic, unmanageable, even incommunicable experience'.[29] Roland Barthes describes the ability of fashion to 'dissolve . . . the myth of innocent signifieds', arguing that 'it does not suppress meaning; it points to it with its finger.'[30] In this way, by deconstructing beauty to levels of niche material detail, Bowen's fetishising language is self-aware and self-referential, creating meaning without denying a sense of the absurd. The triumph of Bowen's prose – its ability to be impressionistic while increasingly specific and elaborate – is indeed an impossible triumph. It ought not to work, but it does. Here, it seems, anything is possible.

In the same way that the polished surfaces of Mansfield's prose led her stories to be misconstrued as saccharine, it is the 'roughness' or 'unacceptability' of Bowen's style that has led her to be considered difficult, and not in the complimentary sense in which one might describe Joyce's *Ulysses* (1922).[31] What Bowen admired so much in Mansfield's language, what she saw as its 'singular beauty', lay in its pellucid quality: 'hardly seeming to *be* language at all, so glass-transparent [was] it to her meaning.'[32] Bowen's prose has, conversely, been perceptively described as of a 'queer, opaque style that realises itself not solely as a style to be looked *through* but a style to be looked *at* as well'.[33] In 1938, Virginia Woolf noted Bowen's appearance as 'cut out of coloured cardboard but sterling & sharp-edged'.[34] Her comments call to mind the plastic arts of Matisse, and there is a sense in which Bowen's literary style indecorously drew too much attention to itself, sidelined even from the modernist avant-garde by being too kaleidoscopic and antagonistic, playing with the tools of realism to undo them, fashioning texts full of 'vitality and mysticism . . . inventive fancy and [an] innate sense of colour'.[35]

Vike Martina Plock has observed that 'the analysis of sartorial styles' in Bowen's literature has often been eclipsed by 'the difficult task of defining Bowen's writing style'.³⁶ Yet their interdependence means that there is no real reason why these tasks should be separated, even if that style continues to shrewdly evade absolute definition. As Lee states in her biography of Bowen, there is a need 'to read "style" as an essential part of what [Bowen] has to say about civilisation and society'.³⁷ Style is not something that should, or can, be separated from the contents of Bowen's fiction – to separate it is almost to commit violence upon it, like the deserted husband in 'Making Arrangements' (1925), tearing Bowen's thoughtfully constructed wardrobe to shreds.³⁸ Bowen believed in art's capacity to bring about the 'reconciliation of the individual with his world'.³⁹ Her brave and unwavering expression of her own style, her dedication to that liminal border between herself and the wider world, is evidence of this commitment.

Material democracy

Bowen writes amusingly of the ways in which, in her youth, her 'trial-and-error' approach to dressing most often resulted in 'errors'.⁴⁰ Yet for the humour in her self-deprecating recollections of these sartorial mistakes, there can be little doubt that Bowen took the matter of clothing seriously. In his mildly insulting obituary (in which he declares Bowen not a 'great' writer but, at best, 'very good'), Phillip Toynbee states that Bowen exhibited 'a certain excessive attention to her clothes' which he outrageously attributes to 'a tormented belief that she was not attractive to men'.⁴¹ Yet it is clear that Bowen saw dress as an art form, observing in a 1937 book review for *The New Statesman and Nation* that while the artist is someone 'disengaged from his own personality to be able to objectify himself or it', dressing is 'the one art the unqualified must practise.'⁴² The unique positioning of dress as a universal art form would doubtless have appealed to Bowen, who descried the 'highfalutin' to embrace the more widely relevant, watching televised sport in her breaks from writing, and equally likely to seek an opinion on her work from her friend Agatha Christie as she was from Virginia Woolf.⁴³ She saw the short story as an egalitarian medium – in an essay on Gorky, she described short fiction writers as forming 'a sort of democracy' – which she compared in turn, in her famous introduction to *The Faber Book of Modern Short Stories*, to the cinema, another populist art form she enjoyed and admired.⁴⁴ If, as Allan Hepburn has stated, the story 'does not take inspiration from heroic or grandiose action' but instead 'its shape and length derive from its implication in ordinariness,' then the fascination displayed in Bowen's short fiction for the vestimentary is an expression of this.[45]

As in the short fiction of her contemporaries Mansfield and Woolf, in Bowen's short stories objects are often treated with equal accord to subjects, documenting revised relationships between humans and things that bore wider philosophical resonance.[46] Like these authors, Bowen was '[a]lways mindful of the furniture of life'.[47] Lee has observed that in Bowen's fiction '[t]hings seems to loom larger than life,' as in the story 'The Tommy Crans' (1934), in which '[p]arts of the body, bits of clothing' might 'separate themselves from their owners'.[48] Like the Dadaists and Surrealists, Bowen's prose refuses 'the ontological distinctions between inanimate objects and human subjects, between people and things.'[49] Her unique style, equally personal as material, equally concerned with persons as materials, also works powerfully to reinforce this view.

Despite these affinities, Bowen's repeated notice of garments and accessories is far more pronounced than in the fiction of her contemporaries, with her texts frequently employing what Barthes would call 'the poetics of clothing'.[50] With a surprising regularity, Bowen's literary mode of thought is vestimentary. She tells us that the modern short story is in danger of becoming 'too much prose draped around an insufficiently vital feeling', elsewhere that it should not succumb to 'high-hat complacency'.[51] 'Had I not been a writer,' Bowen states in a letter to Graham Greene, 'I should probably have struck out in designing and making belts, jewellery, handbags . . . my aim being that these should catch people's fancy, create a little fashion of their own.'[52] Bowen saw writing itself (and particularly the short story) as a craft that should produce physical rather than cerebral objects – her inspiration in writing was not 'to *say*' but 'to *make*'.[53] She saw stories as things to be *fashioned*.

Poetics of shape, colour and texture

Bowen's short stories always germinated from a visual conception; she described them as starting from a 'vision', with characters being brought in last of all as 'carriers' or 'expressers' of the general mood, rather like models employed to show off her visionary designs.[54] In this way, the short fiction in particular demonstrates

Bowen's 'determined devotion to style, forms, and surfaces'.[55] In the preface to her second collection of short stories, *Ann Lee's* (1926), Bowen describes a youthful 'prettiness – prettiness of hats in a shop, of a parrot on a flowing chestnut tree, of the Contessina's juvenile muslins against a glittering lake scene', and there is no evidence of this propensity waning throughout her career. In the same introduction, she evaluates the texts using language which would come to be known as Barthesian, describing them as possessing 'more texture, body, substantiality, than their predecessors'.[56] Bowen saw shape as '*the* important thing' and postulated that it was 'the shape, essentially, that the reader, the mass, the public goes to the story for'.[57] Conceiving of the story structurally and always in terms of the visual and the tactile, she proposed a model for short fiction that would most easily assimilate itself to the materiality of the physical world.

Bowen's stories are full of textile detail, with clothes and accessories bursting voluptuously from the pages like 'miniature glints of genius' and even taking centre stage in the titles of stories like 'Shoes: An International Episode' (1929).[58] Stories take place in hat shops and seamstresses abound, as do bridal trousseaux. We come across characters such as Aunt Marjory, who 'did her hair elaborately, wore remarkable rings, and seemed to have been poured into her tailor-mades', and, in 'Just Imagine . . .' (1926), characters like Noel, who yearns to talk to his grown-up childhood friend about travelling or, 'best of all, clothes'.[59] In 'I Died of Love' (1946), spring and autumn are described not in terms of environmental cycles but as 'the poetical seasons when clothes are being conceived'.[60] It is far more rare that Bowen does *not* tell us precisely what a character is wearing, and in stories such as 'Hand in Glove' (1952), she sees fit (perhaps playing with the literal implications of the phrase 'accessory to murder') to have her protagonist strangled by a pair of haunted 'elbow-length, magnolia-pure white gloves'.[61]

If 'Hand in Glove' goes some way to dramatise the idea that fashion encapsulates a 'despair that nothing lasts', on the whole clothing manages to stay buoyantly animated for the duration of Bowen's story.[62] In the opening paragraphs of 'Daffodils', a piece from her first collection, *Encounters* (1923), Miss Murcheson's skirts are caught by the wind to 'whirl . . . up round her like a ballet dancer's'. This event leads the protagonist to worry most precisely whether 'anyone had witnessed her display of chequered moirette petticoat and the inches of black stocking above her boots'.[63] In 'So Much Depends' (1951), we are presented with a detailed catalogue of a holiday shopping spree, with goods still carrying the hollow magic of advertisement promises:

> Ellen had spent her holiday shopping money on beachwear of the most dazzling kind – supplemented by sunglasses on the Hollywood model, oils that guaranteed a deep, even tan, and a rainbow range of polishes for her toenails. She had bought a smart-looking, second-hand evening dress from a friend who had grown too fat to wear it. Two pairs of sandals, a chalk-white light-woollen coat, and a waterproof lipstick completed her purchases. She had, it is true, tried on one glamorous coral-pink hooded raincoat, with the idea of donning this during a sunshine-shower; but, at this point, she had discovered her purse was empty . . . Was she not going to meet Romance, on the hot gold sands, by a whispering deep-blue sea?[64]

In this passage, Bowen employs all three of the 'styles' Barthes would describe as apparent in fashion photography – the poetic, the romantic and the 'outrageous'.[65] Assonance and alliteration provide the poetry, while the romantic and outrageous protocols combine in the final sentence, with satire undermining the fairytale outcomes that make fashion's seductive power possible. The detail is so intricate it seems inevitable that it was experience that taught Bowen 'the element of fetishism [sic]' where 'certain colours, textures or objects exercise an unholy fascination that reason cannot combat, economy cannot check'.[66] The mysteriousness of this pull is conjured, explored but never explained.

Such unholy fascinations are observable even at the heart of the modernist canon, with Steven Connor citing Samuel Beckett as 'the great, hitherto uncelebrated dramatist of bags'.[67] Yet Bowen would give Beckett a run for his money with the delicate specificity of the prose with which she conjures these receptacles. In 'Candles in the Window' (1958), we are presented with 'a little purse – or, more exactly, reticule: it had a silver drawstring, and silver embroidery outlined the floral scrolls of the pale brocade. The lining was of delicate sea-blue taffeta.'[68] In 'The Evil That Men Do –' (1923) the protagonist is wooed back to her husband from imagined infidelity by a gift:

> It was the most beautiful handbag, silver-grey, with the delicate bloom on it of perfect suede – darker when one stroked it one way, lighter the other. The clasp was real gold and the straps by which one carried it of exactly the right length. Inside it had three divisions;

drawing out the pads of tissue paper one revealed a lining of ivory moiré, down which the light shot into the shadows of the sumptuously scented interior in little trickles like water. Among the silk folds of the centre compartment were a purse with a gold clasp, a gold case that might be used for either cigarettes or visiting cards, and a darling little gold-backed mirror. There was a memorandum-tablet in an outer pocket, and a little book of *papier poudré*.

They sat down on the sofa to examine it, their heads close together.[69]

The fastidiously technical detail here goes beyond the fleeting interest of the dilettante; it also clamours with a multivalent sensuality that is not undermined by the obvious humour of the passage. The handbag functions as an agent, carrying out a seduction of which the husband would otherwise be incapable, and Bowen affects the same enchantment of her reader. When Bowen writes of 'the unique touches [of fashion], the language of the accessories', this is a metaphor she has already literalised in her own fiction.[70]

Dress, stories, mood

Perhaps unsurprisingly, Bowen's critical and personal writings are also stuffed like suitcases with clothing; she wrote for *Vogue* in Britain and America, as well as *Glamour* magazine, and produced a feature article for *Holiday* entitled 'For the Feminine Shopper'.[71] In her introduction to *The ABC of Millinery* by Eva Ritcher (1950), Bowen declares millinery an art, stating that a Ritcher hat is capable of producing an 'unselfconscious happiness' which Bowen 'consider[s] to be the ideal mood'.[72] In a book review entitled 'Dress', Bowen states that clothes 'play such an intimate part in the delicate business of getting oneself across that it seems impossible to discuss them, for long, objectively'.[73] Clothes then, are not autonomous objects; they are so bound up with subjectivity that they preclude the distance necessary to meaningful evaluation. Perhaps more than any other type of object, garments operate within the 'positively charged nexus of personhood and thinghood, subjectivity and objectivity'.[74] Hence in Bowen's stories we might find earrings 'like crystallised tears' or that the 'glass eyes of [a] fox fur glittered some way under her own[er's] with an air of complicity.'[75] Elsa Schiaparelli mourned her lack of control as a clothes designer for precisely this interdependence between subject and object, stating that a dress 'has no life of its own unless it is worn, and as soon as this happens another personality takes over from you and animates it, or tries to, glorifies or destroys it, or makes it into a song of beauty.'[76] If '[h]ow we appear is a great part of what we are,' clothes can be read (or misread) as unique materialisations of identity, subjectivity and mood.[77]

Georg Lukács saw the short story, that literary form which 'pinpoints the strangeness and ambiguity of life', as the 'most purely artistic form' because 'it expresses the ultimate meaning of all artistic creation as *mood*.'[78] Correspondingly, Bowen saw one of the strengths of the short story as its ability to assimilate itself to the wider cultural zeitgeist, to be 'suited to, soaked in the prevailing mood'.[79] 'Of all the arts being practised in England now,' Bowen argued, 'none, I think, responds more quickly to impetus than does the art of the short story.'[80] The high esteem with which Bowen held short fiction is likely corollary to her belief that the purpose of contemporary art was 'to concentrate and to deepen our sense of the "now"', an ambition to which the short story was well suited.[81]

Over the novel, Bowen saw the story as 'now, necessary for expression', capable of reflecting 'contemporary consciousness more immediately, sensitively' and to 'capture what could be transitory, but is not so, quite.'[82] Similarly, she regarded fashion 'not as an order but a response'.[83] In 'Dress', Bowen posits fashion as a cultural barometer, stating that 'new fashion is something we have precipitated, unconsciously,' describing 'the fruit of fancies, tendencies, wishes, reactions to events that are our own', but which are not routinely recognised when 'expressed in hats, dresses, "accessories"'.[84] It is as if fashion knows us more than we know it, incongruously epitomising essences that cannot then be deciphered. If, as Bowen believed, '[i]n dress, in home decoration, shapes, textures, colours, the "I" finds a concrete vocabulary', it is not necessarily a vocabulary third parties are able to read successfully.[85] Like the garment that is capable of meaning without being understood, Bowen located the short story's 'advantage' or 'virtue' in its poeticism – its ability to remain 'non-explanatory'.[86] She described the way in which, writing her stories, she was 'beating [her]self against human unknowableness'.[87] It is this unknowableness which her vestimentary texts work to explore and articulate, simultaneously revealing and obscuring, expressing the instability of fact as personal identity, without disavowing meaning.

Personal style

If identity is for most an unstable, changing construction, it is nonetheless something worth perpetually striving for. If some criticisms of Bowen's style can be seen as bourgeois it is perhaps because her raucous style is vehemently anti-bourgeois; it is weighty, it is active. It works against the vacuous, passive leisurely cycle described in 'Foothold' (1929) where a hollowness or 'room' increasingly blossoms 'underneath' the routine distractions of daily life.[88] It rails against the complacency of the status quo depicted in 'The Easter Egg Party' (1941), where '[n]o one was very rich; nobody was eccentric, and, though few people hunted, nobody wrote letters against blood sports', and 'local families harmonised with the pleasant retired people who had settled there'.[89] If harmony requires stagnation and indistinct orthodoxy, an absence of personality, Bowen's voice clamours and creates discord simply by not being ashamed of being itself. In so doing, it summons propulsion and progression through a spirited individualism. Her stylised prose is not postured but a formalised expression of uniqueness, integrity and artistic commitment.

Charles Ritchie, who would become Bowen's lover, first noticed her clothes. She is on first sight '[w]ell-dressed', while later diary entries notice her 'smart black coat with a pink flower in [the] buttonhole', 'gold chains and bangles', 'a necklace and bracelets of gold and red of the kind of glass that Christmas tree ornaments are made of', which accompany 'a white silk jacket over a black dress'.[90] Later, in June 1942, he asks, '[o]f what is her magic made?' The answer: 'Her uncanny intuitions, her flashes of insight . . . her wit and funniness, the stammering flow of her enthralling talk, the idiosyncracies, vagaries of her temperament'.[91] It is as if Bowen's exterior style conveys her personal meaning before that meaning is conceived of or understood.

In the piece 'How to Be Yourself – But Not Eccentric', she makes a case for self-expression which would favour idiosyncrasy far above 'agreements [made] due to laziness . . . diffidence or humility', such as those to 'dress, behave, run our homes, and conduct our outside existences in the accepted manner'.[92] Bowen argues that the individual voice is stifled too easily by convention and politeness, but need not be; fashion is no longer a 'dictator' but a 'would-be ally of the identity' dealing not in '"musts" but in possibilities', with clothing offering opportunities for individualism to be both nurtured and exposed.[93]

Bowen conceives of small gestures of individualism as having brought about the key triumphs of humanity, but does not limit their importance to those whom posterity has favoured:

> In the best of the world we live in, civilisation, art, we see the splendid achievements of self-expression; countless creative identities, back through time, have greatened our concept of humanity. Not all of us are artists or thinkers, statesmen or pioneers; we are none the less each born with one priceless attribute – we are each unique. In each of us therefore resides the power to leave our own individual marks on life. Small as these may be, they are never trifling: they count.[94]

The material intricacies of Bowen's experimental prose should be seen in this same light – never as irrelevant or extraneous, but as part of the intrinsic fabric of everyday life, its mystery and its meaning.

There is something humane about Bowen's very personal style, so much a hymn to the overlooked and ordinary, which also works against the destruction and generalisation enforced by the brutality of the two wars she lived through. In the preface to *The Demon Lover* collection (1945), Bowen wrote of the ways in which the brutal machinations of war succeeded in quashing individualism:

> And self-expression in small ways stopped – the small ways had been so very small that we had not realised how much they amounted to. Planning pleasures, choosing and buying things, wondering and wandering, dressing yourself up, and so on. All that stopped. You used to know what you were like from the things you liked, and chose. Now there was not what you liked, and you could not choose.[95]

The specificity of Bowen's persistently material style is an outspoken resistance to this overwhelmingly pervasive effect. If, as Lee sees it, Bowen's 'stylishness' betrays 'a deep uncertainty about identity', it equally confirms a profound belief in the importance of it.[96] In 'Summer Night' (1941) Justin complains '[w]e can no longer express ourselves', but these anxieties are balanced by his sister's contentment in what Bowen terms, in 'How to Be Yourself – But Not Eccentric', her 'individual inner world', in the self-expression that finds its way into 'her artless dresses, with their little lace collars . . . mottled over with flowers, mauve and blue' which gesture towards the possibility of creativity and regeneration.[97]

Bowen was aware that during the war people read more; their purpose was to seek out, through literature, 'the communicative touch of personal life' which a faceless violence sought to erase.[98] In seeking to deliver to the public what was necessary to their spiritual survival, Bowen's texts are testament to her belief in 'the important literary function of the reader', as well as the value of the communicative touch implicit in the care she took over her ludic style.[99] Physical destruction had brought with it ramifications that extended far beyond the superficial, as Bowen observed: 'People whose homes had been blown up went to infinite lengths to assemble little bits of themselves – broken ornaments, odd shoes, torn scraps of the curtains that had hung in a room – from the wreckage . . . You cannot depersonalise persons.'[100] Bowen's unashamedly material texts enact a similar process of recuperation and assemblage, weaving their own tender homage to these fierce trophies of ordinariness. Her texts remind us that the 'cry of the self is not egotism' – it is an ethical imperative.[101] If it is 'infinitely rewarding to be oneself', Bowen also knew that it is 'not easy'.[102]

Notes

1. Elizabeth Bowen, 'How to Be Yourself – But Not Eccentric' (1958), in *People, Places, Things*, ed. Allan Hepburn (Edinburgh: Edinburgh University Press, 2008), pp. 412–16 (p. 415).
2. Gilles Lipovetsky states that '[f]ashion as we understand it today emerged during the latter half of the nineteenth century' ('A Century of Fashion', in *Fashion Theory*, ed. Malcolm Barnard (London: Routledge, 2007), pp. 76–86 (p. 76)). Bowen described the modern short story (by which she meant the evolution of the short form proper as innovated by Anton Chekhov, a poetic entity that was more than a condensed novel) thus: 'As an art form, it is still fairly new – roughly, the child of the twentieth century' ('The Short Story in England' (1945), in Hepburn, *People, Places, Things*, pp. 310–15 (p. 310)).
3. Elizabeth Bowen, 'The Faber Book of Modern Short Stories', in *The New Short Story Theories*, ed. Charles E. May (Athens: Ohio University Press, 1994), pp. 252–62 (p. 256).
4. Hermione Lee, *Elizabeth Bowen: An Estimation*, rev. edn (London: Vintage, 1999), p. 127.
5. Sean O'Faolain, *The Short Story* (Cork: Mercier, 1972), p. 256. William Heath's main objection to Bowen's style in the novel *A World of Love* (1958) is that it relies on 'qualities more often associated with the short story than the novel' (*Elizabeth Bowen: An Introduction to Her Novels* (Madison: University of Wisconsin Press, 1961), p. 144).
6. Allan E. Austin, *Elizabeth Bowen* (Boston, MA: Twayne, 1989), p. 12.

7. Cited in Phyllis Lassner, *Elizabeth Bowen: A Study of the Short Fiction* (New York: Twayne, 1991), p. 175.
8. Ibid.
9. Bowen, 'How to Be Yourself', p. 416.
10. Jean Baudrillard, *Symbolic Exchange and Death*, trans. Iain Hamilton Grant (London: Sage, 1998), p. 91.
11. Elizabeth Bowen, cited in Austin, *Elizabeth Bowen*, p. 71. Critics such as William Trevor have remarked on the variance in quality in Bowen's short fiction, asserting that a 'few are slight, several somewhat flat, others tinged with obscurity', suggesting that not every experiment was 'successful' (cited in Lassner, *A Study of the Short Fiction*, p. 172).
12. Austin, *Elizabeth Bowen*, p. 70.
13. Judith Watt, *Vogue on Schiaparelli* (London: Quadrille, 2012), p. 9.
14. Elizabeth Bowen, 'Panorama of the Novel' (1944), in *Listening In: Broadcasts, Speeches, and Interviews by Elizabeth Bowen*, ed. Allan Hepburn (Edinburgh: Edinburgh University Press, 2010), pp. 135–44 (p. 137). In her description of postwar life, Bowen refers specifically to the 1920s.
15. Phyllis Lassner, 'Out of the Shadows: The Newly Collected Elizabeth Bowen', *Modernism/Modernity*, 17.3 (2010): 669–76 (p. 669).
16. Ibid. p. 670.
17. A. G. Macdonell, 'Elizabeth Bowen and Others', *Observer*, 25 August 1935, p. 5.
18. Elizabeth Bowen, 'Introduction' to *The Observer Prize Stories* (1952), in Hepburn, *People, Places, Things*, pp. 318–21 (p. 319).
19. Elizabeth Bowen, 'The Poetic Element in Fiction' (1950), in Hepburn, *Listening In*, pp. 153–61 (p. 161).
20. Dick Hebdige, *Subculture: The Meaning of Style* (London and New York: Methuen, 1979), p. 93.
21. Victoria Glendinning, *Elizabeth Bowen: Portrait of a Writer* (London: Phoenix, 1993), p. 48. Patricia Craig also reports how Hugh Walpole met an extravagantly dressed Bowen at a tea party in 1938: she was wearing 'a hat like an inverted coal scuttle' (*Elizabeth Bowen* (London: Penguin, 1986), p. 89).
22. Elizabeth Bowen, 'The Needlecase' (1934), in *The Collected Stories*, ed. Angus Wilson (London: Jonathan Cape, 1980), pp. 453–60 (p. 456); Elizabeth Bowen, 'Emergency in the Gothic Wing' (1954), in *The Bazaar and Other Stories*, ed. Allan Hepburn (Edinburgh: Edinburgh University Press, 2008), pp. 171–82 (p. 176). This introduces a potential for doubt at Bowen's 'technical competence', which is explored by Susan Osborn in her essay on style and meaning in *The Last September* (1929): 'It is certainly tempting to read these apparently underworked or overworked sentences, as have earlier readers, as inadvertent errors, embarrassing evidence of authorial carelessness that somehow escaped the governing eye of the editor or proofreader'

('"How to Measure this Unaccountable Darkness Between the Trees": The Strange Relation of Style and Meaning in *The Last September*', in *Elizabeth Bowen: New Critical Perspectives*, ed. Susan Osborn (Cork: Cork University Press, 2009), pp. 34–60 (p. 39)).
23. Jean Baudrillard, *For a Critique of the Political Economy of the Sign*, trans. Charles Levin (New York: Telos, 1981), pp. 78–9.
24. Jocelyn Brooke and William Heath, cited in Susan Osborn, 'Introduction' to Osborn, *New Critical Perspectives*, pp. 1–12 (p. 2).
25. Maud Ellmann, *Elizabeth Bowen: The Shadow Across the Page* (Edinburgh: Edinburgh University Press, 2003), p. x.
26. Baudrillard, *For a Critique of the Political Economy of the Sign*, p. 94.
27. O'Faolain, *The Short Story*, p. 256.
28. Elizabeth Bowen, 'The Contessina' (1924), in *Collected Stories*, pp. 136–46 (p. 142).
29. Lee, *Elizabeth Bowen*, p. 3.
30. Roland Barthes, *The Fashion System*, trans. Matthew Ward and Richard Howard (New York: Hill & Wang, 1983), p. 303.
31. Bowen, 'The Poetic Element in Fiction', p. 161.
32. Lee, *Elizabeth Bowen*, p. 219.
33. Osborn, 'How to Measure this Unaccountable Darkness', p. 49.
34. Virginia Woolf, *The Diary of Virginia Woolf*, vol. 5, ed. Anne Olivier Bell and Andrew McNeillie (London: Hogarth, 1977–84), pp. 133–4.
35. Jean Leymarie, *Fauves and Fauvism* (Geneva: Editions d'Art Albert Skira SA, 1987), p. 96.
36. Vike Martina Plock, 'Sartorial Connections: Fashion, Clothes, and Character in Elizabeth Bowen's *To the North*', *Modernism/Modernity*, 9.2 (2012): 287–302 (p. 299).
37. Lee, *Elizabeth Bowen*, p. 3.
38. Bowen stages this scene clearly as one of violence against an individual and individuality itself as what could have been comedic is rendered chilling: 'It seemed to him, as he softly, inexorably approached them, that the swirls, rivers and luxuriance of silk and silver, fur and lace and velvet, shuddered as he came. His shadow drained the colour from them as he bent over the bed' (in *Collected Stories*, pp. 170–9 (p. 178)).
39. Elizabeth Bowen, 'Subject and the Time' (1954), in Hepburn, *Listening In*, pp. 147–52 (p. 149).
40. Elizabeth Bowen, 'On Not Rising to the Occasion' (1956), in Hepburn, *Listening In*, pp. 107–11 (p. 110).
41. Philip Toynbee, 'Elizabeth Bowen', *Observer*, 23 February 1973, p. 36.
42. Elizabeth Bowen, *Collected Impressions* (London: Longmans Green, 1950), p. 112.
43. Elizabeth Bowen, 'Portrait of a Woman Reading' (1968), in Hepburn, *Listening In*, pp. 235–9 (p. 237); Plock, 'Sartorial Connections', p. 288.
44. Bowen, *Collected Impressions*, p. 153, p. 256.
45. Hepburn, *The Bazaar and Other Stories*, p. 15.

46. Critics have most often used Bowen's dispensation towards the world of things as evidence of difference from what Jean Guiget would call Woolf's 'purely psychological' style (*Virginia Woolf and Her Works*, trans. Jean Stewart (London: Hogarth, 1965), p. 253).
47. Ellmann, *The Shadow Across the Page*, p. 5.
48. Lee, *Elizabeth Bowen*, p. 141. At the time she wrote her first collections of stories, Bowen confessed that she 'liked scenes and inanimate objects better than [she] liked people' (Lassner, *A Study of the Short Fiction*, p. 128).
49. R. S. Koppen, *Virginia Woolf: Fashion and Literary Modernity* (Edinburgh: Edinburgh University Press, 2011), p. 3. Martin Heidegger makes these same unhelpful distinctions in *Being and Time* [*Sein und Zeit*, 1926], trans. John Macquarrie and Edward Robinson (New York: Harper & Row, 1962).
50. Barthes, *The Fashion System*, p. 235.
51. Elizabeth Bowen, 'Foreword' to *Tomato Cain and Other Stories*, by Nigel Kneale (1949), in Hepburn, *People, Places, Things*, pp. 250–3 (p. 250); Bowen, *Collected Impressions*, p. 260.
52. Elizabeth Bowen, *The Mulberry Tree*, ed. Hermione Lee (London: Virago, 1986), p. 226.
53. Elizabeth Bowen, 'A Passage to EM Forster' (1969), in Hepburn, *People, Places, Things*, pp. 272–83 (p. 281). In 'Gorki Stories' Bowen asserts that '[t]he craft (it may be no more) of the short story has special criteria' (*Collected Impressions*, p. 153).
54. Elizabeth Bowen, 'How I Write: A Discussion with Glyn Jones' (1950), in Hepburn, *Listening In*, pp. 267–73 (p. 268).
55. Plock, 'Sartorial Connections', p. 298.
56. Lassner, *A Study of the Short Fiction*, p. 128.
57. Bowen, *The Mulberry Tree*, p. 224. Reflecting on her literary achievements in interview in 1950, Bowen would comment: '[a]t their best, my short stories seem to me in good shape: I am less happy as to the shapes of my novels' (Bowen, 'How I Write', p. 272).
58. Bowen, 'How to Be Yourself', p. 413.
59. Elizabeth Bowen, 'The Pink Biscuit' (1928), in Hepburn, *The Bazaar and Other Stories*, pp. 53–65 (p. 54); Elizabeth Bowen, 'Just Imagine . . .' (1926), in Hepburn, *The Bazaar and Other Stories*, pp. 39–52 (p. 44).
60. Elizabeth Bowen, 'I Died of Love' (1946), in Hepburn, *The Bazaar and Other Stories*, pp. 143–51 (p. 144).
61. Elizabeth Bowen, 'Hand in Glove' (1952), in *Collected Stories*, pp. 767–75 (p. 775).
62. Baudrillard, *For a Critique of the Political Economy of the Sign*, p. 88.
63. Elizabeth Bowen, 'Daffodils' (1923), in *Collected Stories*, pp. 21–7 (p. 21).
64. Elizabeth Bowen, 'So Much Depends' (1951), in Hepburn, *The Bazaar and Other Stories*, pp. 152–70 (p. 162).

65. Barthes, *The Fashion System*, p. 302.
66. Bowen, *Collected Impressions*, p. 113.
67. Steven Connor, *Paraphernalia: The Curious Lives of Magical Things* (London: Profile, 2011), p. 17.
68. Elizabeth Bowen, 'Candles in the Window' (1958), in Hepburn, *The Bazaar and Other Stories*, pp. 193–203 (p. 199).
69. Elizabeth Bowen, 'The Evil that Men Do –' (1923) in *Collected Stories*, pp. 83–9 (p. 89).
70. Bowen, 'How to Be Yourself', p. 415.
71. Glendinning, *Portrait of a Writer*, p. 204.
72. Elizabeth Bowen, 'Introduction' to Eva Ritcher (1950), *The ABC of Millinery*, in Hepburn, *People, Places, Things*, pp. 186–9 (p. 187).
73. Bowen, *Collected Impressions*, p. 112.
74. Simon Mussell, 'Object Oriented Marxism?' *Mute* (28 August 2013). Available from: <http://www.metamute.org/editorial/articles/object-oriented-marxism>.
75. Elizabeth Bowen, 'Happiness' (1959), in Hepburn, *The Bazaar and Other Stories*, pp. 204–14 (p. 210); Elizabeth Bowen, 'Flowers Will Do' (undated), in Hepburn, *The Bazaar and Other Stories*, pp. 247–66 (p. 249).
76. Elsa Schiaparelli, *Shocking Life* (London: V&A, 2007), p. 42.
77. Bowen, 'How to Be Yourself', p. 415.
78. Georg Lukács, *The Theory of the Novel*, trans. Anna Bostock (London: Merlin, 2006), p. 51.
79. Bowen, 'Introduction' to *The Observer Prize Stories*, p. 319.
80. Elizabeth Bowen, 'Introduction' to *Chance* (1952), in Hepburn, *People, Places, Things*, pp. 315–17 (p. 315).
81. Bowen, 'Subject and the Time', p. 149.
82. Elizabeth Bowen, 'English Fiction at Mid-Century' (1953), in Hepburn, *People, Places, Things*, pp. 321–4 (p. 321).
83. Bowen, *Collected Impressions*, p. 114.
84. Ibid. In the same essay, Bowen also observed the ability of garments to demarcate societal shifts: 'Women, by bursting out of tailor-mades, grasping handle-bars looking pop-eyed under sailor hats, advised that world that their interests were other than purely sexual' (*Collected Impressions*, p. 115).
85. Bowen, 'How to Be Yourself', p. 415.
86. Bowen, *Collected Impressions*, p. 114.
87. Glendinning, *Portrait of a Writer*, p. 54.
88. Elizabeth Bowen, 'Foothold' (1929), in *Collected Stories*, pp. 297–313 (p. 302).
89. Elizabeth Bowen, 'The Easter Egg Party' (1941), in *Collected Stories*, pp. 529–38 (p. 530).
90. Glendinning, *Portrait of a Writer*, pp. 134–5.
91. Ibid. p. 136.

92. Bowen, 'How to Be Yourself', p. 412.
93. Ibid. p. 415.
94. Ibid. p. 413.
95. Bowen, *Collected Impressions*, p. 49.
96. Lee, *Elizabeth Bowen*, p. 8.
97. Elizabeth Bowen, 'Summer Night' (1941), in *Collected Stories*, pp. 583–608 (p. 590, p. 587); Bowen, 'How to Be Yourself', p. 414.
98. Bowen, *Collected Impressions*, p. 50.
99. Bowen, 'Introduction' to *Chance*, p. 316.
100. Bowen, *Collected Impressions*, p. 50.
101. Bowen, 'How to Be Yourself', p. 413.
102. Ibid. p. 415.

Chapter 2

Elizabeth Bowen: Surrealist

Keri Walsh

Irish literature exerted an enduring fascination for the Surrealists.[1] Not only did the movement's leader, André Breton, name his Skye terrier Melmoth in honour of Charles Maturin's Gothic protagonist, but when the group published their 1929 map of the world, they accorded a place of honour to the land they associated with unusual powers of fantasy and rebellion.[2] For Breton, the Celtic imagination was naturally Surrealist, as were the works of Jonathan Swift and Thomas Moore, both of whom he evoked as precursors to the movement. W. B. Yeats's experiments with automatic writing and his evocations of Celtic mythology, no less than James Joyce's explorations of a night-time world in the 'Circe' section of *Ulysses* (1922) and in *Finnegans Wake* (1939), emerged from the same taste for verbal play and hallucinatory settings that inspired the Surrealists. Like Surrealism, Irish modernism appealed to a notion of the collective imaginary, juxtaposed the banal and the marvellous, and modernised the powers of the Gothic. Declan Kiberd observes how the early twentieth-century Irish dramatists who created the Abbey Theatre's mythical drama were essentially forging a Surrealist aesthetic: they were 'among the first to grasp that fantasy, untouched by any sense of reality, is only decadent escapism, while reality, untouched by any element of fantasy, is merely squalid literalism'.[3] 'The split between modernity and underdevelopment' in Ireland, Kiberd argues, culminated in Joyce's 'almost surreal juxtapositions of affluence and dire poverty, of ancient superstition and contemporary anomie.[4]

Despite the shared pedigree and enduring commonalities between modern Irish and Surrealist art, few critics have explored this mutually fertile relationship, perhaps because the highest-profile Irish writers of the Surrealist era put some distance between themselves and the movement. In Paris in the 1920s, where Joyce's social circles overlapped with those of Breton, Louis Aragon and Philippe Soupault, the great Irish modernist never affiliated himself with the Surrealist group. And a decade later, when Samuel Beckett translated writings by Breton, Paul Eluard and René Crevel for *This Quarter*, he too eschewed any official status in the movement.[5]

In what follows, I approach the emerging notion of Irish Surrealism in a seemingly unlikely corner: the fiction of Elizabeth Bowen. Seldom considered in the context of a modernist avant-garde, Bowen's work has been read – particularly since Hermione Lee's 1981 groundbreaking study – within the history of the novel of manners, with Jane Austen and Henry James as precursors. In the mid-1990s, Irish Studies scholars began to consider Bowen as a chronicler of Anglo-Irish anxiety and ambivalence in the first half of the twentieth century.[6] Underrepresented in the critical literature until recently, however, are the specifically modernist commitments of her art. In 2004 Neil Corcoran observed that Bowen was 'deeply impressed by the ambitions of High Modernism', and a year earlier Maud Ellmann identified a 'prose-style whose reflexivity . . . associates her work with the modernist tradition', singling out Bowen's 'hallucinatory treatment of objects, particularly furniture and telephones'.[7] Bowen's career-long attention to the effects of new technologies on consciousness, her willingness to revise older forms of fiction and to experiment with techniques influenced by painting, cinema and radio as well as her depictions of women struggling to resist inherited Victorian roles and fulfil their desires for autonomy, education, travel and love align her with the modernist tradition of Virginia Woolf, Gertrude Stein and Djuna Barnes. Yet rather than classifying her with such innovators, even those critics attending to her modernist style and technique figure such experiments as idiosyncrasies. Where her prose undermines expectations of realist fiction, Bowen is more often described as an eccentric writer than one participating in modernism. Ellmann, for example, terms her 'one of the strangest' fiction writers of the twentieth century, Lee notes the 'surprising, ambushing oddness of much of her work' and Corcoran devotes himself to 'illuminating her sheer strangeness'.[8] Giving this apparent weirdness an Irish context, Paul Muldoon writes that Bowen's work hinges upon 'a *féth fiada*, the barrier between being and not-being, between this world and some other, wondrous realm'.[9] Uncovering Bowen's dialogue with Surrealism, on the other hand, allows us see her 'strangeness' in a new light, as part of her engagement with avant-garde, continental discourses.

In a direct if fleeting comparison between Bowen's art and Surrealism, Corcoran compares the nocturnal world of her wartime story 'Mysterious Kôr' (1944) to a Surrealist canvas, suggesting that writer's 'mesmeric rhythms and repetitions' conjure 'a mysteriously almost di Chirico-like city-scape'.[10] His observation responds acutely to Bowen's training as a painter, which made her a sensitive reader of visual culture. In what follows, I argue that the Surrealist setting Corcoran notes in one short story is not an isolated moment in her work – and that Bowen's exploration of Surrealist aesthetics in her short fiction led her to critique and even modify tenets of the movement. Her fiction reveals how the brash, imaginative and uncouth behaviour of the Surrealist coterie both energised and irritated her. She adapted the movement's techniques in her own prose, but also challenged its ideology on a range of topics, such as automatic writing, the 'femme-enfant', childhood, 'convulsive beauty' and the uses of shock. During the Second World War, her interest shifted from the automatism of early Surrealism to the veristic techniques typified by Salvador Dali. Stories of the London Blitz, including 'The Happy Autumn Fields' (1944) and 'Mysterious Kôr', are best understood as deriving their haunting effects from Bowen's merging of Surrealist techniques with an Anglo-Irish Gothic tradition.[11] I focus on the short fiction, since for Bowen, that form rather than the novel served as the canvas for her most intense engagement with Surrealism, an engagement paralleling that undertaken by her female colleagues in the art world (including Lee Miller, Dorothea Tanning and Meret Oppenheim), as well as her Irish contemporary, the Belfast-based Surrealist painter Colin Middleton.

The International Surrealist Exhibition of 1936

On 27 June 1936, Elizabeth Bowen wrote to her friend and editor William Plomer: 'I missed you at that Surrealist opening. What chaos.'[12] Not surprisingly, the two had failed to meet earlier that month, when they were among the eleven hundred people huddled into the New Burlington Galleries for London's most sensational art happening of the decade – the opening of the International Surrealist Exhibition of 1936. 'Chaos' aptly describes what Bowen would have witnessed that day, a word communicating the jumbled and hastily assembled nature of the exhibit, the stupefied response of its audience, the overwhelming profusion of artists, viewers and hangers-on it drew, the attending traffic jam that brought central London to a standstill and the media frenzy that followed.[13] But Bowen's remark also betrays her ambivalence about the coherence of the Surrealist project itself. 'What chaos' might as easily describe the works on display, an ambiguity that suggests the conflicted nature of Bowen's rapprochement with the movement.

André Breton's Surrealism, born of disgust with the consequences of the First World War and bred under the influences of Dada and Freud, aimed to produce

> psychic automatism in its pure state, by which one proposes to express – verbally, by means of the written word, or in any other matter – the actual functioning of thought. Dictated by thought, in the absence of any control exercised by reason, exempt from any aesthetic or moral concern.[14]

As a visual technique, Surrealism often relied on the juxtaposition of incongruous objects such as Salvador Dali's *Lobster Telephone* (1936) and photography that belied the eye as in Man Ray's *Le Violin d'Ingres* (1924). In its quest for the dreaming mind, Surrealism sought out the exotic, collecting artefacts from Latin America, Africa, Asia and beyond.[15] Sometimes, practitioners undermined 'reality' through the use of humour and farce; at other times, they borrowed from the tradition of courtly love to seek transcendence through erotic encounter with the female muse. Surrealism proved sensationally popular in London: before the 1936 exhibit closed, over twenty thousand people had come to look at the collection of collages, paintings, sculptures, objects and children's drawings. For figures such as Dylan Thomas, previously unaware of Surrealism, the event marked the beginning of what Valentine Cunningham has termed the English 'honeymoon' with the movement.[16] The Irish painter Colin Middleton began describing himself as a Surrealist in this period; his works throughout the 1930s and 1940s reveal him reimagining Surrealism in Irish terms.[17] The mid-1930s also saw the London publication of David Gascoyne's *A Short Survey of Surrealism* as well as Hugh Sykes Davies's novel-length poem *Petron* (both 1935). Bowen's collection *The Cat Jumps* (1934), which antedated both Gascoyne and Davies's offerings, was one of the first literary responses to the Surrealist phenomenon in English. In *The Cat Jumps*, Bowen emerges as a deft practitioner of Surrealist style, an authority on the ideas in Breton's manifestoes, and a sympathetic as well as sophisticated critic of the movement. But even as she adopts and refines Surrealist techniques, including the use of violent and disjunctive images to provoke shock, she also challenges Breton's pronouncements.

The most explicitly Surrealist story of the collection, 'The Tommy Crans' (1934), depicts a rollicking family Christmas party. Its protagonist Herbert seems to have been playfully named for Herbert Read, the leading English advocate of Surrealism, who was Bowen's colleague at the journal *Night and Day*.[18] Bowen burlesques the nonsensical effects of 'automatic writing' with a series of bizarre and seemingly haphazard images: 'Now into the hall Mrs Tommy Cran came swimming from elsewhere, dividing with curved little strokes the festive air – hyacinths and gunpowder. Her sleeves, in a thousand ruffles, fled from her elbows.'[19] Mrs Tommy's 'swimming' perpetuates the disorienting sense that the story takes place underwater, or more precisely in a fishbowl – 'the room where they all sat seemed to be made of glass' – and after her swim, she goes off 'throwing lollipops to the ducks'.[20] The absurd antics of the story's characters evoke the nonsensical stunts of the Surrealists (such as Dali's plan to give a lecture in a scuba-diving suit at the International Surrealist Exhibition). Bowen ends 'The Tommy Crans' with a vision of 'pink leaflets flutter[ing] into the dark', an ending that Paul Muldoon reads as an allusion to the snowfall of Joyce's 'The Dead' (1914).[21] But the conclusion also evokes a famous chapter of Surrealist history: Breton's practice of distributing promotional leaflets and stickers, often pink, all over Paris, bearing such mottos as 'If you love love, you'll love Surrealism.'[22]

Childhood

If in 'The Tommy Crans' Bowen explores the semiotic disjunctions of Surrealism, she also considers its problematic assumptions, contesting the idealisation of childhood that Breton had emphasised in his 1924 'First Manifesto':

> The mind which plunges into Surrealism relives with glowing excitement the best part of its childhood . . . It is perhaps childhood that comes closest to one's 'real life' . . . childhood where everything nevertheless conspires to bring about the effective, risk-free possession of one's self. Thanks to Surrealism, it seems that opportunity knocks a second time.[23]

Although by playing hide and seek and chasing one another around the room the adults of 'The Tommy Crans' do regain infantile bliss, the story's conclusion condemns their behaviour. By plunging into second childhoods, the Tommy Crans deny their daughter Nancy and her friend Herbert their first ones: forced to marry for money and pregnant with 'a stranger child', Nancy tells Herbert, 'you and I have nothing to do with children'.[24] Throughout the story, moral authority rests unquestionably with the younger generation, as Bowen presents Nancy's reckless, jazz age parents satirically: 'The Tommy Crans had lost all their money – it wasn't fair to expect them to keep it; they were generous and gay. Nancy had to think hard what must they all do.'[25] Allying Nancy's parents with such self-proclaimed grown children as Breton and Dali, she exposes the folly of those who would relive their childhoods without a thought for the consequences.

The conscientious maturity of Nancy and Herbert in 'The Tommy Crans' is unusual in Bowen's fiction, where children are often violent and cruel. But such aggression is generally the result of their victimisation. As with Henrietta and Leopold in *The House in Paris* (1935), and Portia in *The Death of the Heart* (1938), Bowen's children are parentless, simultaneously precocious and arrested in their development, and unloved by the adults charged with their care. Certainly no child in her fiction conforms to Breton's conviction that '[c]hildren set off each day without a worry in the world. Everything is near at hand, the worst material conditions are fine.'[26] Yet if Bowen envisions childhood as a powerless phase to be endured, her insistence on the complex psychological lives of children does not lead her to abjure Breton's claim that they possess extraordinary imaginations. On the contrary, their capacity to imagine intensifies their suffering, as well as their ability to make others suffer. Bowen offers a corrective to Breton's naive estimation of the child by insisting upon all that is unsettling in the mental lives of the young.

The *femme-enfant*

Bowen's scepticism regarding Surrealism's view of childhood extends to the movement's representation of women, a subject that has become prominent in feminist criticism of Surrealism.[27] In 'The Tommy Crans', Nancy epitomises the Surrealist muse, the *femme-enfant*. Although perfectly rational, she seems an automaton to the adults of her family: 'standing up very straight to cut the cake, [she] was like a doll stitched upright in its box, apt, if you cut the string at the back, to pitch right forward and break its delicate fingers'.[28] Fiona Bradley has suggested that the recurrence of such mannequin-like figures in Surrealist art reveals the movement's attachment to a notion of women as dolls. By combining 'two beings with access to the marvellous', she argues, 'the "femme-enfant," young, naive and in touch with her own unconscious, was a role which could be adopted by, or thrust upon, real as well as imagined women.'[29] In 'The Tommy Crans', Bowen turns on its head the formulation of the *femme-enfant* made famous by Breton's *Nadja* (1926); whereas Nadja is a grown woman with the mentality of a child, Nancy is a sensible adult in a child's body. Like Nadja, however, her synthesis of childish and womanly qualities is sexually alluring: she sits 'on her Uncle Joseph's knee, more than politely' and her Uncle Archer comments insinuatingly, '[t]hat was a nice little girl . . . Eh?'[30] Portraying Nancy as a Surrealist puppet, Bowen draws attention to the manipulation of the child's sexuality by the older generation but does not perpetuate the reduction of the *femme-enfant* to a voiceless muse. Nancy emerges, independently of her parents' perceptions, as a sensitive and autonomous character.

The *femme-enfant* also appears in the story 'Her Table Spread' (1930) in the guise of Valeria Cuffe, who, 'at twenty-five, of statuesque development' was 'still detained in childhood'.[31] Whereas the household visitor Mr Alban is initially wary of Valeria because 'he had been warned' that she was 'mad', he comes to learn, as Breton put it, that 'one can love a mad woman more than any other'.[32] What Nadja is to Breton's narrator, Valeria becomes for Alban – a means of transcending his mundane, sterile existence: 'Close by, Valeria's fingers creaked on her warm wet satin. She laughed like a princess, magnificently justified . . . and, in the silence after the laughter, such a strong tenderness reached him that, standing there in full manhood, he was for a moment not exiled.'[33] But Alban's brief redemption is possible only because he has abandoned his attempt to relate to Valeria on human terms. Alban views Valeria as though she were herself a mannequin at a Surrealist exhibition, and in the story's epiphanic moment Bowen metaphorically figures him meandering 'among the apples and amphoras of an art school' when he realises 'he had blundered into the life room: woman revolved gravely'.[34]

Convulsive beauty

As Bowen critiques the notion of women as dolls in her stories of this period, she extends her wariness to another prominent Surrealist motif, the notion of 'convulsive beauty'. The Surrealists believed, as Robert Hughes explains, that '*le merveilleux* – that state of almost sexual excitement which Breton called "convulsive beauty" – was available everywhere, hidden just below the skin of reality.'[35] Bowen's critique of Breton's universal sexualisation is made plain in her empathetic treatments of 'convulsed' characters. For the errant son of 'Last Night in the Old Home' (1934) who cannot transform his sister into a Surrealist muse, no therapeutic redemption through 'convulsive beauty' is possible. Annabelle, the narrator reveals, 'was not "afflicted": she simply did not grow up; inside the big, bustling form of a woman she was a girl of ten.'[36] But Henry's only reaction to her child-like wailing is, '[t]his is intolerable.'[37] Bowen renders the concept of 'convulsive beauty' ridiculous by sending Annabelle into literal convulsions at the end of the tale. Far from confirming Breton's dictum that 'Beauty will be CONVULSIVE or will not be at all', Bowen figures the 'convulsed home-girl' with her 'heaving shoulder' as merely a figure of sympathy, not a conduit for inspiration, arousal, or healing.[38] Convulsions again signal suffering rather than beauty in 'Tears, Idle Tears' (1941); the young protagonist Frederick's 'convulsed face', together with streams of tears, embarrass his mother because they seem 'to be the wounds, in the world's surface, through which its inner, terrible, unassuageable, necessary sorrow constantly bled away and as constantly welled up'.[39]

Whereas in her short stories Bowen exposes the macabre, even pornographic, aspects of the convulsive as applied to human beings, in *The House in Paris* (1935) she draws upon Breton's convulsive *technique*. The novel's climactic scene echoes a well-known passage from Breton's *Nadja*: 'Beauty is like a train that ceaselessly roars out of the *Gare de Lyon* and which I know will never leave, which has not left. It consists of jolts and shocks, many of which do not have much importance, but which we know are destined to produce one *Shock*, which does.'[40] In *The House in Paris*, as the young protagonist Henrietta's train prepares to roar out of the Gare de Lyon, Bowen's narrator merges the perspectives of Ray, Leopold, the author and the reader into the first-person plural:

> Where are we going now? The station is sounding, resounding, full of steam caught on light and arches of dark air, a temple to the desire to go somewhere. Sustained sound in the shell of stone and steel, racket and running, impatience and purpose, make the soul stand still like a refugee, clutching all it has got, asking: 'I am where?'. . . The tramp inside Ray's clothes wanted to lie down here, put his cheek in his rolled coat, let trains keep on crashing out to Spain, Switzerland, Italy, let Paris wash like the sea at the foot of the ramp.[41]

Bowen's insistence on the coexistence of stillness and motion (the soul standing still, the trains rolling out) creates a paradoxical shudder effect. In doing so, she re-enacts Breton's conception of convulsive beauty as that which 'joins an object in movement to the same object in repose', borrowing his example of a train locomotive.[42] The convulsed women and children of Bowen's stories and the convulsively beautiful train scene in *The House in Paris* show her distinguishing between the emotional upheavals of human beings, which merit compassion, and the technique of 'convulsive beauty' that results from the juxtaposition of still and moving objects, a technique she employs to memorable effect.

Shock

While her points of disagreement with the movement were clear, a tendency Bowen did seem to share with the Surrealists was her pleasure in shocking readers through a variety of attacks on conventional modes of perception. As Valentine Cunningham points out, one of Surrealism's most reliable methods for inducing shock was 'doing violence to people within their fictions'.[43] In her short stories, Bowen reveals her own taste for grisly detail. 'Parts of the body, bits of clothing', notes Hermione Lee, 'separate themselves from their owners' in 'The Tommy Crans'.[44] This metaphorical violence becomes literal in 'The Cat Jumps' (1934) when Muriel asks Sara, 'Did you know . . . that one of Mrs. Bentley's hands was found in the library?'[45] In fact, murders abound both in *The Cat Jumps* and in Bowen's following collection, *Look at All Those Roses* (1941): Prothero's smothering of Anita in 'The Disinherited' (1934), the mysterious disappearance of Josephine's father in 'Look at All Those Roses' (1941) and Henrietta Post's suspicious history in 'Reduced' (1935). Although the grotesque tale that unfolds in 'The Cat Jumps' owes much to Bowen's Anglo-Irish Gothic roots, as the work of Margot Gayle Backus suggests, the Surrealist influence is also apparent. Bowen signals her modern context through her characters' appeal to the authority of well-known psychoanalysts and sociologists. This confrontation between traditional Gothic terror and contemporary Surrealist models of the mind animates the plot of 'The Cat Jumps', for the more the Harold Wrights repress their interest in the murderous history of the house they have just purchased, the more virulent the revenge of the unconscious becomes. The soothing rationality of 'Krafft-Ebing, Freud, Forel, Weiniger and . . . Havelock Ellis' is no match for the power of paranoia or the ill will of unquiet spirits.[46] By refusing to deconstruct her ghosts, Bowen separates herself from both Freud and the Surrealists. Of 'ghost stories, harrowing tales, terrifying dreams, prophecies', Breton declares, 'I abandon you', denying supernatural influence of all kinds.[47] In 'The Cat Jumps', on the other hand, Bowen refuses such an abandonment of the supernatural. Although the ghostly presences at the newly purchased house at Rose Hill may be explicable in psychoanalytic terms as 'group' neurosis, Bowen hedges her bets: there is no answer to a guest's question about the lingering odour of the murdered woman's perfume – 'Who uses "Trèfle Incarnat?"' – no rational explanation for the dimming of the lights, except Harold's lame remark, 'Funny stuff, electricity.'[48] Resisting the Surrealists, Bowen draws on the Irish Gothic tradition to explore the power of the ghost story, recognising in its shock effects the ability to 'expose . . . our susceptibilities, which are partly personal, partly those of our time'.[49]

But for all the shocking violence that haunts her stories, Bowen's characters are as frequently alarmed by improper social conduct as by grim physical detail. The word *shock* appears in nearly every story, but it is usually socially shocking behaviour that startles her characters – particularly her male characters – from their complacency. The revelation of female sexual activities consistently catches men off guard. In 'The Last Night in the Old Home', Henry, 'having no idea [his sister Delia] was such a bad woman, violently registered shock'; Robertson meets the news of Connie's pregnancy in 'Firelight in the Flat' (1934) with 'a dull shock'; in 'The Man of the Family' (1934), William says, 'Aunt Luella . . . you shock me. How can you let a person like that marry Rachel?'[50] Female characters, meanwhile, are largely immune from such reactions. Insisting upon 'shock' as a moral rather than a physical or aesthetic response, Bowen places men in the position of the receivers, not the perpetrators of that assault on bourgeois values that the (mostly male) Surrealists took on as their charge. Bowen is again on the offensive here, suggesting how deeply invested her male characters are in preserving the sexual status quo.

The victim of a hoax

Bowen consolidates her critique of the Surrealists' approach to women, as well as her sense that the movement's promise of sexual liberation was only skin deep, in the comic story 'No. 16' (1939).

Here, she confronts the figure of the Surrealist artist. Maximilian Bewdon, a fictional composite of various prominent Surrealists, inhabits a derelict home called Medusa Terrace: 'to approach' it was to 'fancy oneself... the victim of a hoax'.[51] Bowen dates 'the splash' that Maximilian had made on the art world to 1924, the year of the appearance of Breton's 'First Manifesto'.[52] In addition to this coordinate, Maximilian shares a name with the Dadaist-cum-Surrealist Max Ernst, originator of collage and signatory to the group's declaration of 1925 that proclaimed 'we have nothing to do with literature' and warned of the fate awaiting renegades from the movement: 'beware of your deviations and *faux-pas*; we shall not miss a single one'[53] One of the chief targets of Bowen's satire is Breton's practice of publicly 'excommunicating' members who broke ranks with the movement. In 'No. 16', Bewdon has committed the ultimate faux-pas of participating in the literary establishment. Yet when Jane, a young poet whose book he has reviewed, turns up on his doorstep looking for a mentor, Maximilian bombards her with Surrealist rhetoric, even as he concedes his status as a pariah. As she hands him her poems, he begs that she '[b]urn them. You'll only lose your way.' And when she reminds him of his encouraging review, he replies: 'I've got to live. How could I write, in a paper, "She should have burned her hands off before she wrote?"'[54] Bewdon expresses his frustration with the impossibly high demands of Surrealism, an artistic doctrine that repudiated art, and in doing so, banned its members from any activity by which they could make a living. Breton was notorious for casting members of the group out of the fold when they became commercially successful or seemed too interested in worldly approbation: Louis Aragon and Philippe Soupault were dismissed in the mid-1920s, Salvador Dali after a mock trial in 1939 (the same year Bowen published 'No. 16' in the *Listener*) and Max Ernst in 1954 when he accepted the grand prize at the Venice Biennale.[55]

The sexual life of the Surrealist male becomes another target of satire of 'No. 16', as the story juxtaposes Max's amorous pursuits against his otherwise utterly conventional domestic life. Bowen contrasts Maximilian and Jane's adolescent behaviour with the realistic presence of Mrs Bewdon, whose actions draw attention to the practical services required by even the least worldly of artists:

> She fumbled her way to the kitchen, where she put on the kettle, then into the back room, where she turned the light on and saw Jane and Bewdon asleep with their foreheads together: he lying, she kneeling

twisted beside the sofa. They looked like a suicide pact. The room smelled of the scorching of Bewdon's rug. Mrs. Bewdon, when she had drawn the curtains, stooped and gave Jane's shoulder a light pat. 'Tea-time,' she said.[56]

When the impressionable Jane at last realises just how humiliated and 'demoralised' Mrs Bewdon is by her husband, her infatuation with the older artist vanishes: 'the indifference in Mrs Bewdon's voice, and her half-understanding, [bring] everything low. "He has lost me too, she thought."'[57] Given her ambivalence about Surrealist artists and their understanding of gender, we might notice that Bowen's name is a near anagram of both the overwrought Surrealist artist and his underwhelmed wife. In 'No. 16', Bowen wittily spoofs the wifely services upon which the Surrealists relied as they went about their rebellion against middle-class sexual mores.

Surrealism at war

Until the late 1930s, Bowen's approach to Surrealism remained equally amused and detached; she exposed the naiveties of Surrealist practice while adapting the movement's techniques to her own purposes. But during the Second World War years, Bowen drew on Surrealist aesthetics in earnest to present the psychological trauma of the Blitz. Beginning in the 1940s, characters in Bowen's short fiction increasingly express desires to locate more authentic modes of being. In the story of Irish neutrality, 'Summer Night' (1941), Justin despairs over the 'impossibility *of* living – unless we can break through to something else'.[58] This feeling of staleness and claustrophobia becomes even more acute for the heroines of Bowen's London wartime stories, who find 'something else' in Breton's concept of 'voluntary hallucination': the exercise of mental powers to the point at which 'everything that might exist destroys at each step whatever does exist.'[59] Bowen's female protagonists of this period, with their penchant for sleeping and dreaming, find in hallucination a buttress against reality. Often their visions parallel Lee Miller's Surrealist photographs of the London Blitz, in which bombed out buildings evoke mysterious, ancient ruins. In 'Mysterious Kôr' (1944), the mass destruction of the bombing liberates Pepita from the rationality of prewar life into the strange logic of the dream; as she enacts an imaginative reversal of the destruction, she tells her soldier boyfriend, '[i]f you can blow whole places out of existence, you can blow whole places into it.'[60] Here Bowen investigates Breton's suggestion that it 'remains for us only to hurl on the ruins of the ancient world the foundations of our new terrestrial paradise'.[61] By conjuring a consoling vision of the lost city of Kôr, Pepita, in true Surrealist fashion, works to the 'point where the distinction between subjective and objective ceases to be necessary or useful'.[62]

The plight of the lovers in 'Mysterious Kôr', confined for the duration of Arthur's leave to a tiny flat shared with the virginal Callie, echoes that described by Breton in his 'Discourse on the Paucity of Reality' (1924). The 'Discourse' envisions an apocalyptic city in which the pressure of space thwarts the possibility of desire:

> Even if only a few days remain for us to love, since we are alone after this much-talked-of earthquake, and the accumulation of ruins is so great that we may never get loose, there remains but one recourse: for us to love . . . A few square metres would be enough for us . . . Paris crumbled yesterday. We are at the bottom of a heap, where there is no room at all.[63]

In 'Mysterious Kôr', however, Bowen modifies Breton to suggest that hallucination itself, not love, offers Pepita her only escape from the trauma of war. The unlikely alliance of Pepita and Arthur provides solace to neither, and as she sleeps in solitude, Pepita dreams him into a male version of the Surrealist muse: 'She still lay, as she had lain, in an avid dream, of which Arthur had been the source, of which Arthur was not the end . . . He was the password, but not the answer: it was to Kôr's finality that she turned.'[64] That Pepita can enter her 'abiding city' either through waking fantasies or through dreams emphasises the thinness of the partition between her conscious and unconscious minds.[65]

In other wartime stories, Bowen engaged the veristic Surrealism made famous by Salvador Dali, whose extraordinarily detailed paintings created 'an accuracy more than photographic'.[66] Veristic Surrealism, a growth of the movement that dispensed with automatic composition in favour of academic discipline and form to express the unconscious, was a style brilliantly suited to Bowen's methodical craftsmanship. As Hughes suggests, Dali 'discovered that realism, pressed to an extreme of detail, could subvert one's sense of reality'.[67] In 'Summer Night', Bowen opens with a Dali-inspired vision of a melting, strangely inhospitable landscape:

As the sun set its light slowly melted the landscape, till everything was made of fire and glass. Released from the glare of noon, the haycocks now seemed to float on the aftergrass . . . [I]t would be a pleasure of heaven to stand up there, where no foot ever seemed to have trodden, on the spaces of wood soft as powder dusted over with gold.[68]

Similarly, the nineteenth-century sequences of 'The Happy Autumn Fields' (1944) depict a strange, unearthly atmosphere reminiscent of the canvases of Dali, René Magritte and Dorothea Tanning, in which the irrationality of objects is belied by the careful verisimilitude of their presentation. In an autobiographical note, Bowen revealed that she tried 'to make words do the work of light and colour . . . Much (and perhaps the best) of my writing is verbal painting.'[69] 'The Happy Autumn Fields' contains several descriptive set pieces easily imagined as Surrealist paintings. In the story's opening paragraphs, the specificity of the 'beetle-green, mole [and] maroon skirts' and the sound of the 'distant soft stiff scrunch' made by the family walking party lend sensory credence to the scene, even as the merging and blurring of the characters' psyches radically undermine conventional notions of identity.[70]

The plot of 'The Happy Autumn Fields' is as confounding as a Dali canvas. The timeline jumps back and forth between a bombed, crumbling London apartment inhabited by a somnambulistic character named Mary, and an older, lyrical Irish Victorian world in which two sisters, Sarah and Henrietta, experience perfect telepathy and mutual devotion until Sarah's suitor Eugene threatens to come between them. During a family walk led by their father around their large property, Sarah's clairvoyant imagination allows her to share perfect communion with Henrietta, but also to know 'the thoughts of Constance', experience 'the depths of Emily's pique at Cousin Theodore's inattention' and 'rejoice . . . with Digby and Lucius at the imaginary fall of so many rooks'.[71] But her strange sensitivity turns malevolent when it inexplicably transports her to war-torn London of the 1940s, where she becomes 'saddled with Mary's body and lover'.[72] The bombing of Mary's apartment has unearthed a box of old mementoes, including photographs and letters from Sarah's family. To Mary, the most compelling of these is 'a *carte de visite* of two young ladies hand-in-hand in front of a painted field': she sustains a 'personal shock' when she identifies them as Sarah and Henrietta of her hallucinatory voyage.[73] As Phyllis Lassner has pointed out, neither Sarah's Victorian world nor Mary's contemporary one is 'real', but neither are they dreams.[74] More than any of Bowen's other stories, 'The Happy Autumn Fields' embodies the ultimate aim of the Surrealist movement in regard to the conscious and unconscious, as described by Breton:

> ... we have assigned ourselves the task of confronting these two realities with one another on every possible occasion, of refusing to allow the pre-eminence of one over the other ... of acting on these two realities not both at once, then, but one after the other, in a systematic manner, allowing us to observe their reciprocal attraction and interpenetration.[75]

In order to show the interpenetration of the Victorian and modern worlds, Bowen uses modernist narrative modes to present the nineteenth-century setting. 'We surmount the skyline: the family come into our view, we into theirs', she writes, adopting the conventions of the screenplay.[76] Another disjunctively modern element in the Victorian sequences and one of the most puzzling elements of the story is the language used to describe Henrietta's curse on her rival. Henrietta's 'pain, which, like a scientific ray, passed through the horse and Eugene to penetrate Sarah's heart', gains comprehensibility in light of Breton's famous statement that Surrealism is the '"invisible ray" that shall enable us one day to triumph over our enemies'.[77] Although in 'The Happy Autumn Fields' Bowen never reveals 'what made the horse shy in those empty fields' to throw Eugene, it seems that it is Henrietta's prophecy ('whatever tries to come between me and Sarah becomes nothing'), combined with the power of her 'scientific ray' that enables her to destroy him.[78] The sense of dread that permeates both Victorian and modern sections of 'The Happy Autumn Fields', imaged by the continual circling of rooks overhead, evokes Dali's skies. As Breton remarks:

> The art of Dali, the most hallucinatory known until now, constitutes a real menace. Absolutely new and visibly mal-intentioned beings hereupon enter into play. It is with a sinister joy that we watch them pass by unhindered, and realise, from the way in which they multiply and swoop down, that they are beings of prey.[79]

'The Happy Autumn Fields', the most complex and enigmatic of Bowen's wartime stories, brings the influences of Dali and Breton to the Anglo-Irish Gothic tradition of Sheridan Le Fanu. The result is a particularly unsettling combination of menace, lyricism and hallucination.

In 'The Happy Autumn Fields' and 'Mysterious Kôr', Bowen reaped the rewards of her apprenticeship in Surrealism throughout the 1930s. Employing the compositional techniques of the veristic Surrealists, combined with Breton's insights on the interpenetration of waking and sleeping states, she created distinctively modern, ghostly effects. Bowen would continue to explore the altered, oddly communal consciousness of Londoners during the Second World War in her novel *The Heat of the Day* (1949); in later years, pursuing the linguistic implications of Surrealism, she would produce increasingly experimental novels, such as *A World of Love* (1955) and *Eva Trout* (1968).[80] Surrealism was both a source of creative inspiration and an ideological movement demanding critique for Bowen, and her work provides a rich archive of the complex and fruitful dialogue between French Surrealism and Irish modernism. When the Surrealists redrew the map of the world in 1929, they wiped out nearly all of Europe but preserved Ireland. Their fascination with all things Irish was reciprocated by artists such as Middleton and Bowen. Reading Bowen's critical engagement with the Surrealist movement gives us a new paradigm for understanding her 'strangeness' and illuminates her importance within the Irish modernist canon.

Notes

1. My thanks are due to Hermione Lee and Vera Kreilkamp for their careful reading of several drafts of this project. This article is reproduced with the permission of *Éire-Ireland* where it first appeared (42.3/4 (2007): 126–47).
2. Mark Polizzotti, *Revolution of the Mind: The Life of André Breton* (New York: Farrar, Straus & Giroux, 1995), p. 303; ed. Neil Matheson, *The Sources of Surrealism: Art in Context* (Aldershot: Lund Humphries, 2006), p. 626.
3. Declan Kiberd, *Inventing Ireland* (London: Jonathan Cape, 1995), p. 339.
4. Ibid. p. 338.
5. Anthony Cronin, *Samuel Beckett: The Last Modernist* (New York: HarperCollins, 1997), p. 132. Whatever the wariness of both writers, however, recently critics have traced the Surrealist qualities of Joyce and Beckett, with Lois Gordon (*Reading Godot* (New Haven, CT: Yale University Press, 2002)) discussing the Surrealists' influence on the psychological landscape of *Waiting for Godot* (p. 26), and Annette Shandler Levitt (*The Genres and Genders of Surrealism* (New York: St. Martin's, 1999)) suggesting that *Finnegans Wake*

'may well mark the beginning of the second generation of Surrealist art' (p. 139).
6. See Margot Gayle Backus, *The Gothic Family Romance: Heterosexuality, Child Sacrifice, and the Anglo-Irish Colonial Order* (Durham, NC: Duke University Press, 1999), pp. 155–8, pp. 179–94; Kiberd, *Inventing Ireland*, pp. 364–79; Vera Kreilkamp, *The Anglo-Irish Novel and the Big House* (Syracuse: Syracuse University Press, 1998), pp. 141–73.
7. Neil Corcoran, *Elizabeth Bowen: The Enforced Return* (Oxford: Clarendon, 2004), p. 4; Maud Ellmann, *Elizabeth Bowen: The Shadow Across the Page* (Edinburgh: Edinburgh University Press, 2003), p. x, p. xi.
8. Ellmann, *The Shadow Across the Page*, p. x; Hermione Lee, *Elizabeth Bowen*, rev. edn (London: Vintage, 1999), p. 12; Corcoran, *The Enforced Return*, p. 11.
9. Paul Muldoon, *To Ireland, I* (Oxford: Oxford University Press, 2000), p. 24.
10. Corcoran, *The Enforced Return*, p. 166.
11. For further reading on the history and development of the Gothic tradition in Ireland, see W. J. McCormack, 'Irish Gothic and After', in *The Field Day Anthology of Irish Writing*, ed. Seamus Dean (Derry: Field Day, 1991); R. F. Foster, *Paddy and Mr Punch: Connections in Irish and English History* (New York: Viking, 1994), pp. 212–32; and Terry Eagleton, *Heathcliff and the Great Hunger* (London: Verso, 1995), pp. 187–99.
12. Elizabeth Bowen, *The Mulberry Tree: Writings of Elizabeth Bowen*, ed. Hermione Lee (London: Virago, 1986), p. 201.
13. Paul C. Ray confirms Bowen's sense of disorder: 'The exhibition was somewhat chaotic in its presentation . . . The exhibition had been hung, the items numbered, and the catalogue printed when André Breton arrived from Paris: he declared the exhibition a disaster and ordered it rehung' (*The Surrealist Movement in England* (New York: Cornell University Press, 1971), p. 135).
14. André Breton, *What Is Surrealism? Selected Writings*, ed. Franklin Rosemont (New York: Pathfinder, 1978), p. 308.
15. Louise Tythacott's *Surrealism and the Exotic* (London: Routledge, 2003) chronicles Surrealism's anthropological impulses.
16. Valentine Cunningham, *British Writers of the Thirties* (Oxford: Oxford University Press, 1988), p. 67.
17. The influence of Middleton's Surrealism on contemporary Irish poetry is registered in Michael Longley's 'A Working Holiday'. Subtitled 'For Colin Middleton', the poem includes recollections of a 'very eccentric' classics master and a Mrs Quirk 'gliding towards us like a huge balloon' (*Collected Poems* (London: Jonathan Cape, 2007), pp. 26–7). Seamus Heaney used Middleton's drawings as illustrations for *Sweeney Astray* (London: Faber & Faber, 2001).

18. Surrealism receives numerous mentions in *Night and Day* after 1936. In a theatre review of July 1937, Bowen pokes fun at the musical *Revudeville* in a manner that remains reserved about the merits of Surrealism: 'The *Tableau*, which I hear is quite a feature, is very pretty, against a Dali sky; it is much less inexplicit than a Dali' (*Night and Day*, ed. Christopher Hawtree (London: Chatto & Windus, 1985), p. 65).
19. Elizabeth Bowen, 'The Tommy Crans' (1934), in *Collected Stories*, ed. Angus Wilson (London: Vintage, 1999), pp. 349–54 (p. 349).
20. Ibid. p. 349, p. 352.
21. Ibid. p. 354; Muldoon, *To Ireland, I*, pp. 23–4.
22. Breton, *What Is Surrealism?*, p. 52.
23. André Breton, 'First Manifesto of Surrealism', in *Modernism: An Anthology of Sources and Documents*, ed. Vassiliki Kolocotroni, Jane Goldman and Olga Taxidou (Edinburgh: Edinburgh University Press, 1998), pp. 307–11 (p. 310).
24. Bowen, 'The Tommy Crans', p. 354.
25. Ibid. p. 352.
26. Breton, 'First Manifesto', p. 307.
27. See Mary Ann Caws, *Surrealism and Women* (Cambridge, MA: MIT Press, 1991); Katherine Conley, *Automatic Woman: The Representation of Women in Surrealism* (Lincoln: University of Nebraska Press, 1996); and Fiona Bradley, *Surrealism* (London: Tate Gallery, 1996).
28. Bowen, 'The Tommy Crans', p. 351.
29. Bradley, *Surrealism*, pp. 47–8.
30. Bowen, 'The Tommy Crans', p. 351.
31. Elizabeth Bowen, 'Her Table Spread' (1930), in *Collected Stories*, pp. 418–24 (p. 423).
32. Ibid. Breton, *What Is Surrealism?*, p. 11.
33. Bowen, 'Her Table Spread', p. 424.
34. Ibid. p. 423.
35. Robert Hughes, *The Shock of the New: Art and the Century of Change* (London: BBC, 1980), p. 243.
36. Elizabeth Bowen, 'Last Night in the Old Home' (1934), in *Collected Stories*, pp. 371–4 (pp. 371–2).
37. Ibid. p. 374.
38. Ibid. André Breton, *Nadja* (London: Penguin, 1999), p. 159.
39. Elizabeth Bowen, 'Tears, Idle Tears' (1941), in *Collected Stories*, pp. 481–7 (p. 486).
40. Breton, *Nadja*, p. 159.
41. Elizabeth Bowen, *The House in Paris* (London: Vintage, 1998), p. 237.
42. Breton writes, 'In my opinion, there can be no beauty – convulsive beauty – except at the price of the reciprocal relationship that joins an object in movement to the same object in repose. I am sorry not to be able to reproduce here a photograph of a very handsome locomotive

after having been abandoned for many years to the fever of a virgin forest' (*Nadja*, p. 39).
43. Cunningham, *British Writers of the Thirties*, p. 66.
44. Lee, *Elizabeth Bowen*, p. 141.
45. Elizabeth Bowen, 'The Cat Jumps' (1934), in *Collected Stories*, pp. 362–70 (p. 362).
46. Backus, *The Gothic Family Romance*, p. 366.
47. Breton, *What Is Surrealism?*, p. 35.
48. Bowen, 'The Cat Jumps', p. 364, p. 366.
49. Elizabeth Bowen, *Afterthought: Pieces about Writing* (London: Longman, Green, 1962), p. 104.
50. Bowen, 'The Last Night in the Old Home', p. 372; Elizabeth Bowen, 'Firelight in the Flat' (1934), in *Collected Stories*, pp. 435–40 (p. 437); Elizabeth Bowen, 'The Man of the Family' (1934), in *Collected Stories*, pp. 441–52 (p. 450).
51. Elizabeth Bowen, 'No. 16' (1939), in *Collected Stories*, pp. 547–54 (p. 547).
52. Ibid.
53. Breton, *What Is Surrealism?*, p. 421.
54. Bowen, 'No. 16', pp. 552–3.
55. Polizzotti, *Revolution of the Mind*, p. 591.
56. Bowen, 'No. 16', p. 553. Léonor Fini's recollections provide an illuminating historical context for 'No. 16': 'I met Max Ernst and we soon became lovers . . . One day in his studio in the disordered flat in the rue des Plantes, which he shared with his long-suffering wife Marie-Berthe, he presented me with a copy of his "Semaine de Bonté" series with the inscription: "*à Léonor Fini. Plus je pense à elle, plus j'oublie le Diable. Max Ernst*"' (cited in Peter Webb and Léonor Fini, 'The Surreal Life of Léonor Fini', *Tate: The Art Magazine*, 26 (2001): 34–9 (p. 34).
57. Bowen, 'No. 16', pp. 553–4.
58. Elizabeth Bowen, 'Summer Night' (1941), in *Collected Stories*, pp. 583–608 (p. 590).
59. Breton, *What Is Surrealism?*, p. 62, p. 32.
60. Elizabeth Bowen, 'Mysterious Kôr' (1944), in *Collected Stories*, pp. 728–40 (p. 730).
61. Breton, cited in Franklin Rosemont, *André Breton and the First Principles of Surrealism* (London: Pluto, 1978), p. 40.
62. Breton, *What Is Surrealism?*, p. 147.
63. Ibid. p. 34.
64. Bowen, 'Mysterious Kôr', pp. 739–40.
65. Ibid. p. 730.
66. Hughes, *The Shock of the New*, p. 237.
67. Ibid.
68. Bowen, 'Summer Night', p. 583.
69. Bowen, cited in Victoria Glendinning, *Elizabeth Bowen: Portrait of a Writer* (London: Phoenix, 1988), p. 41.

70. Elizabeth Bowen, 'The Happy Autumn Fields' (1944), in *Collected Stories*, pp. 671–85 (p. 671).
71. Ibid.
72. Ibid. p. 677.
73. Ibid. p. 678.
74. See Phyllis Lassner, *Elizabeth Bowen: A Study of the Short Fiction* (New York: Twayne, 1991). Lassner insists on the independent existence of the two timelines, writing that 'neither scene is weighted as the key to the significance of the other' (pp. 105–6).
75. Breton, *What Is Surrealism?*, p. 156.
76. Bowen, 'The Happy Autumn Fields', p. 675.
77. Ibid. Breton, *What Is Surrealism?*, p. 168.
78. Bowen, 'The Happy Autumn Fields', pp. 683–5.
79. Breton, *What Is Surrealism?*, p. 29.
80. For a study of the postmodern developments in Bowen's later fiction, see Andrew Bennett and Nicholas Royle, *Elizabeth Bowen and the Dissolution of the Novel: Still Lives* (Basingstoke: Macmillan, 1994).

Chapter 3

Elizabeth Bowen and the Pleasure of the Text

Jessica Gildersleeve

The English novel, from its beginning on, has been the subject of so much critical writing that one may feel there remains little to add. Its characteristics have been defined; its development has been noted; influences upon it have been traced. In so far as all this may enlarge our pleasure in reading, we owe thanks to the critic. I do, however, see one danger – that too much information about great novels may make us less spontaneous in our approach to them – though they offer entrancing subjects for study, they were in the first place written to be enjoyed.[1]

The pleasure of the text is when my body pursues its own ideas – for my body does not have the same ideas I do.[2]

One does not usually refer to Elizabeth Bowen and Roland Barthes as literary theorists in the same breath. Yet, for both writers, reading is a process that is not simply or not only intellectual, but one which draws on the body as independent of the mind. While several authors in the extant criticism have used various lenses of critical theory through which to analyse Bowen's work, a case for Bowen as a theorist herself has not yet been made. Through an analysis of Bowen's critical essays, reviews and depictions of reading and writing in her fiction, this chapter proposes a logic of literary theory as it emerges in her work. Bowen's theory of reading does anticipate in some ways poststructuralist theory as it appears in the work of Roland Barthes, particularly in terms of her syntactical evocations of trauma. Where her work differs (or defers) from his, however, is in her insistence upon a kind of mindless and 'spontaneous' work of reading which describes the impact of the reader and the text upon each other and the production of pleasure engendered through this relationship. It is in the process of this mutual engagement, Bowen's work suggests, that each comes into being, through which identity is formed, particularly for her women characters, and by which the ethical act of narrative comes into being. This essay will thus argue for the innovation present in Bowen's understanding of reading and writing as an anticipation and an inflection of later poststructuralist theory, as well as considering the nature of reading pleasure in the often grim context of difficult Modernist reading and writing.

The strangeness of Bowen's writing, her breaches of syntax, her diction and the oddly stilted yet lyrical forms of her prose are often commented upon by critics. Susan Osborn, for example, characterises Bowen's writing as exhibiting a 'lack of cooperation' with the reader, thereby 'interrupt[ing] the easy concord between the reader and the writer'.[3] Yet, this 'easy concord' is not one which is top of the mind, as it were, for either Bowen's texts or their reader. Indeed, Bowen's disruptions, I argue here, are precisely to do with both the pleasure and the bliss of reading. In this way, they anticipate the poststructuralist debates of the late 1960s and 1970s, bringing modernism into play with its theoretical descendants. Roland Barthes has famously distinguished between the text of pleasure and the text of bliss:

> Text of pleasure: the text that contents, fills, grants euphoria; the text that comes from culture and does not break with it, is linked to a comfortable practice of reading. Text of bliss: the text that imposes a state of loss, the text that discomforts (perhaps to the point of a certain boredom), unsettles the reader's historical, cultural, psychological assumptions, the consistency of his tastes, values, memories, brings to a crisis his relation with language.[4]

Bowen's disruptive, uneasy narratives might be characterised, then, as texts of 'discomfort', texts that 'unsettle', that 'bring to a crisis'. Indeed, Bowen once said that the short story itself could be described as a 'crisis'.[5] These affective qualities aroused by a text, moreover, Barthes explains, are 'not an attribute of either product or production'; rather, they link 'the reading neurosis to the hallucinated form of the text' – that is, they occur where the text and the reader interact, where the mind meets the magic wrought by the material object.[6] And too, those pleasures are of the body, as if it were written, Barthes says, '*aloud*' – its aesthetic is an 'articulation of the body, of the tongue' rather than 'of meaning, of language.[7] But more than this, the text of bliss intensifies those aesthetics: 'it granulates, it crackles, it grates, it cuts, it comes: that is bliss'.[8] Bowen's articulations of reading and writing, however, bring Barthes's two kinds of textual pleasure into view at the same time; her writing, I will show, upholds these as an aporia, a perpetual interplay between pleasure and bliss, between mind and body, in the production of meaning.

In her essay, 'How Should One Read a Book?' (1926), Bowen's contemporary Virginia Woolf outlines two distinct aspects of the reading experience:

> The first process, to receive impressions with the utmost understanding, is only half the process of reading; it must be completed, if we are to get the whole pleasure from a book, by another. We must pass judgement upon these multitudinous impressions; we must make of these fleeting shapes one that is hard and lasting. But not directly. Wait for the dust of reading to settle . . . Then suddenly without our willing it . . . the book will return, but differently.[9]

Pleasure, the 'whole pleasure' of reading, for Woolf, is not simply understanding the words on the page, but making meaning from them; in other words, pleasure is precisely the process identified by poststructuralist theorists like Barthes. Woolf's two stages of reading are also recalled in J. Hillis Miller's model of ethical reading, in which meaning is produced through the interaction of, or in the space between, our 'fast' and 'slow' reading of a text – our impression of Woolf's 'fleeting shapes' and the book's later 'return'. This meaning-making, or what some theorists refer to as deconstruction, is, Miller argues, 'nothing more or less than good reading as such'.[10] There emerges, then, a connection between pleasurable reading and good reading – reading well, reading fairly, reading ethically: taking pleasure in a text demands that we make meaning of it; making meaning of a text demands that we read it well – that we 'pass judgement' upon the two sets of 'impressions' we receive. Pleasure, then, has little to do with the content of a book, and everything to do with what we make of that content – the ways in which we respond to the text and take that response into the world. As Miller has it, '[l]iterature must be in some way a cause and not merely an effect.'[11]

But what of the modernist text, renowned for its difficulty, its harsh view of the world, its distinctly unpleasurable subject matter? Indeed, as Richard Poirier has it, the two could not be more opposed: '[m]odernism . . . happened', he says, 'when reading got to be grim.'[12] Far from inviting the reader to simply receive impressions, or to wait for the return of meaning, Laura Frost argues, 'modernists offer a challenging and even hostile reading experience that calls into question the most axiomatic premises of what literature and pleasure can do ... Modernism, in short, instructs its reader in the art of unpleasure.'[13] More than this, Frost points out, in modernist writing pleasure is a suspicious, risky business, so that in an inversion of Sigmund Freud's pleasure principle, '[w]hat would usually register as pleasure often becomes empty, dangerous, or even anhedonic.'[14] The suspicion of pleasure is a product of its association with the sensual body, rather than the intellectual mind, so celebrated during the modernist period. Frost explains that in Greek philosophy, '*hedone* (pleasure) is only one unruly factor in *eudaimonia* (happiness). Pleasure is integrally tied to bodily, sensual experience, while happiness is more abstract and metaphysical, correlated with truth, contemplation, and wisdom.'[15] Pleasure, she adds, 'can get out of hand; happiness, never.'[16] Pleasures of the body, modernist writing makes clear, are fleeting and false, opposed to the certainty of the mind and intellectual thought. What is instinctive, therefore, is to be regarded with suspicion; what is difficult is reliable and careful.[17] Pleasure, paradoxically, is a product of 'tension, difficulty, and obstacles' – 'aesthetic practices that require extraordinary kinds of reading practices and often entail a hostile relationship to the reader'.[18] Bowen's observations of pleasure would seem to align with this model:

> All pleasure is of the moment: what we desire actually is the 'now'. During the moment in which we draw the breath, we cast round for what shall pierce us, elate us. The enhanced sensation, the dazzling image, the enjoyable regret, the tear shed looking at a sunset – from our nostalgia we gather an easy harvest.[19]

Pleasure for Bowen, it seems, is immediate, thoughtless, tinged perhaps by the romance of memory. More than this, it is 'easy', unworthy of the difficult aesthetic engagement demanded by modernist reading. Strikingly, Bowen also argues that the 'aim of art' is 'to concentrate and to deepen our sense of the "now"'; it 'is not merely a statement not made *till* now; it is in essence a statement *of* now'.[20] For her, then, the art work or text is nothing more or less than a capturing of the elusive present, itself synonymous with pleasure.

In this sense, Bowen might be seen to escape the bounds of typical modernist definitions. 'I read for pleasure', she notes, 'and it must be remembered that I write as a pleasure-seeker and not a judge.'[21] In 'The Fear of Pleasure' (1951), she makes this opposition explicit – her title is 'challenging – not to say truculent', she notes.[22] It is the modernist 'demand for a plan of life' which 'militate[s] against pleasure', she says – indeed, which militates against the 'human': 'to cease to envisage pleasure, or to desire it, must involve a distortion of outlook, a misdirection, even a dereliction of our inherent power to live well.'[23] In fact, 'to educate the faculty for pleasure', she says, should be 'part of the response to the threat of atrophy of the rational faculties'.[24] Her apparent position could not be further from that of perhaps the most prominent critic of pleasure in the period, Aldous Huxley. In his essay, 'Pleasures' (1923), Huxley argues that pleasure is a kind of modern poison, more dangerous than the war from which the world has just exited. Drawing on the modernist elevation of mind over body, he suggests that '[t]he most alarming dangers are those which menace [civilisation] from within, that threaten the mind rather than the body and estate of contemporary man.'[25] In contrast to previous generations, who preferred 'distractions requiring the expense of a certain intellectual effort', he notes, modern pleasure demands 'no personal participation and no intellectual effort of any sort'.[26] Huxley's argument finds resonance in Sigmund Freud's essay 'Beyond the Pleasure Principle', published the previous year; like Huxley, writing in the context of the social and individual traumas which occurred in the wake of the First World War, Morag Shiach observes, Freud develops 'a compelling argument for the importance of forces and energies that lay "beyond" the pleasure principle, including not only the reality principle, but also the compulsion to repeat and the death instinct as fundamental aspects of the human psyche.'[27] What is strange to note, however, is that while Bowen's critical commentary suggests her belief in reading as pleasure, her works of fiction bear the effects of trauma, suggesting that her writing is working far harder for and at the reader than her statements might appear.[28] While pleasure is a fundamental aim of art, as she has it, this is not to say that reading and writing are, in her work, to be understood to be without challenge, without effort. Instead, it is precisely through the interaction of pleasure and unpleasure that Bowen's narratives not only posit the ethical function of reading and writing in the modernist period, but also show how Bowen exceeds or expands our definitions of modernist literature.

Bowen's women are particularly expressive of the pleasures and unpleasures of reading, especially insofar as reading (or not reading) is associated with the formation or expression of identity and agency. In *The Heat of the Day* (1949), young drifter Louie devours a 'diet' of newspapers, nourished by their reassurance of her multiple identities as a worker, a soldier's lonely wife, a war orphan, a pedestrian, a Londoner, a home- and animal-lover, a thinking democrat, a movie-goer, a woman of Britain, a letter writer, a fuel-saver, and a housewife . . . Louie now felt bad only about any part of herself which in any way did not fit into the papers' picture; she could not have survived their disapproval.[29]

That Louie feels herself to survive only within the pages of the newspaper text is ironic considering the fact that she does exist only within the pages of the novel text, but what is more, the novel emphasises the way in which she is filled up by, nourished by, created by the words she reads. In the absence of true connection with other people during the war (her husband is away serving as a soldier), the newspapers fill the gap:

> Louie came to love newspapers physically; she felt a solicitude for their gallant increasing thinness and longed to feed them; she longed to fondle a copy still warm from the press, and, in default of that, formed the habit of reading crouching over her fire so as to draw out the smell of print. (*HD*, p. 153)

Pleasure, for Louie, then, is to be found in the mere presence of the text as a kind of mirror or reassurance of her own existence: without them, she and they would both cease to be. Although she expresses a distaste for reading, in *The Last September* (1929) the young and glamorous Marda's attitude aligns with Louie's when she declares that she will 'give up reading – I'm sick of their personal elephants'.[30] The writer's personality, Marda expresses, is an imposition on her own: whereas the weak and lonely Louie depended on that adoption of other ideas in order to nourish her own sense of self, the confident Marda has no need for such a crutch. In *The Death of the Heart* (1938), too, Daphne, a young librarian, is not 'fond of reading' – 'but that's not so much what they want', her stepmother affirms. 'They want a girl who *is* someone . . . A girl who – well, I don't quite know how to express it – a girl who did not come from a nice home would not do at all, *here* . . . Personality counts for so much here.'[31] Harriet S. Chessman has argued that 'Bowen scatters her novels with female figures who not only resist the narratives they see around them, but who themselves have no language, and who therefore cannot generate other texts'; she adds that these figures 'represent the unarticulated and inchoate femaleness which must in some sense be betrayed or at least abandoned, in the very act of entering language to tell stories'.[2] Indeed, it seems that the most confident women in Bowen's work do *not* read: reading pleasure appears to be a kind of opiate (as Huxley has it) for impersonality. The book cannot compete with the assured self.[32]

In part this is to do with the uncanny qualities of reading, which Bowen acknowledges in one of the planned sections of her autobiography, *Pictures and Conversations*.[33] As I have argued elsewhere, for Bowen, to 'read without the brain', as she puts it in 'Out of a Book' (1946), 'is to seek consolation in fantasy, to read without knowledge, without thought, to throw oneself entirely into the world of fiction and of life outside death'.[34] Reading, then, has sympathetic, even healing properties. At the same time, however, Bowen shows reading to be dangerous or destructive. Chessman has made the point that Bowen's fiction 'compels a recognition of the danger inherent in all fiction-making. Stories are, quite simply, untrue; they capture us . . . in their nets.'[35] Neil Corcoran, too, has recognised that Bowen's descriptions of these 'seem virtually occult . . . often ambivalently poised between affection and infection, poison and salve'.[36] This kind of danger is exemplified in one of her wartime short stories, 'Mysterious Kôr' (1944), in which a couple's moonlit walk becomes a journey into the fictional city of Kôr, which Pepita remembers from her reading of Rider Haggard's novel, *She* (1886–7). 'Her own fiction validates her theories' in notes on writing a novel.[37]

To imagine themselves in Kôr is not simply to imagine an escape from their oppressive world of war, however: it is to imagine Kôr as a replacement for that world. 'If you can blow whole places out of existence, you can blow whole places into it', Pepita tells her lover.[38] That Bowen offers up Kôr as this site of fantasy is no accident. *She* was her own favourite novel of childhood: as a child it had on her 'the effect of well-sugared cocoa laced with some raw and subtle intoxicant' – an intensely soothing, even hypnotic pleasure, a psychological and an oral incorporation of story into the self.[39] Later she realised the 'magic' power of that pleasure was the text itself: 'Writing – that creaking, pedantic, obtrusive, arch, prudish, opaque, overworded *writing* . . . what it could do! That was the revelation; that was the power in the cave.'[40] Reading in Bowen, Andrew Bennett and Nicholas Royle note, is a 'ceaseless "machinery of agitation" . . . [that] has to do with forms of trance or of what Bowen calls [in *The Death of the Heart*] "dream wood".'[41] The same might be said of another of Bowen's stories of war, 'The Happy Autumn Fields' (1944), in which Mary falls asleep one night during the Blitz and dreams herself to be Sarah, a young woman in prewar Ireland. The fantasy threatens a hallucinatory collapse between past and present when something unknown, something occult perhaps, appearing in an empty field, causes the accidental death of Sarah's lover. As in 'Mysterious Kôr', the text (Mary's dream is instigated by her discovery of a series of old letters) enables a kind of portal between fantasy and reality, but more than this, it dissolves the distinctions between them so that the world of fantasy has the capacity to replace the world of the real. Even in Bowen's reflections on her writing of her first short stories, she notes that '[t]he room, the position of the window, the convulsive and anxious grating of my chair on the board floor were hyper-significant for me: here were sensuous witnesses to my crossing the margin of a hallucinatory world.'[42]

However, the point is underscored in *The Little Girls* (1963). Mrs Piggott's entire absorption in her novel does not so much enable her to disappear, as it were, into the story as it does obliterate the world around her:

> To disturb Mrs Piggott once she was *in* a novel was known to be more or less impossible . . . But for the periodic flicker as she turned a page, Mrs Piggott, diagonal on the sofa, might have been a waxwork . . . The scarlet, brand-new novel, held up, masked its wholly-commanded reader's face. Though nominally she was 'lying' on the sofa, the upper part of the body of Mrs Piggott was all but vertical, thanks to cushions – her attitude being one of startled attention, sustained rapture, and, in a way, devotion to duty. The more flowing remainder of her *was* horizontal: feet, crossed at the ankles, pointing up at the end. She was as oblivious of all parts of her person as she was of herself. As for her surroundings, they were nowhere. Feveral Cottage, the sofa, the time of day not merely did not exist for Mrs Piggott, they did *not*, exist. This began to give Clare, as part of them, an annihilated feeling. She burned with envy of anything's having the power to make *this* happen. Oh, to be as destructive as a story![43]

Mrs Piggott's attention is entirely sustained by the book: true, in Bennett and Royle's interpretation, her reading 'trance' 'points up the significance of the body, from head to feet, in reading'.[44] Entranced in body and mind, she is 'commanded' by the novel, 'devot[ed]' to her work of reading, and caught in a kind of hypnotic 'rapture'. It is also true, however, that this transition is not just from the real to the fantastic: just as she enters the world of the book, the novel replaces her surroundings, so that the external world, the world of the real, is not just forgotten, but 'nowhere'. This uncanniness is compounded, Shannon Wells-Lassagne reminds us, by the fact that the narrative's 'reality' is itself a fiction, an 'artifice' which, in a 'typically modernist' move, demands the reader's participation in the process of meaning-making.[45] Indeed, the work of reading, Bowen clarifies in 'Books that Grow Up With One' (1949), is a work both on and on behalf of the book itself. The book does not only

> c[o]me into existence ... at times of reading. On the contrary, its existence within us, when it has been even *once* read, is continuous. Absorbed into the consciousness of the reader, the book is at work in him all the time. As, also, the reader's memory is at work on the book.[46]

The point is echoed in 'Out of a Book' (1946): 'The child lives in the book; but just as much the book lives in the child.'[47] Reading's pleasures are absorbing, to the point of annihilation, of infiltration, of parasitism.

Writing, on the other hand, is associated with the pleasure of mastery and manipulation, even outright rebellion. If reading is a kind of mindless pleasure of the body, then writing, it seems, harnesses the pleasure of the mind. Chessman argues that women in Bowen's work occupy only one of two positions in relation to language and narrative:

> Certain women become objects of narration, in stories told both by the primary narrators and by characters who act as narrators. Yet, as objects, these women tend to resist their forced entrance into narrative, and to desire the presence of another narrative form. Usually these figures are either silent or inarticulate, and point to a desire for a new language based on models of silent and symbiotic union – a desire which emerges in the work of many other modern women writers, especially Virginia Woolf. Other female figures, however, assume a place as author, or co-author, of a story. These women, who become alter egos of the inarticulate female figures, have the capacity to author, through their mastery of language, these other women; yet often, as with Iseult's half-authoring of Eva in *Eva Trout*, such creation comes freighted with danger.[48]

For Chessman, the movement between these two positions constitutes what she calls 'a radical schizophrenia' – in other words, 'an apparently unbridgeable gap exists between woman as subject and woman as object'.[49] I want to suggest, however, that the movement of this kind is not (or not only) between 'woman as subject and woman as object', but between woman as manipulative, even aggressive, writer and woman as either impressionable reader or defiant non-reader. Indeed, the writer herself positions her own (adult) reading as one of opportunity, noting in the preface to her first short story collection that 'it would not be too much to say that my attitude to literature was brigandish; I could not wait to rifle its vocabulary.'[50] Yet the point does not align with other claims Bowen makes about reading and writing, including, as I have noted, that she claims to 'write as a pleasure-seeker and not a judge'. It may be the case that this is part of the way in which Bowen differentiates between the form and function of the short story and the novel: the short story, for her, is a kind of free zone, a genre far 'more liberated than the novel', a perception which explains her permission of the supernatural in her short fiction.[51] Despite this caveat, we might see in Bowen's work a real 'self-consciousness about reading and writing', Corcoran notes, identifying 'a nervousness in this, an anxiety that the mere writer herself may not remain in control of the riot'.[52] It is in her final novel, *Eva Trout, or Changing Scenes* (1968), however, that this anxiety comes to the fore: Eva's language not only exceeds the efforts of her teacher and guardian, Iseult Arble who, although she had, on first meeting Eva, 'proposed to tackle Eva's manner of speaking', must finally admit that she 'had come too late on the scene; she had had to give up.'[53] Indeed, Iseult is not alone: '[i]t took Dickens not to be eclipsed by Eva' (*ET*, p. 120). Writing, language, Iseult confesses under Eva's influence, is always already an arbitrary tool; writing, she says, is 'hopelessly distant' (p. 120). Eva, in renée c. hoogland's terms, occupies the bliss of the pre-oedipal: she 'has taken the Law into her own hands' and 'has assumed the position of master/God over a world ostensibly unaffected and unconstrained by the phallogocentric symbolic'.[54] As such, Bowen's expression of inconsistent views suggests not so much a vacillation of her own ideas but, and in a powerfully postmodern move, a hovering between Barthes's conceptualisations of pleasure and bliss, between presentations of her own work as literary or popular, and between considerations of language as bound by or free from the phallogocentric order. To be in control of the text might adhere to the Victorian conceptualisation of the omniscient author-narrator, but to admit to its riot, and to the bliss of the riot, is to bring the novel screaming into the twentieth century, into conversation with the constructs of literary theory.

Pleasure, Frost has argued, 'is a narrative punctuation that is also, apparently, the end of theoretical and critical speculation.'[55] Opposed to desire, that is the 'work in progress' of epistemophilia, pleasure is usually seen to mark the end point of literary engagement.[56] In this sense, as an apparently passive rather than active engagement with the text, pleasure would also be seen to fail as an ethical act of reading. Bowen's representations of the (often uncanny) power of both reading and writing, however, position pleasure in reading as an absorption which might be said to meet Miller's requirements of the 'ethical moment in the act of reading': 'On the one hand it is a response to something, responsible to it, responsive to it, respectful of it . . . On the other hand, the ethical moment in reading leads to an act. It enters into the social, institutional, political realms.'[57] In Bowen, Eluned Summers-Bremner has argued, 'an act of reading is seldom neutral', and writing itself is 'a starter of new events'.[58] What I have suggested here is that rather than upholding a Modernist unpleasure of reading bliss, so often associated with work and distinguished from the pure, childlike pleasure of simple story, Bowen upholds both kinds of reading as occurring at the same time. What she 'want[s] to do to [her] readers', she says, is 'to experience a series of reactions . . . I desire, in fact, that when my reader has finished the book or story, all the reactions experienced in its course shall run together within him, to form *something*. I want my book to crystallise, in and for the reader.'[59] It is that crystallisation of reactions, the crystallisation of the book, which causes it to act on the reader and on the world as an ethical act. Without that interaction between fiction and reality, enabled by both the pleasure and the work of reading, ultimately neither book nor reader can 'act'.

Notes

1. Elizabeth Bowen, *English Novelists* (Bahamas: Britain in Pictures, 1942), p. 7.
2. Roland Barthes, *The Pleasure of the Text* (1973), trans. Richard Miller (New York: Hill & Wang, 1975), p. 17.
3. Susan Osborn, '"How to Measure this Unaccountable Darkness between the Trees": The Strange Relation of Style and Meaning in *The Last September*', in *Elizabeth Bowen: New Critical Perspectives*, ed. Susan Osborn (Cork: Cork University Press, 2009), pp. 34–60 (p. 41, p. 40).
4. Barthes, *The Pleasure of the Text*, p. 14.
5. Elizabeth Bowen, 'Preface to *Stories by Elizabeth Bowen*' (1959), in *The Mulberry Tree: Writings of Elizabeth Bowen*, ed. Hermione Lee (London: Harcourt Brace Jovanovich, 1986), pp. 126–30 (p. 128).

6. Barthes, *The Pleasure of the Text*, p. 63.
7. Ibid. pp. 66–7 (original emphasis).
8. Ibid. p. 67.
9. Virginia Woolf, 'How Should One Read a Book?' (1926), *The Common Reader: Second Series*. University of Adelaide eBook. 27 March 2016. <https://ebooks.adelaide.edu.au/w/woolf/virginia/w91c2/chapter22.html> 27 August 2016.
10. J. Hillis Miller, *The Ethics of Reading: Kant, de Man, Eliot, Trollope, James, and Benjamin* (New York: Columbia University Press, 1987), p. 10.
11. Ibid. p. 5.
12. Richard Poirier, cited in Laura Frost, *The Problem with Pleasure: Modernism and Its Discontents* (New York: Columbia University Press, 2013), p. 6.
13. Ibid. p. 3, p. 6.
14. Ibid. p. 2.
15. Ibid. p. 7.
16. Ibid. p. 8.
17. Ibid. p. 24.
18. Ibid. p. 24, p. 10.
19. Elizabeth Bowen, 'The Cult of Nostalgia' (1951), *Listening In: Broadcasts, Speeches, and Interviews by Elizabeth Bowen*, ed. Allan Hepburn (Edinburgh: Edinburgh University Press, 2010), pp. 97–102 (p. 101).
20. Elizabeth Bowen, 'Subject and the Time' (1954), in Hepburn, *Listening In*, pp. 147–52 (p. 149).
21. Bowen, *English Novelists*, p. 8.
22. Elizabeth Bowen, 'The Fear of Pleasure' (1951), in Hepburn, *Listening In*, pp. 178–80 (p. 178).
23. Ibid. p. 179, p. 178.
24. Ibid. p. 180.
25. Aldous Huxley, 'Pleasures' (1923), *On the Margin: Notes and Essays* (London: Chatto & Windus, 1971), pp. 45–52 (p. 46).
26. Ibid. p. 47, p. 48.
27. Morag Shiach, '"Pleasure Too Often Repeated": Aldous Huxley's Modernity', *The Modernist Party*, ed. Kate McLoughlin (Edinburgh: Edinburgh University Press, 2013), pp. 210–27 (p. 211).
28. For further explanation of Bowen's writing of trauma, see Jessica Gildersleeve, *Elizabeth Bowen and the Writing of Trauma: The Ethics of Survival* (Amsterdam and New York: Brill/Rodopi, 2014).
29. Elizabeth Bowen, *The Heat of the Day* (1949; London: Vintage, 1998), p. 152.-Hereafter cited parenthetically as *HD*.
30. Elizabeth Bowen, *The Last September* (1929; New York: Anchor, 2000), p. 142.
31. Elizabeth Bowen, *The Death of the Heart* (1938; London: Vintage, 2012), pp. 173–4 (original emphases).

32. Harriet S. Chessman, 'Women and Language in the Fiction of Elizabeth Bowen', *Twentieth Century Literature*, 29.1 (1983): 69–85 (p. 71).
33. Bowen's notes for that final section read: 'V. WITCHCRAFT: A QUERY. Is anything uncanny involved in the process of writing?' (*Pictures and Conversations* (London: Allen Lane, 1974), p. 63).
34. Elizabeth Bowen, 'Out of a Book' (1946), in Lee, *The Mulberry Tree*, pp. 48–53 (p. 50); Gildersleeve, *Elizabeth Bowen and the Writing of Trauma*, p. 106.
35. Chessman, 'Women and Language in the Fiction of Elizabeth Bowen', p. 69.
36. Neil Corcoran, *Elizabeth Bowen: The Enforced Return* (Oxford: Clarendon, 2004), p. 10.
37. Hermione Lee also notes that Bowen's 'fiction validates her theories', expressed in *Pictures and Conversations* (*Elizabeth Bowen*, rev. edn (London: Vintage, 1999), p. 213).
38. Elizabeth Bowen, 'Mysterious Kôr' (1944), in *The Collected Stories of Elizabeth Bowen*, ed. Angus Wilson (London: Vintage, 1999), pp. 728–40 (p. 730).
39. Elizabeth Bowen, 'Broadcast: Rider Haggard, *She*' (1947), in Lee, *The Mulberry Tree*, pp. 246–50 (p. 247); see Mary Jacobus, who posits: 'Suppose, for a moment, that oral incorporation really is the unconscious aim of reading – the way we imagine putting the world inside us, disposing of its dangers by making its meanings ours, cannibalistically consuming it, recycling it, savouring its borrowed sweetness as our own' (*Psychoanalysis and the Scene of Reading* (Oxford: Oxford University Press, 1999), p. 31).
40. Bowen, 'Rider Haggard, *She*', p. 250 (original emphasis).
41. Andrew Bennett and Nicholas Royle, *Elizabeth Bowen and the Dissolution of the Novel: Still Lives* (Basingstoke: Palgrave, 1995), p. xvii.
42. Elizabeth Bowen, 'Preface to *Encounters*' (1949), in Lee, *The Mulberry Tree*, pp. 118–22 (p. 118).
43. Elizabeth Bowen, *The Little Girls* (1963; New York: Anchor, 1991), pp. 94–5 (original emphasis).
44. Bennett and Royle, *Elizabeth Bowen and the Dissolution of the Novel*, p. 129.
45. Shannon Wells-Lassagne, '"*She*-ward Bound": Elizabeth Bowen as a Sensationalist Writer', in Osborn, *New Critical Perspectives*, pp. 96–112 (p. 109, p. 112).
46. Elizabeth Bowen, 'Books that Grow Up with One' (1949), in Hepburn, *Listening In*, pp. 92–6 (95, original emphasis).
47. Elizabeth Bowen, 'Out of a Book' (1946), in Lee, *The Mulberry Tree*, pp. 48–53 (p. 51).
48. Chessman, 'Women and Language in the Fiction of Elizabeth Bowen', p. 70.
49. Ibid. p. 71.

50. Bowen, 'Preface to *Encounters*', p. 120.
51. Lee, *Elizabeth Bowen*, p. 209.
52. Corcoran, *The Enforced Return*, p. 3.
53. Elizabeth Bowen, *Eva Trout, or Changing Scenes* (1968; New York: Anchor, 2003), p. 10. Hereafter cited parenthetically as *ET*.
54. renée c. hoogland, *Elizabeth Bowen: A Reputation in Writing* (New York: New York University Press, 1994), p. 250.
55. Frost, *The Problem with Pleasure*, p. 11.
56. Ibid.
57. Miller, *The Ethics of Reading*, p. 4.
58. Eluned Summers-Bremner, 'Dead Letters and Living Things: Historical Ethics in *The House in Paris* and *The Death of the Heart*', in Osborn, *New Critical Perspectives*, pp. 61–82 (p. 65, p. 77).
59. Elizabeth Bowen, 'How I Write: A Discussion with Glyn Jones' (1950), in Hepburn, *Listening In*, pp. 267–73 (pp. 271–2; original emphasis).

Chapter 4

Obnoxiousness and Elizabeth Bowen's Queer Adolescents

renée c. hoogland

In one of her autobiographical sketches collected in the appropriately titled and posthumously published *Pictures and Conversations* (1974), Elizabeth Bowen writes about adolescence as a kind of affliction, a nasty disease, the 'onslaught' of which she herself was fortunately spared.[1]

> I never did have adolescence at all badly. Chicken-pox, measles, German measles, mumps, whooping-cough in turn took their toll of me, and heavily, but with the last of those my afflictions ceased. Adolescence apparently, by-passed me – or if I ever did have it, I got off light . . . At around sixteen I dabbled in introspection, but hardly more. Tormenting nameless disturbances, conflicts, cravings were not experienced by me. I had never heard of them.[2]

The sentence closing this passage is telling. Bowen at once acknowledges what we have, post-deconstruction, learned to recognise as the discursive construction of (gendered) subjectivity, in one or all of its modulations (among which, crucially, at least in Western cultures, that of adolescence), and points up the complex interrelations between meaning and materiality, between signification and corporeality, in the experience of (one's) self. Bowen takes this founding constructivist notion a step further, however, by including not only formalised thought and ideologemes into the (discursive) 'constitutive outside', but also that which remains 'nameless', that is the 'disturbances, conflicts, cravings' commonly associated with adolescence. Feelings one has never heard of, she appears to suggest, will not be part of one's experience, will not go into the making of one's self, but once one has heard of them, once they have been articulated, they become available to one's consciousness, either to embrace and incorporate into one's being – perhaps more accurately: into one's becoming – or, indeed, to be (retroactively) rejected.

Bowen's claim to imperviousness with regard to the 'onslaught' of adolescence may strike readers familiar with even only a few of her works as somewhat puzzling. For throughout a writing career that spanned forty years, in which she published ten full-length novels, dozens of short stories, a history of her family, many critical and varied shorter journalistic essays, Bowen was obsessed with children and adolescents. The figure of, especially, the *female* adolescent is of such central importance to her work that one of its earliest permutations has occasionally been hailed by critics as a 'prototype' that would set the pattern for all of the author's subsequent heroines, irrespective of their age.

Bowen's dismissal of the phenomenon of adolescence with respect to her own pre-adult experience is thus quite remarkable, even more so because for her the distinction between fact and fiction, imagination and reality, is impossible to maintain. In her essay 'Out of a Book' (1946), for example, the author admits to having 'layers of synthetic experience' and concedes that the 'most powerful of [her] memories are only half true'.[3] Such 'layers of fictitious memory', she explains, are the result of the 'overlapping and haunting of life by fiction', a process that began for her at an early age and that clearly complicates any traditional distinction between the imaginary and the real, between fact and fiction, or, in effect, between meaning and being. Bowen's recognition that such layers of fictitious memory 'densify as they go deeper down', in that they find their origins in a moment way 'before there was anything to be got from the printed page', additionally locates the joint emergence of these two modalities of the (experience of) self, in their very inextricability, in a moment before she could read, before articulation, and thus in a preverbal domain: in the domain of perception and sensation, rather than that of (conscious) thought or discourse. As such, the early aesthetic encounters with stories and pictures in books, quite literally constitute the 'structures of feeling' from which, she acknowledges, 'today's chosen sensations and calculated thoughts' continue to arise.[4] These reflections on the intermingling of preverbal and verbal, inarticulate and articulate thoughts and feelings indicate that Bowen's attitude towards adolescence, in life as in fiction, is rather more complex than her emphatic rejection of its afflictions in the former may, at first glance, convey. What her comments on adolescence do indisputably suggest, however, is that feelings, as much as thoughts and ideas, are fundamentally social in character, hence culturally present even if not fully acknowledged, and, as such, available to our experience as aesthetic objects in, among others, literary texts.

What I wish to do in this essay, then, is to bring together the constitutive operations of language (or discourse) and the critical function of feelings in questions of meaning and be[com]ing, by connecting the figure of the queer adolescent in Bowen with the equally queer operations of her writing, with her novels as aesthetic events. My purpose is to posit adolescence as a particular structure of feeling that, in the assemblage of Bowen's writing, at once mobilises the stylistic operations of her prose and that, no less forcefully, (over)determines the singularity and materiality of her novels' aesthetic effects.

On the one hand, I suggest, Bowen's fascination with children and adolescents, as 'sensationalists', has to do with her insight into young persons' ability to read 'deeply, ravenously, unthinkingly, sensuously', before the 'brain is to stand posted between his [*sic*] self and the story', and the loss of such a primary sensibility, or 'virgin susceptibility' is compromised – even if it is not ever fully supplanted – by the desire for meaning, for form, 'to be unmistakably demarcated, to *take shape*' as an adult human being, as a subject.[5] An avowed 'sensationalist' herself, the author incessantly returns to that which has not become quite lost, that which can be 'unconsciously remembered', the 'magic stored up in those years', the pre-cognitive, affective dimensions of being or becoming that are essential to life: '[p]robably children, if they said what they thought, would be much franker about the insufficiency of so-called real life to the requirements of those who want to be really alive'.[6]

On the other hand, it should be noted that in her refusal to draw a clear line between fact and fiction or between imagination and reality, Bowen reverses the terms in relation to which such distinctions are conventionally cast. Her insistence on the 'continuity . . . between living and writing' hence does not mean that the characters in her novels originate in real life: '[i]f anything, the contrary was the case'.[7] Whereas 'persons playing a part in [her] life . . . had about them something semi-fictitious', the characters in her stories, as soon as they 'made themselves known' to her, were 'instantly recognisable, memorable, from then on': 'Nominally "imaginary," these beings made more sense, were more convincing, more authoritative as humans, than those others, consisting of flesh-and-blood, that I had wasted years in failing to know.'[8]

Trying to 'know' humans, then, it seems, does not work very successfully through cognitive means, on a rational level, but rather requires the imaginary, the power of the imagination, which primarily works through *aesthesis* in the literal sense of perception and sensation. It is this belief in, or susceptibility to her (imaginary) characters' creative force – 'I became, and remain, my characters' close and intent watcher: their director, never. Their creator I cannot feel that I was, or am' – which allows me to propose that the figure of the adolescent in Bowen's work functions as an aesthetic object or, even, an aesthetic event; an event or force which, in its singularity, inscribes itself not only in both the content and the form of her writings, expressing itself on the narrative level as much as in the style of her prose, but also – and this is what concerns me here – imposes itself on us, her readers, in our own encounter with her novels' unsettling operations.[9]

The novels are unsettling because neither Bowen's characters nor the narratives in which they obtain are necessarily reassuring, or even fully fathomable. On the contrary, as she continues her reflections on the relation between her own childhood reading and its effects on her living/writing: 'The characters who came out of my childish reading to obsess me were the incalculable ones, who always moved in a blur of potentialities. It appeared that nobody who mattered was capable of being explained. Thus was inculcated a feeling for the dark horse.'[10] This preoccupation with the 'dark horse', with characters that defy explanation, has not, at least not until recently, contributed to Bowen's critical reputation. Her stories and novels often leave readers annoyed and exasperated, frustrated with the irreducible affectations of her style and with characters and events that at once invite us to project 'meaning' onto them and that refuse to be captured in straightforwardly hermeneutic terms.

While considered one of the most prominent writers in Britain and the United States during her lifetime, Bowen has occasionally been dismissed as the author of modest drawing-room dramas or, as one critic would have it, 'delicate small-scale post-Jamesian studies, mostly of children and adolescent girls'.[11] In her more recent and much more thorough and appreciative study of Bowen's novels, even Maud Ellmann cannot but admit that the author's work is, decidedly, strange: '[a]lways entertaining – funny, moving, suspenseful . . . it is also profoundly disconcerting.'[12] As Ellmann positions herself in the wake of a 'larger reconsideration of the place of women writers on the map of modern literature', her careful close readings, informed as they are by psychoanalysis and deconstruction, primarily serve to contextualise Bowen's writing in various literary traditions to 'reveal unexpected affinities' with some, and 'intertextual skirmishes' with other modernist writers – male and female, Irish, British and European.[13] This overall purpose may explain why Ellmann refers what she designates the 'arresting oddness' of Bowen's prose to the idiosyncratic blend of literary forms, and to the 'reflexivity and the material intrusiveness' of her writing style, rather than to the author's investment in the oddball character of the female adolescent.[14] In an 'estimation' pre-dating the 'overdue revival' of Bowen's works of the past fifteen years or so, Hermione Lee offers a less-approving gloss on Bowen's mannered prose by, in contrast, explicitly connecting what she regards as the failure of the early novels to the ungainliness they share with the author's favourite character-type.[15] Exempting Bowen's second novel, *The Last September* (1929) (even though this also revolves around an adolescent girl), from her illuminating verdict, Lee writes that '[t]he other early novels, like her own awkward adolescent characters, are rather affected.'[16]

Affected, odd, strange, awkward and disconcerting. As qualifications of both a prose style and a peculiar character obsession, these terms suggest a convergence of the figure of the (female) adolescent and the operations of a feeling that I would like to qualify as obnoxiousness. In light of Bowen's insistence on the creative force of fiction and on the 'continuity between living and writing', I propose the obnoxious as an unruly and disorderly feeling that equally obtains on the level of narrative events and in the operations of her language. While I have elsewhere focused on the queer potential of the figuration of adolescence in her work, I will here foreground its operations as at once a structure of negative, uncontainable feeling – of unfeeling and of feeling anew – and as the site of unbecoming, or of becoming otherwise, that is to say a dual and ambivalent force that is expressed in the performative process of aesthetic experience.[17]

Obnoxiousness and adolescence would appear to go seamlessly together. Both are marked by a curious ambivalence. As a historically and culturally specific phenomenon, the inter-stage between childhood and adulthood takes up a peculiar position in our collective consciousness. The phrase 'obnoxious adolescent' evokes culturally sanctioned, unpleasant behaviour and wayward attitudes that in humans falling outside the category of adolescence – that is to say as a distinct period of life that we have learned to define as one of transition, in-betweenness and relative lawlessness – would be considered unacceptable and inappropriate. Actually, in its current usage, 'obnoxious', my various (online) dictionaries tell me, means anything ranging from extremely unpleasant, objectionable and offensive to disagreeable, nasty, distasteful, unsavoury, unpalatable, awful, terrible, dreadful, revolting, repulsive, repellent, disgusting, odious, vile, foul, abhorrent, loathsome, sickening, hateful, insufferable, intolerable, detestable, abominable, despicable and contemptible. Yet, in combination with adolescence, things do not seem nearly so bad. I may be wrong in my assessment here, but it seems clear that 'we' – that is to say so-called adults in the Western cultural hemisphere – tend to accept, endure or forbear modes of being and behaviour in unruly and unwieldy teenagers and youngsters that would provoke disapproval, protest and punishment if exercised by ourselves and other members of our age group. Interestingly, these divergent assessments of the same type of behaviour can be linked to the ambivalence at the heart of the word obnoxious itself. First emerging in the English language in the sixteenth century, obnoxiousness finds its origins in the Latin adjective *obnoxiosus*, meaning 'vulnerable or exposed to harm'. It is only in the seventeenth century that it – both as a word and as a state of being or a mode of behaviour – became additionally associated with 'noxious', in the sense of harmful, pernicious, deadly and unwholesome. Whereas, with respect to adolescence, 'obnoxious' thus appears to have retained its original sense, its connotations in other contexts reflect the influence of the later associations.

Such etymological ambivalence is carried over into the contemporary notion of adolescence, which, it will be clear, is (and not only in Western cultures) an equally inherently contradictory phenomenon. Socio-historically and culturally specific, adolescence is not the same as puberty. Different cultures assign different meanings to the biological transition from childhood to adulthood, and the period of adolescence may range from anywhere between ten to twenty-one years of age.

In the Grand Narratives of the West, the process of adolescence primarily serves to set subjects, male and female, on their way to a successful acquisition of one of two gender identities. Coming into one's own as a qualified adult means to have accepted, adopted and internalised a socio-culturally viable identity as man or woman. The most immediately effective route to earning this certificate of social viability is to play one's proper role in the plot of heterosexual romance, that is to say in somewhat less attractive but more explicit terms, to subject oneself to the system of 'compulsory heterosexuality', or to assume one's place in the 'heterosexual matrix'.[18] In one constitutive moment, the initiation into the realm of carnal knowledge, if enacted in properly binary fashion, thus at once (re)establishes 'natural' sexual difference and produces individual human beings in relation to its terms, that is as male and female subjects (before the law) and as ontologically stable, gendered human beings, as men and women. From the 'invention' of sexuality in the eighteenth century onwards, but especially since the early twentieth century, *pace* Sigmund Freud, and a couple of decades later, Erik Erikson, adolescence has come to be regarded as a crisis structure that serves to 'discipline' – in a Foucauldian sense – the relatively un- or ambi-sexed child into gendered and sexualised adulthood defined in oppositional, binary terms.[19] Intriguingly, in this scenario, once one has eaten from the tree of knowledge, the entry into adulthood is irreversible. And it is this, I believe, that makes the obnoxious adolescent at once so attractive and disconcerting, especially, if not precisely, in the context of novelistic writing.

In an influential and largely psychoanalytically informed essay published in 1990, Julia Kristeva embraces the ambivalence of adolescence as 'less an age category than an open psychic structure' that 'opens itself to the repressed at the same time that it initiates the reorganisation of the individual – thanks to a tremendous loosening of the superego'.[20] Kristeva links the open structure of the adolescent figure to the emergence of the open structure of the novelistic genre, which she describes as largely 'tributary, in its characters and the logic of its actions, to the "adolescent" economy of writing'.[21] Not surprisingly, in view of the historical coincidence of their joint emergence, it is the novel, as opposed to the epic and the courtly romance, Kristeva goes on to claim, which allows for the imagination and inscription of 'this in-between space, this *topos* of incompleteness that is also that of all possibilities, of the "everything-is-possible"'.[22]

Where and when everything is possible, nothing is realised – or, at least, not yet. As a space of the not-yet, of the not-yet-being, of the not yet-being-anything-in-particular, and thus, as a site of indeterminacy and non-being, the figure of the adolescent is as abhorrent and repellent as it fascinating and attractive. In so-called real life the adolescent, without the protection of a relatively stabilised gendered or sexualised identity, is a decidedly queer figure, and as such at once alluring and vulnerable to harm. Yet, within prevailing systems of gender and sexuality, which critically depend on the determination and maintenance of clearly defined and definable modes of normative being, the site of the not-yet is simultaneously insufferable and unwholesome.

Bowen's refusal to maintain a firm distinction between writing and living, between fiction and reality, in conjunction with Kristeva's psychoanalytically informed ideas about the adolescent novel, encourage me to take the figure of the female adolescent beyond its significance as an unruly figuration of specific aspects of normative identities. What I would like to do is to try to think about the inherent ambivalence of the adolescent, or, more particularly, of the *writing* of adolescence within the open structure of the novel, as a figuration of a more fundamental, if not ontological site of unbecoming, of the dissolution and loss of subjectivity, but also as a zone of great intensity, of creative potential and thus, simultaneously, as a *topos* 'of all possibilities' and a locus of *im*possibility. The convergence of the contradictory valences that adolescence and obnoxiousness have in common allow me to elaborate on the operation of the figure of the queer adolescent in Bowen's work as not so much, or not only, a particular character type but, as suggested before, primarily a structure of feeling.

Obnoxiousness, unlike other forms of negative affect such as anger, aggression, aggravation, is not in-your-face: you cannot simply fight off its effects by yelling, screaming, fighting or defying it. Obnoxiousness lurks and lingers, it takes possession of you in stealthy ways, it permeates and affects you almost unnoticeably until it is simply there in you, toxic, nasty. As a structure of unpleasure, obnoxiousness contaminates, it clings. This, I suggest, is the expressive force of Bowen's prose, as much as it is enacted by and in the figure of the unruly adolescent in her novels – most of them orphaned or with no parent in sight, and thus bequeathed upon a fictional world in which they have no clear, formally recognisable place. Funny, entertaining and moving they may be, but these figurations also produce what Ellmann senses to be the 'arresting oddness', the disconcerting strangeness, indeed the queerness characterising the author's prose.

Take, for example, the heroine of Bowen's first novel, *The Hotel* (1927), Sydney Warren, 'a probable twenty-two', described as an over-intelligent and neurotic young woman who does not really know what to do with the adult life facing her.[23] The hotel on the Italian Riviera, the novel's setting, comes across as a site immobilised in time and space and, as such, forms an adequate reflection of the protagonist's suspension in limbo. Despite her apparent state of dormancy, Sydney throws the entire company of British vacationers staying at the hotel into disarray by attracting a great many suitors, male and female, while remaining indifferent, appearing to be 'subject to a deplorable kind of paralysis' herself (p. 12). Ellmann quite rightly draws a parallel between Sydney's 'strange anaesthesia' and Lois Farquar, the protagonist of Bowen's second novel *The Last September*. Both girls, she maintains, are unable to 'work [themselves] up into the passion traditionally required of a heroine'.[24] Placing such inability within the overall structure of their respective narrative contexts, and within her own psychoanalytic interpretive perspective, Ellmann infers from this that these, Bowen's first two novels, do not so much 'lack a *subject* of desire' as they 'question the very possibility of a desiring subject'.[25] Andrew Bennett and Nicholas Royle similarly point to the disconcerting effects of Sydney's 'stillness', her 'interior quietness' and the pervasive atmosphere of 'abeyance' of the novel which, in their view, presents a 'dissolution of writing in a dissolution of thought'.[26] Underlining what I have suggested above regarding Bowen's insistence on the 'continuity between living and writing', they foreground the ways in which such a 'dissolution' of writing in thought in the first place involves a 'dissolution of the boundaries between so-called people in real life and characters in fiction'.[27] (This line of argument will, in the course of their fascinating reading of Bowen's novelistic *oeuvre*, extend to include the 'dissolution of the novel' as such.)

While this is clearly not her immediate intention, Ellmann's view on Sydney's and Lois's 'stillness', on the operation of their characters as topoi of abeyance, allows us to see the function of the adolescent figure as, emphatically, *not* a subject of desire, but as a site of ambivalence or a structure of feeling and as such as something that ultimately remains 'incalculable', defying explanation and/or articulation. Lois's anxiety, when overhearing a conversation between her aunt Myra and a friend talking about her in the next room adequately reveals both the power of language in defining meaning and being and Bowen's 'dark horse' characters' defiance of such power:

> But when Mrs Montmorency came to: 'Lois is very –' she was afraid suddenly. She had a panic. She didn't want to know what she was, she couldn't bear to: knowledge of this would stop, seal, finish one. Was she now to be clapped down under an adjective, to crawl round lifelong inside some quality like a fly in a tumbler?[28]

The figure of the adolescent 'moving in a blur of potentialities' structures but does not carry meaning and actively resists finalisation. Bowen articulates this in a comment on the protagonist of what is perhaps her best-known novel, Portia Quayne in *The Death of the Heart* (1938):

> I have heard [*The Death of the Heart*], for instance, called a tragedy of adolescence. I never thought of it that way when I wrote it and I must say I still don't see it in that way now. The one adolescent character in it, the young girl Portia seems to me to be less tragic than the others. She at least, has a hope, and she hasn't atrophied. The book is really . . . a tragedy of atrophy, not of *death so much as of death sleep* . . . And the function of Portia in the story is to be the awake one, in a sense therefore she was a required character. She imparts meaning rather than carries meaning.[29]

As a similarly functional textual object, the figure of Sydney evokes rather than produces a response from other characters as much as from the novel's readers. She obtains, in short, as an aesthetic object under which humans can be assembled.

This is confirmed in Bowen's observations in 'Out of a Book' about her own childhood reading, that is that 'characters in the books gave prototypes under which, for evermore, to assemble all living people'.[30] As we have seen, Bowen considered figures and characters in books at once 'more convincing, more authoritative as humans' and, furthermore, in their incalculability and inexplicability, infinitely more compelling than actual human beings. Marking the constitutive or creative, if not the *poietic* power of fictional characters, these reflections suggest that it is not the possibility of a 'desiring subject' so much as the viability and/or desirability of subjectivity per se, that is at stake in our encounter with the figuration of adolescence qua aesthetic object.

Bowen's writings point up the operation of what Kristeva defines as the open structure of the novel as a site of imagination and inscription: an 'adolescent economy of writing', in which everything is possible, nothing ever fully to be completed, a textual/aesthetic realm of indeterminacy. Instead of adopting this container model of the novel, as a space somehow already in existence but always and ever ready to be newly inscribed, I prefer to approach novelistic writing as a specific kind of assemblage, in the sense suggested by Gilles Deleuze and Félix Guattari, in their opening comments on (and in) their book, *A Thousand Plateaus: Capitalism and Schizophrenia* (2003). Generally speaking, an assemblage is any number of things (animate and inanimate, real and imaginary, material and immaterial) gathered into a single context. As such, it can bring about any number of effects – aesthetic, productive, destructive, consumptive and so on. A book equally constitutes such an assemblage with, potentially, any number of effects:

> In a book, as in all things, there are lines of articulation or segmentarity, strata and territories; but also lines of flight, movements of deterritorialisation and destratification. Comparative rates of flow on these lines produce phenomena of relative slowness and viscosity, or, on the contrary, of acceleration and rupture. All this, lines and measurable speeds constitutes an assemblage. A book is an assemblage of this kind, and as such is unattributable. It is a multiplicity – but we don't know yet what the multiple entails when it is no longer attributed, that is, after it has been elevated to the status of the substantive.[31]

So described, the book is an untidy mixture of parts or pieces, a 'blur of potentialities' in its own right, which is capable of producing a variety of effects, rather than a tightly organised and coherent whole generating one particular (set of) meaning/s. Lacking overall organisation, an assemblage can attract and incorporate all sorts of disparate elements, so that a book, qua assemblage, can itself enter into new assemblages (with readers, other books, bookstores and so on).

Bowen's novels, in and of themselves assemblages of facts and fictions, incorporating disparate elements from both so-called real life and from the imaginary domain in which the author learned to dwell from an early age onwards, grant a privileged position to the indeterminate, the in-between space, the 'dark horse' figure of the adolescent. Taken as not so much a character type – or even a prototype – but as a distinct element in an assemblage with which we as readers forge our own connections with an aesthetic object that affects us in any variety of ways, but also, if not primarily, on a visceral level (obnoxiousness clings, sticks, unconsciously), the obnoxious adolescent operates as a key and, undeniably, as a creative force or function in the Bowenesque novelistic assemblage.

As a structure of feeling, a site or locus of attraction-cum-unpleasure, the adolescent in Bowen's novels, we have seen, evokes decidedly contradictory and not always altogether positive critical responses. As a disturbing, unwieldy element in a range of different narrative contexts such responses to the figuration of the obnoxious are neither surprising nor to be deplored let alone 'rectified' or 'corrected'. After all, a book is a 'multiplicity' and as such enables, like all other things, 'lines of flight, movements of deterritorialisation and destratification' that can provoke any number of responses, produce any number of effects. The beauty of an assemblage is that it can and will always open up to new possibilities, newly 'emergent properties'.

Thus writes Jane Bennett, in an altogether different context, about assemblages:

> Ad hoc groupings of diverse elements, of vibrant materials of all sorts. Assemblages are living, throbbing confederations that are able to function despite the persistent presence of energies that confound them from within ... assemblages are not governed by any central head: no one materiality or type of material has sufficient competence to determine consistently the trajectory or impact of the group. The effects generated by an assemblage are, rather, emergent properties.[32]

Bennett's project, obviously, is very different from what I am trying to think about in this essay. Nonetheless, I believe that her supposition of the *agency* of assemblages, her proposal of *material* agency in order to counter the human exceptionalism that denies agency to anything or anyone not so defined is helpful to approach the agency of the character of the adolescent as a non-human yet material force in the open structure of novelistic discourse. What I have been trying to get at in the preceding paragraphs is a notion or a conception of the novelistic character as not so much a copy of a human being or a textual effect that resembles a human being, but rather as an element in an ad hoc shifting configuration, a force field or an assemblage, whose expressive actualisation is affective and, hence, ultimately aesthetic in nature.

Nowhere is this more clear than in Bowen's final novel, *Eva Trout, or Changing Scenes* (1968), with its eponymous heroine as the Ur-model of many, if not all, of her obnoxious predecessors, the disparate assemblage of other wayward children and adolescent girls that space constraints, alas, do not allow me to discuss. Eva Trout, orphaned and thus at large in the world, is described as 'larger than life', and remains, in the words of Victoria Glendinning, 'largely unexplained'.[33] Dismissed in 1981 by Hermione Lee as an 'illustration of Elizabeth Bowen's late *malaise*' and as an 'unfocussed and bizarre conclusion to her *opus*', *Eva Trout*, in the eyes of Patricia Craig, proved that at the end of her writing career Bowen had 'let her mannered manner run away with her', while the novel's 'formidable' heroine represents to her an 'impossibly inflated version of the Bowen destructive innocent'.[34]

Several other of Bowen's critics, including Ellmann, Bennett and Royle, and myself, have offered different, if not necessarily more reassuring assessments of the novel and the figure of its 'amazing, gawkish and overgrown' heroine.[35] Such critical dismissals as Lee's and Craig's nonetheless testify to the disconcerting effects of both *Eva Trout*'s protagonist and the author's prose and furthermore expose the novel's expressive power as an assemblage whose effects are 'emergent properties', in which the 'monstrous' adolescent figure functions as 'vibrant material', as an 'element' with agentic power, rather than as a character-agent resembling a human being.

To be sure, Eva Trout is not a character with a recognisable 'interiority'; she is not a subject endowed with thoughts or feelings, but exists, or comes into existence, exclusively in her encounters with others – that is other characters (whose thoughts and feelings we, as readers, do in fact share) and every single one of whom she leaves profoundly affected. As Henry, the young, precocious vicar's son, points out to her:

> You know, Eva . . . you leave few lives unscathed. Or at least, unchanged . . . Ethically, perhaps, you're a Typhoid Mary. You plunge people's ideas into deep confusion . . . You roll around like some blind indeflectible planet. *Sauve qui peut*, those who are in your course.[36]

To be sure, these are the words of a character who actually *likes* Eva and who is willing to participate in the staged event of their marriage at the end of the novel – an event that, even as a stage-act, is never realised, because Eva's adopted son Jeremy shoots her before the pair can embark on the train that is supposed to take them on their honeymoon. Henry, young and 'emergent' in his own right, is interested in Eva or, rather, in how she makes him feel, a site of experience as a singular structure of feeling that is, as such, primarily aesthetic in nature.

Aesthetic experience, which need not be 'good', let alone edifying or ethical, as Henry's gloss on Eva's being makes brilliantly clear, has to do with the way we feel in response to an object. Aesthetics engages affect and singularity because it is preverbal, embodied, visceral and comes before cognition. Aesthetic experience is thus not so much subjective as it draws the subject out of her/himself.

The aesthetic encounter, in Stephen Shaviro's words, is an 'event, a process, rather than a condition and a state' and, what is more, particularly relevant to what I am suggesting here: '[a]esthetic experience is a kind of *communication without communion* and *without consensus*.'[37]

As an element within the textual assemblage, a textual object in the 'throbbing confederation' of novelistic discourse, the figure of the adolescent in Bowen functions as a lure that draws us out, without our consensus, without communication and without communion. It remains disinterested in us, and our only interest lies in how it makes us feel. In aesthetic contemplation, Shaviro explains, 'I don't *have* particular feelings, so much as my very existence is suspended upon these feelings.'[38] As a figuration of openness, incompleteness, unfinishedness or even of unfinishability – after all, the textual adolescent never grows up, never leaves the space of in-betweenness behind – the adolescent figure lures us as a 'locus of all possibilities', of indeterminacy, of not-yet-being, and thus, I would say, as a figure of hope. As an aesthetic object, however, the unruly figuration in the novelistic assemblage animates us with feelings upon which our existence is suspended, feelings that as subjects we cannot ultimately outlive, and thus also makes us consciously aware of the very *im*possibility of subjectivity, of being (anything-in-particular) as a state or condition per se. To cite Shaviro one more time: '[t]he subject is solicited by the feelings that comprise it; it only comes to be through those feelings. It is not a substance, but a process. And this process is not usually conscious; it only becomes so under exceptional circumstances.'[39]

This, I submit in conclusion, is what happens in the experience of our aesthetic encounter with the figure of Bowen's obnoxious, queer adolescents. The figure's utter ambivalence lies not so much in its sexual ambiguity – although this is clearly a central and undeniable aspect of both its attraction and its repulsiveness – but in its operation as a structure of feeling, as a creative agent, animating us with feelings that we have not had before (and will not have again, at least not in exactly the same way). In this experience of becoming, of becoming otherwise, we are at the same time forced to reflect on the instability, the perishability, the factual impossibility of a stable, sustainable subjectivity as such – that is to say, and to be more precise, of our own subjectivity. The unbecoming operations of the adolescent figure do not leave us unaffected and, inscribed in the open structure of novelistic discourse, provide us with the exceptional circumstances under which we become conscious of this process. An obnoxious creature indeed.

Notes

1. This article is reproduced with the permission of *Genders* where it first appeared (1.2 (2016): n.p.).
2. Elizabeth Bowen, *Pictures and Conversations* (London: Penguin, 1975), p. 53. The title *Pictures and Conversations* is drawn from the first page of Lewis Carroll's *Alice's Adventures in Wonderland*, whose 'play of sense and nonsense' invites Deleuze to call Carroll's world a 'chaos-cosmos' or 'chaosmos' (Gilles Deleuze, *The Logic of Sense*, ed. Constantin V. Boundas, trans. Mark Lester with Charles Stivale (New York: Columbia University Press, 1990), p. xiii).
3. Elizabeth Bowen, 'Out of a Book', in *The Mulberry Tree: The Writings of Elizabeth Bowen*, ed. Hermione Lee (San Diego, New York and London: Harcourt Brace Jovanovich, 1985), p. 48, p. 49.
4. Ibid. p. 49. I am borrowing and slightly distorting Raymond Williams's influential concept 'structures of feeling' to foreground the activity of reading as a formative process, as an emergent event that always takes place in a specific present. Williams introduced the term to identify 'changes of presence' in society as it is lived, and as distinct from already formed institutions and ideological formations. Structures of feeling, he writes, may be 'emergent or pre-emergent, [but] they do not have to await definition, classification, or rationalisation before they exert palpable pressures and set effective limits on experience and on action.' See Raymond Williams, 'Structures of Feeling', *Marxism and Literature* (Oxford: Oxford University Press, 1977), p. 132. Both these key inflections of the term shed light on Bowen's complex investments in the phenomenon of adolescence and at the same time help us account for the uneasy and contradictory critical reception of her work.
5. Bowen, 'Out of a Book,' p. 49; Bowen, *Pictures and Conversations*, pp. 58–9 (original emphasis).
6. Bowen, 'Out of a Book', p. 49.
7. Bowen, *Pictures and Conversations*, p. 58.
8. Ibid.
9. Ibid. p. 60.
10. Bowen, 'Out of a Book', p. 51.
11. Douglas Hewitt, *English Fiction of the Early Modern Period* (London: Longman, 1988), pp. 196–7.
12. Maud Ellmann, *Elizabeth Bowen: The Shadow Across the Page* (Edinburgh: Edinburgh University Press, 2003), p. x.
13. Ibid. p. xi.
14. Ibid. p. x.
15. Ibid.
16. Hermione Lee, *Elizabeth Bowen: An Estimation* (London: Vintage, 1981), p. 58.

17. Elsewhere, I make a crucial theoretical difference between feeling and affect, especially in relation to visual forms of art; see, for example, *A Violent Embrace: Art and Aesthetics after Representation* (Hanover, NH: University Press of New England, 2014). In order to allow for the aesthetic productivity of precisely the ambivalence characterising both adolescence and obnoxiousness in a literary and narrative context, I here take Sianne Ngai's lead in assuming that the difference between them is a 'modal difference of intensity or degree, rather than a formal difference of quality or kind'. See Sianne Ngai, *Ugly Feelings* (Cambridge, MA: Harvard University Press, 2005), p. 27.
18. See Adrienne Rich, 'Compulsive Heterosexuality and Lesbian Existence', *Desire: The Politics of Sexuality*, ed. Ann Snitow, Christine Stansell and Sharon Thompson (London: Virago, 1984), pp. 212–41; Judith Butler, *Gender Trouble: Feminism and the Subversion of Identity* (New York and London: Routledge, 1990), p. 5.
19. See, for instance, Jeffrey Weeks, *Sexuality*, 3rd edn (New York and London: Routledge, 2010); see Sigmund Freud, *On Sexuality: Three Essays on Sexuality*, trans. and ed. James Strachey (Harmondsworth: Penguin, 1953); Erik Erikson, *Identity: Youth and Crisis* (London: Faber & Faber, 1968); see Michel Foucault, *The History of Sexuality*, vol. 1, trans. Robert Hurley (New York: Vintage, 1990).
20. Julia Kristeva, 'The Adolescent Novel', *Abjection, Melancholia, and Love: The Work of Julia Kristeva*, ed. John Fletcher and Andrew Benjamin (London and New York: Routledge, 1990), p. 5.
21. Ibid. p. 11.
22. Ibid. p. 14.
23. Elizabeth Bowen, *The Hotel* (1927; Harmondsworth: Penguin, 1984), p. 11. Hereafter cited parenthetically as *TH*.
24. Ellmann, *The Shadow Across the Page*, p. 141.
25. Ibid. p. 71.
26. Andrew Bennett and Nicholas Royle, *Elizabeth Bowen and the Dissolution of the Novel* (Basingstoke: Palgrave, 1995), p. 2.
27. Ibid. p. 3.
28. Elizabeth Bowen, *The Last September* (1929; New York: Random House/Anchor, 2000), p. 83.
29. Elizabeth Bowen, 'Interview with Jocelyn Brooke', broadcast 3 October 1950, MS (Harry Ransom Humanities Research Centre, University of Texas at Austin).
30. Bowen, 'Out of a Book', p. 51.
31. Gilles Deleuze and Félix Guattari, *A Thousand Plateaus: Capitalism and Schizophrenia*, trans. Brian Massumi (Minneapolis: University of Minnesota Press, 2003), pp. 3–4.
32. Jane Bennett, *Vibrant Matter: A Political Ecology of Things* (Durham, NC and London: Duke University Press, 2010), p. 24.

33. Victoria Glendinning, *Elizabeth Bowen: Portrait of Writer* (Harmondsworth: Penguin, 1977), p. 225.
34. Lee, *Elizabeth Bowen*, p. 206; Patricia Craig, *Elizabeth Bowen* (Harmondsworth: Penguin, 1986), p. 135.
35. Bennett and Royle, *Elizabeth Bowen and the Dissolution of the Novel*, p. 140.
36. Elizabeth Bowen, *Eva Trout, or Changing Scenes* (1968; New York: Random House/Anchor, 2003), pp. 196–7.
37. Steven Shaviro, *Without Criteria: Kant, Whitehead, Deleuze, and Aesthetics* (Cambridge, MA: MIT Press, 2009), p. 4, p. 6 (original emphasis).
38. Ibid. p. 13 (original emphasis).
39. Ibid. p. 12.

Chapter 5

Tender Ties: Elizabeth Bowen and Habit

Ulrika Maude

Portia, the orphaned and unnervingly impassive adolescent protagonist of Elizabeth Bowen's *The Death of the Heart* (1938), has spent her early life on the Continent in hotels 'before the season, when the funicular was not working yet'.[1] More recently, she has been living with her half-brother Thomas and his wife Anna in London. Shunted off to stay at Waikiki, the Hawaiian-sounding house of Anna's erstwhile governess Mrs Heccomb in Seale-on-Sea in Kent, Portia reflects on her adoptive London home, observing '*I am not there*':

> She began to go round, in little circles, things that at least her senses had loved – her bed, with the lamp turned on on winter mornings, the rug in Thomas's study, the chest carved with angels out there on the landing, the waxen oilcloth down there in Matchett's room. Only in a house one has learnt to be lonely does one have this solicitude for *things*. One's relation to them, the daily seeing or touching, begins to become love, and to lay one open to pain.

The memory of the London house seems to reside in Portia's eyes and skin and nerve endings, in 'the daily seeing or touching', in pre-reflective experiences that dissolve any clear demarcation between object and self. The salving memory of a house in which Portia feels herself to have been, even so, hardly at home, resides not in her yearning for the company of its inhabitants, but in the everyday objects that form Portia's habits. '[W]hen one remembers habit it seems to have been happiness', the narrator observes: 'Habit is not mere subjugation, it is a tender tie' (p. 139).

In this essay, I want to investigate the 'tender ties' of habit in Bowen's writing, and to suggest that an appreciation of the functions and mechanism of habit is key for an understanding of Bowen's work.

Furthermore, I will argue that in making the loss of and therefore desire for the habitual central, Bowen was drawing both from cultural and from more directly personal experience, for in cultural and political terms, habit was a luxury that had become increasingly and indeed violently compromised for the Anglo-Irish during Bowen's lifetime. Her 'Irish' novels *The Last September* (1929) and *A World of Love* (1955) record most clearly the predicament of a class that is about to lose, or has already lost, its status and traditions with the inauguration of the Irish Free State in 1922, but that therefore clings, more and more desperately, to residual habits. But the question of habit – habit as a problem, a dilemma even – was also highly personal for Bowen. After losing her father to mental illness at the age of six, she lived with her mother in various boarding houses in Kent. When her mother died some seven years later, Bowen was left even more seriously homeless and adrift, and was condemned to an adolescence spent boarding in schools and with relatives. What began as the life of an outsider, born in Ireland without being of Irish ancestry, was perpetuated by the incessant travelling Bowen experienced with her mother, and her subsequent years in boarding schools and the houses of relatives. Thereafter, Bowen spent much of her adult life travelling between England and Ireland, experiencing the radical displacement resulting from the bombing of her London home in the Second World War and undertaking frequent, almost compulsive international trips, especially from the early 1950s onwards. For someone so often and so much on the move, habits were not necessarily a habit: hers was a life in perpetual motion and in near-constant flux.

Habits, therefore, are seldom transparent in Bowen's writing, which, as critics have acknowledged, focuses distinctively on the things that go to make up one's habits and one's habitual space. The habit-forming effects of spaces and of things are even emphasised in Bowen's account of her own practice of writing. In the 1949 preface to her first collection of short stories *Encounters* (1923), for example, Bowen recalls the experience of writing the stories in terms of 'that first uncanny complicity with one's physical surroundings', commenting on the 'objects, sounds, colours and lights-and-shades comprehensively known as "the writing-table"'. What Bowen stresses are '[t]he room, the position of the window, the convulsive and anxious grating of my chair on the board floor', all of which were 'hyper-significant to me'.[2] The 'tables, chairs, lamps' of Bowen's writing practice themselves mark the extent to which the habit of the quotidian is a luxury, a privilege.[3] Habit in Bowen's writing is a way of holding oneself together; it constitutes what might even be termed a minimal ontology. The 'habits, desire, and ruling trends of the inner person', Bowen comments in a 1947 essay for *Vogue* magazine, are 'the real mysteries': they 'work within one, make one, in fact, *are* one', she remarks.[4]

Habit

Conventionally conceived, habit presents a challenge to our received understanding of what it is to be human because it seems to entail an absence of reflection, agency and intentionality, to constitute an alienation from the self, and to be closer to a form of automatism. Habit appears therefore to be antithetical to what we value in ourselves: critical reflection, intentional actions and an Aristotelian capacity for wonder. For this reason, habit features prominently in the work of philosophers such as Immanuel Kant and Friedrich Hegel, who tend to view it with deep suspicion. But there is an alternative line of thinking that can be traced back at least to the work of Aristotle and that finds perhaps its fullest articulation in the nineteenth-century French philosopher, Félix Ravaisson, whose 1838 essay, *Of Habit*, influenced prominent modernist and later twentieth-century writers and thinkers such as Henri Bergson, Marcel Proust, Maurice Merleau-Ponty, Paul Ricoeur and Gilles Deleuze.

The noun 'habit' comes to the English language from the Old French, 'habit' or 'abit', which in turn originates in the Latin noun 'habitus', from the verb 'habere', to have – or in its reflexive form, 'to be constituted; to be'. The noun therefore seems to suggest that habits contain something essential to subjective experience – to suggest, even, that habits are *what we are*.[5] In his extended essay, *Of Habit*, Ravaisson's analysis seems to accord with this etymology. His book advances one of the most sophisticated and detailed analyses of habit, steering a path between materialism and idealism. Ravaisson divides habits into two main groups: firstly, there are the habits that originate in an intentional act, such as learning to play a musical instrument or to speak a foreign language, to practise certain sports or to dance – actions to which we may dedicate considerable attention and effort. Secondly, there are the habits that originate in 'passivity', in which the organism is bombarded by stimuli, to which it then habituates itself and gradually begins to crave. Devoid of intentionality, this second kind of habit constitutes an addiction. However, intentional habits – Ravaisson's primary concern – are formed as 'an idea that gradually naturalizes, an action that, as a result of repetition, imperceptibly moves from the understanding and the will to nature'.⁶ What originates in effort becomes, by insensible degree, second nature, like an instinct that paradoxically has been learned. Habit, in this analysis, bridges the gap between will or consciousness on the one hand and matter and the automated functions of the body on the other, forming a kind of complex ontology in which virtually everything integral to the subject can be traced back to it. In this respect, Ravaisson's thinking radically departs from the philosophical understanding of habit as 'an obstacle to knowledge'.⁷ Instead, his theory forges a connection between will and habit as an aspect of the connection between will and nature. Following Aristotle, Ravaisson argues that '[h]abit is an acquired nature, a *second nature* that has its ultimate ground in primitive nature'.⁸ Becoming second nature, habit takes the place of instinctual behaviour, which in humans has all but been lost.

For Ravaisson, habit is a source of grace as well as of addiction: it results in ease, facility and power, and can even produce exceptional physical elegance, beauty and style. But it is also conceived of in terms of the machinic and at times in terms of pathological repetition, characterised by '[i]nflammations, spasms, convulsions', which make 'regular reappearances' without any 'determining cause in the material of the organism'.⁹ For Ravaisson, chronic illness is a habit, and his essay draws substantially from medical textbooks of his time. As he argues, '[a] fever that has come by chance to manifest itself in regular bouts tends to convert itself into periodic affection' such that 'the periodicity becomes essential to it'.¹⁰

Writing some fifty years after Ravaisson, William James argues in *The Principles of Psychology* (1890) that habit reveals both the weakness and the strength inherent in organisms, which yield to outside forces but are not broken by them. This is particularly evident in nervous tissue, James argues, which is remarkable for its plasticity. For James, the effect of habit on the organism can be linked to the effect of habitual actions on inanimate objects. Quoting the nineteenth-century philosopher of sensibility, laughter and habit Leon Dumont, James offers a number of positive examples of the effects of habit on objects, including the 'sounds of a violin', which 'improve by use in the hands of an able artist', or a lock, which may initially feel stiff and awkward to open but adapts and improves with use. These effects of habit are likened to sensory impressions in the nervous system, the plasticity of which is epitomised by the fact that in the brain, 'currents pouring in from the sense-organs make with extreme facility paths which do not easily disappear'.¹¹ James argues that habits, like other nervous events, are 'mechanically, nothing but a reflex discharge; and its anatomical substratum must be a path in the system'. For James, the most complex habits are 'nothing but *concatenated* discharges in the nerve-centres, due to the presence there of systems of reflex paths'.[12]

In its inherently material quality, habit for James is not simply attributable to living beings, as his examples of the violin and the lock attest. Musical instruments that have once belonged to great masters, for instance, are invaluable because they seem to bear, in their molecular structure, their very material constitution, the traces of their previous playing. Objects, then, also have their habits – or rather, they contain and record the habits of their users, as if they were extensions of the owners' central nervous systems which have themselves been engraved in turn by the imprints of their objects.

In an extended essay on Marcel Proust from 1931, Samuel Beckett analyses habit in the great French modernist writer in terms that endow it with a similar material grounding to that in James's thinking. For Beckett, habit is 'a compromise effected between the individual and his environment', or between the individual and his or her particular 'organic eccentricities'.[13] Habit 'consists in a perpetual adjustment and readjustment of our organic sensibility to the conditions of its worlds', he argues.[14] But Beckett conceives of habit in exceedingly negative terms: it 'drugs those handmaidens of perception whose co-operation is not absolutely essential'; it stunts our perceptions, since the 'creature of habit turns aside from the object that cannot be made to correspond with one or other of his intellectual prejudices'.[15] Habit, he remarks caustically, organises thought on 'labour-saving principles'.[16] And yet, although Beckett's early theorising of habit in his reading of Proust has profoundly negative overtones, it is often treated in his own writing in a much more sensitive, even fond way – one might think of Winnie's ritualistic laying out of the contents of her handbag in *Happy Days* (1961), for example, or of Molloy's intricately organised and regularly undertaken act of sucking stones in the *Trilogy* (1951): it is this longing for habit, this habit-forming longing, that has a particular resonance with the work of Beckett's Anglo-Irish contemporary, Bowen.

Habitus

From the outset, Bowen's writing devotes much attention and a great deal of care to the habits of her characters and to the nature of their habituatedness and their general habitus. At the beginning of *To the*

North (1932), for example, Cecilia returns to her house in St John's Wood in London after a train trip to Italy. '[N]ot knowing where to begin', she inspects the house, registering objects that are 'out of place' as the unfamiliarity and the habit-forming familiarity of the room gradually merge:

> Cecilia, her senses still running ahead from the speed of the journey, looked round. The drawing-room, still clearly seen as though strange, but already misting across with her sense of her life here, was exceedingly dear to her: two or three things, she noticed, were in the wrong place.[17]

As she looks around the uncannily familiar room, her eyes gaze over 'a whole array of dear objects, sentimental and brittle' on the mantelpiece. The sentimental objects have a prosthetic function: they embody Cecilia's past life and habit and, as the word 'brittle' suggests, delicately but tenuously succeed for a moment in making it whole. 'In these first few glances', we learn, Cecilia 'seemed to visit herself' (p. 20). As she returns to her home, in other words, she gradually begins to coincide with, to re-habituate herself to, the person that has earlier inhabited this space. Habits allow for the (re-)formation of an identity that has become dissipated.

As Cecilia's return home suggests, the relationship with inanimate objects allows for a habitual connection to be forged between what is present and that which is absent. In a 1958 essay on Bowen's Court, the Irish home that had been owned by her family since the late eighteenth century, Bowen records her relationship to her family's Big House. Sold in 1959 to a local famer, the house was demolished in 1961, and in the essay Bowen is already writing elegiacally of the house and of the way that the things of it offer her a direct link with people who are no longer there:

> ... between those who were here and me there is a physical link, forged of touch and sight – a matter of handling the same door knobs, mounting the same stairs, looking out at the same scene through the same windows.[18]

In this passage, habit transgresses individual experience and acquires a historical dimension. It constitutes a tender transgenerational tie that in its effects seems to exceed and surpass both blood and heritage. Experience is encoded in the nerve-endings of each generation through shared sensuous experience, transmitted through tactile objects or visual impressions afforded by the house itself. In Bowen's writing, the habits associated with the spaces that one inhabits result in a fond transgenerational haunting.

As this suggests, historical continuity is itself a crucial dimension of Bowen's work of habit, her habitus, so to speak, and in this respect it is the historical discontinuity of early twentieth-century Ireland that produces both a crisis in and a near-obsession with habit in Bowen's work. The problem is perhaps most clearly articulated in Bowen's two 'Irish' novels, *The Last September* and *A World of Love*. Set in September 1920 during the Irish War of Independence, Bowen's second novel, *The Last September*, was 'nearest my heart', as she put it.[19] The novel stages the life of Lord and Lady Naylor and their niece and heir, Lois Farquar, along with the numerous visitors to their Big House, Danielstown. The Naylors and their visitors play tennis, hold tea parties and dances, and wander around the gardens, while the Black and Tans patrol the countryside and Irish rebels lurk in ambush and store guns nearby. The key events of the narrative occur off-stage, and what is foregrounded instead, throughout the text, is the Naylors' habit, custom, wont. For this is a novel not of 'clearly discernible climaxes', but of manners and of habits.[20] What sustains the Anglo-Irish – whose life is already an afterlife – is no longer bloodlines (Lord and Lady Naylor have no children of their own) or the guarantee of enduring political and financial privilege, but a set of habits and customs that affirms them as a class and as a people. The unifying centre of habit and custom is Danielstown, which Maud Ellmann has referred to as the novel's 'central consciousness', as if the house itself contained and perpetuated the habits of its previous inhabitants.[21] That life in Danielstown is already an afterlife, and that the Anglo-Irish Ascendancy, by the 1920s, was 'a ghost only' is epitomised in the house itself, not least in its coldly staring 'window sockets' which anticipate its final annihilation.[22] The novel's ghost, Laura, the dead mother of Lois, haunts the text by inhabiting Lois's habitus: her expressions, her gestures and her manner. Lois's habits establish her as 'the ever-living Laura' (p. 80) and for Mrs Montmorency the very 'image of Laura' (p. 8). The novel concerns the ways in which such transgenerational haunting can sustain the habits of a lost era.

A World of Love is also dominated by a ghost, haunted as it is by the memory of Guy, the cousin of Lady Antonia, who has fallen in the war. The novel's protagonist, Jane, is an adolescent whose deceased mother, Lilia, was once Guy's lover. In a striking evocation of the way the dead are forgotten, de-habituated, the narrator informs us that '[l]ife works to dispossess the dead, to dislodge and oust them. Their places fill themselves up; later people come in; all the room is wanted.'[23] And yet this is far from true of Guy, whose curiously forceful phantasmatic presence permeates the text. Jane receives an invitation to visit the 'haunted' Lady Latterly in her 'unusually banal Irish castle', which, like its owner's name, seems to be lodged in the past (p. 57). At dinner, there is an empty place at the table, which in the guests' eyes, comes to be occupied by the ghostly Guy: 'Now more than living, this face had acquired a brightened cast of its own from the semi-darkness, from which it looked out with easy conviction of being recognized ... Invisibly concentrated around him was all the time he had ever breathed: his todays, his yesterdays, his anticipated tomorrows' (pp. 68–9). Guy's presence at the party is portrayed as a matter of perceptual habit: 'his death seemed ... an invented story ... it was unlike him to be dead' (pp. 44–5). He is, as his ghost anticipates, recognised and more intensely present at the party than the living, as is acknowledged in the 'recoil of the others' and 'the reflection of crisis in each face' (p. 65). The dead Guy continues to inhabit Castle Trent, the Big House of the novel, because its '[o]bstinate rememberers of the dead seem to queer themselves or show some signs of a malady; in part they come to share the dead's isolation, which it is not in their power to break down' (p. 44). When mourning becomes habitual, Bowen powerfully suggests, it transforms into melancholia, the condition in which we share our habitation with those who have departed.

In Bowen's Second World War novel, *The Heat of the Day* (1949), something like a reversal of this habituation occurs when Roderick visits his mother Stella in her rented flat with its alien furniture. While Roderick reckons that the place doesn't 'look like home', he nevertheless acknowledges that '[s]omewhere between these chairs and tables must run the spoor of habit, could one but pick it up.'[24] The sofa he sits on, for instance, seems to be 'without environment': 'it might have been some derelict piece of furniture exposed on a pavement after an air raid or washed up by a flood on some unknown shore.' The visit is uncomfortable because of the very 'absence of every inanimate thing they had in common', and we learn that 'no benevolence came to [the meeting] from surrounding things'. The narrator goes on to stress the importance of the familiar, of the habitual, in intimacy, commenting that it is 'the music of the familiar that is awaited, on such occasions, with most hope; love dreads being isolated, being left to speak in a void.' 'Even lovers can feel this', the narrator goes on: 'how many passions have not been daunted by the hotel room?' (p. 55).

It is for this reason, perhaps, that it is for Stella her repeated return with Robert to the flat that gives the place its significance:

> Repetition gave increasing magic to those returns – to stepping over and leaving disregarded letters on her doormat, to the hasty blacking-out of windows already black with night, to the blind course back through the dark in which Robert waited till her fingers found the switch of a lamp. (p. 100)

It is as if the apartment itself were part and parcel of the relationship, and as if the habits and sensuous moments of the love affair were encoded in its very fabric. One of the armchairs, for instance, bears the imprint of Robert, the physical mark or trace of his habit, and thus suggests his continuing presence in the room. Stella instinctively looks at the empty 'armchair proper to Robert' (p. 133) while Harrison is in the kitchen preparing her a drink: the chair itself is an extension of her lover, a prosthetic marker of his absent presence and a reminder of the intrinsic impropriety of Harrison's actual, unwanted presence in the flat.

As James observed, however, habits can also have a negative effect, and in Bowen, this too, like the more fortunate associations, is imprinted on the objects that clutter and determine our lives. Stella, for instance, dislikes the part of her room which registers the memory of Harrison's first visit:

> It was imperative that she should overcome, with the unconscious aid of Roderick's presence, her aversion from that part of the room where, forced to listen to Harrison, she had been forced to sit. Even the papers, letters, among which she had rested her elbow, listening to him, seemed to be contaminated; she shrank, even, from phrases in purple type on which, in the course of the listening, her eyes had from time to time lit. (p. 57)

The objects themselves seem to have registered Harrison's abrasive presence and now bear the 'contaminated' traces of the encounter. In this way, as Elizabeth Inglesby remarks, Bowen's 'characters fasten their fears and desires' onto objects.[25] But the objects also have a hold over these emotions: they have scarred her characters, leaving their own inscriptions on the nerves and the senses. Bowen's writing seems to suggest, in line with Maurice Merleau-Ponty's thinking, that we bury our intentions in objects which, although they exist externally, exist *for us* only to the extent to which they arouse in us volitions, thoughts or emotions.[26] In Bowen's writing, objects acquire near-sentience because they have grown onto the characters: in objects are encoded the habits of thought and action, just as objects themselves have been incorporated into the very nervous constitution of her characters.

Ellmann has stressed the porousness of the characters in *The Heat of the Day*. She cites a passage in Bowen's postscript to *The Demon Lover*, in which Bowen writes about the effects of war: 'Sometimes I hardly knew where I stopped and somebody else began', she comments; 'Walls went down.'[27] As the narrator of *The Heat of the Day* puts it, war works as a 'thinning of the membrane between this and that' (*HD*, p. 195). But this thinning and the osmosis that it allows is in fact a feature of all of Bowen's writing, and it helps to explain the hypersensitivity towards objects and places that characterises her work. This is also why Bowen's attitude to objects and things is duplicitous, for while on the one hand her writing reveals 'a piety for solid things', their loss, on the other hand, affords what Ellmann calls 'an intoxicated dream of weightlessness'.[28] Bowen writes of how, during the Second World War, '[t]he violent destruction of solid things, the explosion of the illusion that prestige, power and permanence attach to bulk and weight, left all of us, equally, heady and disembodied.'[29] Losing one's possessions results in a kind of amnesia, an undoing, a release from the self. The process embodies what Sigmund Freud calls the death-drive, which Jonathan Dollimore glosses as the 'desire to *become unbound*; . . . the desire for oblivion, for a dissolution of consciousness, the irresistible desire to regress back to a state of zero tension before consciousness, before life, before effort, before lack'.[30] Losing objects, then, involves an unravelling of the self, as is starkly envisioned in Michael Haneke's film *The Seventh Continent* (1989), in which the destruction of possessions functions as the prerequisite for death. But Haneke's also unveils why we so often refrain from parting with things: both habits can be understood to be ways of preparing for what Freud refers to in 'Beyond the Pleasure Principle' (1920) as 'the aim of all life': death.

In Bowen's writing, much emphasis is in fact placed on the *wonder* of motor and sensory habits – habits that can be indicative of what, in an essay from 1968, 'Ecstasy of the Eye', Bowen refers to as 'a figure's unknowing grace'. 'One *can* stand stone-cold before a "beautiful" object', she comments: 'Ecstasy's sources are *not* always ethereal: light, air, fire, and water.' The sensation can also, she writes, 'take off' from 'chance revelations of human comeliness', from '[h]uman mystery' that is evoked in the habit-induced 'turn of a head' or in a 'smile reflected fleetingly in a mirror'.[31] In a striking evocation in *The Heat of the Day* of the gracefulness of habitual action or 'mechanical reflex', Harrison watches Stella answer the telephone in a dark room:

> In the dark she took up the receiver with the unfumbling sureness of one who habitually answers a telephone at any, even the deepest, hour of the night. Her hand would have reached its mark before her eyes opened; before her brain stirred her ear would be ready, so that the first word she heard, even the first she spoke, would be misted over by some unfinished dream. This mechanical reflex of hers to a mechanical thing suggested to Harrison, standing there aware in the other room, the first idea he had had of poetry – her life. (*HD*, p. 44)

As Andrew Bennett has pointed out, poetry, falling in love and answering the telephone congregate in this passage around what we might see as a mechanistic telephone habit.[32] In answering the telephone, Stella's graceful habit accords with Merleau-Ponty's phenomenological evocation of the body's habit-formed relationship with the world that it inhabits: 'My body has its world, or understands its world, without having to make use of my "symbolic" or "objectifying function"', Merleau-Ponty remarks.[33] It is the body's grace, its 'unfumbling sureness', as Bowen fumblingly puts it, its embodied actions set loose from any governing consciousness or thought, that are evoked in Stella's habitual act of picking up the receiver: it is a reflex or automatic action, learnt through long practice, that occurs even before the 'brain stirred'. And it is a mechanical action that also bears witness to a certain poeticity, a certain conception of what it is that goes to produce poetic language – not so much a thought-induced, calculated process of reasoning but an impulsive habit of word-formation that is largely instinctive, mechanical, gracefully reflexive.

It is when habit is lost or wrecked that things tend to disintegrate in Bowen's narratives. Thus, at one of the crisis points in *Friends and Relations* (1931), when the heretofore implicitly understood limits on family association have been disastrously breached, Lady Elfrida melodramatically 'braces herself' to 'dash in and extricate Janet and Rodney from the wreckage of habit'.[34] Less cataclysmically, in Bowen's first novel, *The Hotel* (1927), as Colonel Duperrier enters the 'isolating vastness' of the Italian Riviera's hotel lounge, he forlornly confronts the unfamiliar and friendless room with its 'groves of chairs' through which he wanders aimlessly, missing the 'tug of association and habit towards one chair.'[35] Habit in Bowen, then, can reveal itself in its absence, and it can become painfully apparent through loss. In *The Heat of the Day*, when Robert and Stella meet after a bomb has exploded close to her apartment and they have had an uncanny near-telepathic experience of one another, Stella reflects on Robert's countenance: 'To miss from his eyes, mouth, forehead the knowable unguarded play of his nature was for her, for the first time, to be made to feel its force. In the unfamiliar the familiar persisted like a ghost' (*HD*, pp. 98–9). Indeed, love itself in Bowen is often perceived as habit: 'Habit, of which passion must be wary, may all the same be the sweetest part of love' (p. 99). It is, perhaps, the paradoxical intimacy of habit that also accounts for the novel's strikingly colloquial tone. Daniel George, Bowen's editor at Cape, commented that 'unless the reader is lucky enough to coincide with [Bowen] in placing a stress on the key word of a sentence, he may be baffled completely.'[36] It is as if the novel itself demanded from the reader the appropriate Bowenesque habit of reading. And Bowen refused to change her prose, replying in a letter that 'I'd rather keep the jars, "jingles" and awkwardnesses – e.g. "seemed unseemly," "felt to falter." They do to my mind express something. In some cases I *want* the rhythm to jerk or jar – to an extent, even, which may displease the reader.'[37] In order to adopt the Bowen habit of reading, in other words, we may need to be jerked or jarred out of our own well-established reading habits. If poetry (or poetic prose) is, in part, instinctual, the proper response to it in Bowen's often jarring prose requires a relinquishing of our habitual or cosily familiar ways of reading.

Habit and (dis)comfort

For James, as for Ravaisson, habit can also become pathological, like a scar which is 'more liable to be abraded, inflamed, to suffer pain and cold, than are the neighbouring parts'.[38] Similarly, a sprained ankle is more liable to sprain or dislocate again, while each fresh attack of rheumatism, gout or catarrh leaves the organism more prone to a relapse. This is particularly true of what James calls 'functional diseases', such as 'epilepsies, neuralgias, convulsive affections' and 'insomnias'.[39] In Bowen's writing, these negative habitual experiences present themselves most prominently as disturbances in spatial configuration, in the agoraphobia and claustrophobia that figure so prominently in her work, and which in the early twentieth century were diagnosed precisely as forms of neurasthenia. Responding to the violently chaotic environment of wartime London, spaces in *The Heat of the Day* such as Stella's tiny flat in Waymouth Street or Louie's boarding-house in Chilcombe Street are notably constricted and claustrophobic. In her essay, 'London, 1940', we get a sense of Bowen's own wartime claustrophobic relationship to space, as she recalls her experiences of the Blitz: 'We *can* go underground – but for this to be any good you have to go very deep, and a number of us, fearful of being buried, prefer not to.'[40] The fear of being buried alive, even if it is not an unreasonable one under the conditions of war, is a classic symptom of claustrophobia, in which the sufferer, Benjamin Ball argued in 1879, experiences 'a panic fear of being alone in a closed space, a sensation of being in a passage getting narrower and narrower', which triggers in the sufferer a flight into open spaces.[41] As Bowen adds in her essay, 'Our own "things" – tables, chairs, lamps – give one kind of confidence to us who stay in our own paper rooms.'[42] There is, or can be, Bowen suggests, more shelter and security in the consolations of the habitual, even in rooms that are effectively made of paper, than there is in the tangible and very real safety of the underground; people like her, she seems to propose, prefer the 'protection' of familiar objects, tables, chairs and lamps. They are prepared to risk the dangers of 'paper houses' for the consolations of the quotidian and for the habit-formed comfort of the domestic space.

The character who suffers most from spatial phobias in Bowen's fiction, however, is Emmeline in *To the North*. Emmeline is presented as both claustrophobic and agoraphobic, and descriptions of the nerves and nervousness of Emmeline and other characters feature prominently in the novel. It is partly in this way, indeed, that *To the North* stages the disintegration and transformation of its protagonist's habits. Her lover's dark and oppressive London room creates a 'touch of strangeness upon her nerves' (*TN*, p. 180); in Paris she experiences an 'oppressive contraction of space' (p. 144); and in her Bloomsbury travel agency, she finds 'herself crowded in the office . . . she no longer had the power to fill her own desk' (pp. 223–4). The novel focuses on the thrills and dislocations of metropolitan life and international travel, in which various communication networks – telegrams, telephones, motorcars, trains and aeroplanes – feature prominently, reconfiguring and even disfiguring the text's temporal and spatial coordinates. As her relationship with her lover Markie finishes, and as her life in Oudenarde Road comes to an end with Cecilia's impending marriage, Emmeline takes to street-haunting:

> One day, scared by a sudden darkness over the sunshine, by an intensification of London's roar in her brain, she turned into an empty teashop and sat down, pressing the palms of her hands to a marble table ... That week her hair went darker and dull, her face white: if anyone looked at her in the streets, it was to wonder from what she was running away. Broken up like a puzzle the glittering summer lay scattered over her mind, cut into shapes of pain that had no other character. Walking the streets blindly she did not know that she thought, till a knuckle grazed on a wall, a shout as she stepped off into the traffic recalled her from depths whose darkness she had not measured. The bleeding knuckle, the angry face of a man shouting down from a lorry were like bright light flashed in her eyes: the nightmare drew back, waiting. One note held her ears through the hollow thunder of traffic: in shells of buildings the whirr of unanswered telephones. These were insistent: she put her hands to her head ... (p. 225)

Spatial phobias, like all phobias, seem to hollow out, to de-habituate, conceptual, intellectual meaning, revealing instead, as Adam Phillips has argued, the body's capacity 'to be gripped by occult meaning'.[43] Phobias tell us virtually nothing about the object of fear, 'except its supposed power to frighten'.[44] The phobic object, therefore, triggers merely paralysis or flight.[45] The nineteenth-century French architectural philosopher Julien Guadet identified agoraphobia as 'an anxiety of the body and the senses, not of the mind'.[46] To be overcome by a phobia is therefore a state of somatic possession, a loss of agency, a form of submission, which chimes with, or has itself become, a pathological habit.[47] 'It is as though the object [itself were] issuing the orders', and it is indeed space in *To the North*, 'the richest [source] of the novel's power', which becomes the carrier of agency in the text, an effect that is anticipated in the lengthy final sentence of the novel's opening paragraph, which so strikingly registers an absence of human subjects.[48] The scene prefigures Emmeline's final car ride, in which speed can be understood as a means of transgressing space, the source of the novel's fear. For the nineteenth-century neurologists Jean-Martin Charcot and George Miller Beard, in fact, both claustrophobia and agoraphobia constituted a more generalised fear of space. Both were seen as characteristically urban, middle-class and predominantly female neurasthenias, and both can be read as a failure to sustain one's habitual sense of self, either alone or in the company of other people.⁴⁹ It is as if the very disintegration and loss of habit, of familiar 'tables, chairs, lamps', ultimately deprives Emmeline of a sense of self, of solid ground, triggering the novel's final, fatal car crash.

Final habits

For Maurice Merleau-Ponty, habit reveals 'the organic relationship between subject and world, the active transcendence of consciousness, the momentum which carries it into a thing and into the world by means of its organs and instruments'.⁵⁰ Both Merleau-Ponty and James see habits, once they have been formed, as belonging to the realm of pre-reflective experience, before the separation of subject and object – before, that is, the subject's entry into an objective, or what later theorists would call 'symbolic', realm. The profound engagement with habitual objects, places and actions in Bowen attests to the prominence of a similar understanding in her work. For Bowen, as for Merleau-Ponty, objects and places are so integral to the self that they acquire near sentience and are endowed with the capacity to console, pierce or wound. Bowen's work is characterised by a porousness in which boundaries between the animate and inanimate, and between self and non-self, are tenuous and prone to collapse. As such, her work is haunted by a subjectivity and agency that insistently foregrounds the instinctive, the unreflective and the ineradicably habitual.

Notes

1. Elizabeth Bowen, *The Death of the Heart* (London: Vintage, 1998), p. 34. Hereafter cited parenthetically as *DH*.
2. Elizabeth Bowen, 'Preface' to *Encounters* (1949), in *The Mulberry Tree: Writings of Elizabeth Bowen*, ed. Hermione Lee (London: Virago, 1986), pp. 118–22 (p. 118).
3. Elizabeth Bowen, 'London, 1940' (1950), in *The Mulberry Tree*, pp. 21–5 (p. 23).
4. Elizabeth Bowen, 'A Way of Life' (1947), in *People, Places, Things: Essays by Elizabeth Bowen*, ed. Allan Hepburn (Edinburgh: Edinburgh University Press, 2008), pp. 386–91 (p. 386).
5. The word 'habit' can mean: external deportment, constitution, or appearance; habitation; bodily condition or constitution; the bodily 'system'; the outer part, surface, or external appearance of the body;

habitation, abode; mental constitution, disposition; custom, usage, use, wont; an automatic, 'mechanical' reaction to a specific situation which usually has been acquired by learning and/or repetition; 'Fashion or mode of apparel, dress' (*OED*, 'habit', n.).

6. Leandro M. Gaitán and Javier S. Castresana, 'On Habit and the Mind-Body Problem: The View of Félix Ravaisson', *Frontiers in Human Neuroscience*, 8 (2014): 1–3 (p. 1).
7. Clare Carlisle and Mark Sinclair, 'Editor's Introduction', in Félix Ravaisson, *Of Habit*, trans. Clare Carlisle and Mark Sinclair (London: Continuum, 2008), pp. 1–21 (p. 16).
8. Ravaisson, *Of Habit*, p. 59.
9. Ibid. p. 35.
10. Ibid.
11. William James, *The Principles of Psychology*, vol. I (Cambridge, MA: Harvard University Press, 1981), p. 112.
12. Ibid.
13. Samuel Beckett, *Proust and Three Dialogues with Georges Duthuit* (London: Calder, 1999), pp. 18–19.
14. Ibid. p. 28
15. Ibid. p. 20.
16. Ibid. p. 23.
17. Elizabeth Bowen, *To the North* (London: Vintage, 1999), p. 18, pp. 19–20. Hereafter cited parenthetically as *TN*.
18. Elizabeth Bowen, 'Bowen's Court' (1958), in *People, Places, Things*, pp. 140–50 (p. 148).
19. Elizabeth Bowen, 'Preface' to *The Last September* (1952), in *The Mulberry Tree*, pp. 122–6 (p. 123).
20. Susan Osborn, '"How to Measure This Unaccountable Darkness Between the Trees": The Strange Relation of Style and Meaning in *The Last September*', in *Elizabeth Bowen: New Critical Perspectives*, ed. Susan Osborn (Cork: Cork University Press, 2009), pp. 34–60 (p. 36).
21. Maud Ellmann, *Elizabeth Bowen: The Shadow Across the Page* (Edinburgh: Edinburgh University Press, 2003), p. 60.
22. Elizabeth Bowen, *Bowen's Court* (New York: Ecco, 1979), p. 430; Elizabeth Bowen, *The Last September* (London: Vintage, 1998), p. 124. Hereafter cited parenthetically as *LS*.
23. Elizabeth Bowen, *A World of Love* (London: Vintage, 1999), p. 44.
24. Elizabeth Bowen, *The Heat of the Day* (London: Vintage, 1998), p. 47, p. 52. Hereafter cited parenthetically as *HD*.
25. Elizabeth C. Inglesby, '"Expressive Objects": Elizabeth Bowen's Narrative Materialises', *Modern Fiction Studies*, 53.4 (2007): 306–33 (pp. 312–13).
26. Maurice Merleau-Ponty, *Phenomenology of Perception*, trans. Colin Smith (London: Routledge, 1994), p. 82.

27. Elizabeth Bowen, 'Postscript' to *The Demon Lover* (1945), in *The Mulberry Tree*, pp. 94–9 (p. 95).
28. Ellmann, *The Shadow Across the Page*, p. 168
29. Bowen, 'Postscript' to *The Demon Lover*, p. 95.
30. Jonathan Dollimore, 'Death and the Self', in *Rewriting the Self: Histories from the Renaissance to the Present*, ed. Roy Porter (London: Routledge), pp. 249–61 (p. 256).
31. Elizabeth Bowen, 'Ecstasy of the Eye' (1968), in *People, Places, Things*, pp. 40–1 (p. 41).
32. See Andrew Bennett, 'Elizabeth Bowen on the Telephone', below.
33. Merleau-Ponty, *Phenomenology of Perception*, pp. 140–31.
34. Elizabeth Bowen, *Friends and Relations* (London: Penguin, 1943), pp. 99–100. Hereafter cited parenthetically as *FR*.
35. Elizabeth Bowen, *The Hotel* (London: Penguin, 1987), p. 46. Hereafter cited parenthetically as *TH*.
36. Victoria Glendinning, *Elizabeth Bowen: A Portrait* (Harmondsworth: Penguin, 1985), pp. 152–3.
37. Elizabeth Bowen to Daniel George, 2 June 1948, Harry Ransom Humanities Research Center, Elizabeth Bowen Collection, box 10, folder 4. The author wishes to acknowledge the support of the C. P. Snow Fellowship she held at the HRHRC in 2010.
38. James, *The Principles of Psychology*, p. 111.
39. Ibid.
40. Bowen, 'London, 1940', p. 23.
41. Anthony Vidler, *Warped Space: Art, Architecture, and Anxiety in Modern Culture* (Cambridge, MA: MIT Press, 2001), p. 32.
42. Bowen, 'London, 1940', p. 23.
43. Adam Phillips, 'First Hates: Phobias in Theory', in *On Kissing, Tickling, and Being Bored: Psychoanalytic Essays on the Unexamined Life* (Cambridge, MA: Harvard University Press, 1993), pp. 12–26 (p. 22).
44. Ibid. p. 21.
45. Ibid. p. 19
46. Guadet, cited in Vidler, *Warped Space*, p. 35.
47. Phillips, *On Kissing*, p. 22
48. Hermione Lee, *Elizabeth Bowen: An Estimation*, rev. edn (London: Vintage, 1999), p. 73.
49. Paul Carter, *Repressed Spaces: The Poetics of Agoraphobia* (London: Reaktion, 2002), p. 33.
50. Merleau-Ponty, *Phenomenology of Perception*, p. 153.

Chapter 6

'One Is Somehow Suspended': Elizabeth Bowen, Katherine Mansfield and the Spaces in Between

Emma Short

Writing to her cousin from her room at Queen's College, London, Katherine Mansfield recounts a teacher's dismissal of her as 'a little savage from New Zealand', and thus recognises the way in which her colonial status precludes her from truly belonging either to her now-distant birthplace or to the Imperial centre of London.[1] Elizabeth Bowen's Anglo-Irish national identity is similarly hybrid. Bowen never felt that she fully belonged to either nationality, existing instead in a liminal sphere between the two. The impact of this geographical hybridity can be traced in the work of both Bowen and Mansfield: both of them demonstrate a preoccupation with spatiality, and specifically with those spaces that exist in between one location and another. Their writing is scattered with a preponderance of characters who exist primarily in these in-between spaces of everyday existence. Staircases, windows, hallways and corridors haunt the fiction of both authors, alongside the larger, more complex spaces such as the hotel that exists in between the public chaos of modernity and the private confines of the domestic. In this chapter, I sketch out a taxonomy of such spaces in Bowen and Mansfield's narratives, and in doing so trace a clear line of narrative influence from Mansfield to Bowen. Charting the persistence of in-between spaces in their work, I draw on recent postcolonial approaches to modernism to consider how their shared, complex histories of hybridity, mobility and dislocation shape and direct their fiction. Crucially, I consider the relationship between the fractured histories of Bowen and Mansfield and the focus on and exploration of women's lived experience in their work. Forging a literature of the in-between, the work of these two writers at once complicates conventional notions of home and belonging and interrogates the shifting position of women in modernity.

The striking parallels between the biographical details of Bowen and Mansfield arise in their shared histories of a colonial birthplace: each was been born into a family that formed part of the colonising tradition. Born in Dublin to Anglo-Irish parents, Bowen's affection for Ireland is clear in her personal writings, referring to it as 'this small vivid country', and as a place that 'haunts the memory'.[2] Bowen also occasionally leans towards including herself within the Irish community, seen, for example, in her affectionate criticism of Irish cooking, whereby she remarks that '*we* are bad at pastry, poor at sauces; and our coffee-making notably is abominable'.[3] Yet Bowen also felt the cultural distance between the Anglo-Irish and the Irish, and referred to them as two distinct nationalities.[4] Born in Wellington, New Zealand in 1888, Mansfield was similarly part of a colonising family that, according to her husband John Middleton Murry, 'had been in Australia and New Zealand for three generations'.[5] Mansfield was fully aware from an early age of the differences between herself and the Maori people – she was, Claire Tomalin notes, 'fascinated by the exoticism of the Maoris and happy to pretend to Maori blood herself on occasion', though this was never anything more than a knowing, if ethically problematic, performance.[6] Yet while Mansfield and Bowen openly acknowledged the differences between themselves and those native to their birthplaces, they did not identify with the English roots of their colonial tradition when, in later life, they relocated to England and to the Imperial centre of London.

Although now widely acknowledged as a key modernist writer, Mansfield was nevertheless never fully accepted by many of her modernist literary peers in the Bloomsbury group. According to Andrew Bennett, 'as a "colonial" from a family connected to commerce and as the mistress of the lower-middle-class Murry . . . Mansfield was always to remain on the fringes of this august grouping.'[7] Indeed, as Bowen herself points out, 'amid the etherealities of Bloomsbury', Mansfield 'was more than half hostile, a dark-eyed tramp'.[8] Recalling the barbed comments of Mansfield's teacher, this description of the author bears more than a trace of prejudice and thus hints at the deeply troubling sentiments that lurked beneath the surface of the Bloomsbury set. Mansfield's current and relatively central position within the modernist canon is at the very least a testament to the quality of her writing, as well as to her refusal to be professionally intimidated by such intolerance. Yet, as Anna Snaith points out, a key consequence of Mansfield's integration 'into accounts of

European, literary modernism' is 'a delay in exploration of the complexities of her colonial origins and their impact on her writing', an apparent critical blind spot when it comes to interrogating how her hybrid identity shaped her work.[9] Postcolonial readings of Mansfield's writing have begun to proliferate in recent years, though the focus of such work has primarily been her earlier stories set in New Zealand: Snaith highlights the fact that '[c]ritics have been unsure how to read a colonial background into her European-based short stories.'[10] What I suggest here is that it is precisely in those in-between spaces that one might begin to trace the impact of this colonial heritage in both Bowen's and Mansfield's works.

Unlike Mansfield, Bowen was never the victim of outright hostility, though there was nevertheless a trace of the same prejudice that Mansfield had previously faced from the Bloomsbury set, and from Virginia Woolf in particular. Woolf, who visited Bowen a number of times at Bowen's Court, her family home in County Cork, commented in a letter written in 1934 to Vanessa Bell that the house was 'merely a great stone box . . . full of decayed eighteenth-century furniture', in which Bowen 'insisted on keeping up a ramshackle kind of state, dressing for dinner and so on'.[11] Woolf's cutting remarks are particularly revealing of the prejudices of the English upper classes and an attempt to insidiously position the Anglo-Irish as outsiders. Never feeling fully at home in either Ireland or England, Bowen shared with Mansfield a sense of estrangement, which she describes as 'a cleft between my heredity and my environment'.[12] Hermione Lee refers to this 'cleft' as a 'particularly acute form of the Anglo-Irish split between confidence and ambivalence, the sense of dislocation and alienness'.[13] The split is further encapsulated by Shannon Wells-Lassagne, who describes the Anglo Irish as 'the personification and the locus of tension created by the phenomenon of Empire', a characterisation that is, she maintains, entirely attributable to their peculiar existence in between the English and Irish identities.[14] Of colonial women writers like Mansfield and Bowen, Snaith argues that 'their movement between nations parallels the lack of any stable national imaginary in their writing'.[15] Perpetually caught between countries and between identities, this instability, along with that same sense of dislocation and alienness that Lee identifies in the Anglo-Irish, seeps through the writing of both Bowen and Mansfield, manifesting in the liminal spaces that their characters pass through or in which they are momentarily suspended. In particular, it is both writers' female characters who are habitually positioned between one place and another. As Snaith points out, 'gender has always been central to the ways nations and empires are imagined into being and sustained.'[16] To attend to nationhood in Mansfield and Bowen is therefore also to attend to gender. In their fiction, the conventional bond between woman and the home – which is in itself so central to imperial narratives concerning gender and nation – is disrupted and in some cases severed entirely, replaced with the shifting, uncertain and uncanny space of the in-between. The repercussions of this disruption are at times positive – offering characters moments of liberation, sexual or otherwise – but they can also be negative, threatening and occasionally fatal. Through an examination of the in-between spaces of their work, I show how Mansfield and Bowen challenge and interrogate the position of women in early twentieth-century society.

While there are undoubtedly connections, then, between the works and lives of Bowen and Mansfield, it is important to acknowledge that influence between the two writers only flowed one way. Mansfield's death on 9 January 1923 precludes her from having read any of Bowen's writings, the first of which – a collection of short stories entitled *Encounters* – was not published until the summer of that same year. In her preface to *Early Stories* in 1951 (a collection which combined the stories of *Encounters* (1923) and *Ann Lee's* (1926)), Bowen recalls that she first read Mansfield's work soon after the completion, and crucially before the publication, of her own first collection. While she later became an avid reader of Mansfield's work, she admits that her initial response was one tinged by jealousy and a sense of competition: 'admiration and envy were shot through by a profound dismay: I thought: "If I ever am published, everybody will say I imitated her." I was right.'[17] However, Bowen's admiration for her predecessor soon overtook any dismay or envy she might have felt, and is demonstrated not least in the care and consideration she took in editing a 1957 collection of Mansfield's stories, and in the depth of analysis she bestows upon Mansfield's writing in her introduction to that same collection. Mansfield's influence is detectable in the stylistic and formal qualities of Bowen's own fiction – indeed, as Allan Hepburn observes, '[o]f all influences on Bowen's short stories, none is stronger than . . . Mansfield's', and this influence extends beyond Bowen's short stories to her novels.[18] Many of the observations Bowen makes regarding Mansfield's work could well be ascribed to her own. The 'isolated . . . claustrophobic . . . dream-fastness of a solitary person' which she argues is so well depicted in Mansfield's characters is also true of Bowen's own protagonists, such as Portia in *The Death of the Heart* (1938) and Lois in *The Last September* (1929).[19] Present too in Bowen's writing is the 'backbone' she attributes to Mansfield's stories, and the 'objectiveness', the 'quick, sharp observations' and the 'adept presentations' are all features which characterise her own novels and short stories.[20] Yet perhaps the most prominent connection between the writing of the two authors arises in their use of space – more specifically, the types of spaces in which they choose to situate the key events of their narratives.

Bowen herself was the first to admit the essential role of spatiality in her writing. In *Pictures and Conversations*, her unfinished autobiography, she remarks that 'what gives fiction its verisimilitude is its topography'.[21] Of the specific topography of her own fiction, she maintains that 'the Bowen terrain cannot be demarcated on any existing map; it is unspecific. Ireland and England, between them, contain my stories.'[22] Bowen's choice of the word 'between' is particularly pertinent here, suggesting that not only she but also her narratives exist in a strange limbo between Ireland and England. She thus locates her stories in the same in-between space that she herself occupies. Although Bowen at times comments on the importance of an 'inner landscape', on the 'recognisable world, geographically consistent' to which, she argues, any writer must have recourse, it is ultimately in the 'unfamiliar' that she finds her inspiration: she has 'thrived . . . on the changes and chances, the dislocations and . . . the contrasts which have made up so much of my life.'[23] For Bowen, then, there is a direct connection between her own disrupted national identity and the spatiality of her own writing.

Given her fascination for the spatiality of dislocation and the unfamiliar, it is unsurprising that Bowen was drawn to the prevalence of in-between spaces in Mansfield's work. For Bowen, the spaces that stand out in Mansfield's writing are those that exist between one place and another. She comments, for example, on the way in which the 'quayside, café, shop interior, tea-time terrace, or public garden' – all spaces connected by their liminality – 'stand concretely forward into life' in Mansfield's short stories.[24] These same spaces make regular appearances in Bowen's own work, such as the idyllic tea-garden in *The Hotel* (1927), 'with its lit-up lawns, its bulging lemons and oranges hanging down in the sun', or the forbidding interior of the chemist at Market Keaton in *Friends and Relations* (1931), 'a dark shop like the inside of a camera', which unnerves Lady Elfrida, making her wish 'she had not come into town at all'.[25] Critical commentary on Bowen and Mansfield has also picked up on the prevalence of the in-between in their writing. In a particularly pertinent passage from one of Mansfield's letters, the author remarks upon the unique nature of stairs, an archetypal in-between space:

> One is somehow suspended. One is on neutral ground – not in one's own world nor in a strange one. They are an almost perfect meeting place. Oh Heavens! How stairs do fascinate me when I think of it . . . People come out of themselves on stairs – they issue forth, unprotected.[26]

Indeed, Angela Smith argues that Mansfield's writings 'show an intimate knowledge of overcrossing, being suspended, sitting on strange stairs, inhabiting an in-between place, a state of liminality'.[27] Louise Edensor also notes that 'Mansfield often places characters at thresholds such as windows or on staircases', while Antony Alpers remarks that Mansfield's stories 'achieve that intricate delineation of the spaces between people'.[28] Regarding Bowen, Maud Ellmann similarly maintains that 'it is characteristic of Bowen's fiction that the narration zeroes in on liminal spaces' and, writing on Bowen's coastal narratives, Edwina Keown notes that 'Bowen was always alert to the significance of crossing-points and boundary spaces.'[29] This tendency of both authors to focus on the in-between spaces of life, and the preponderance of characters who exist neither here nor there, in a perpetual state of liminality, can be traced back to the shared colonial histories of Mansfield and Bowen. Through her short stories, Bowen recognises Mansfield as a fellow exile, as one who, like her, did not appear to belong anywhere. Commenting on Mansfield's London stories, she suggests that Mansfield lived in the city in the way that 'strangers are wont to do, in a largely self-fabricated world'.[30] That this observation is drawn from personal experience is confirmed in 'Coming to London' (1956), an essay first published in *The London Magazine*, in which Bowen refers to her own 'protracted London half-life', and describes the unreal, daydream-like nature of the capital for her young self.[31] The ubiquitous and often illusory in-between spaces in Bowen and Mansfield's writing are thus firmly connected to their own rootless and suspended existence.

The trope of the in-between operates in a number of different ways across the writing of both Mansfield and Bowen, not least at a textual level. Mansfield's style, combined with the conventions of the short story – which, as Bowen herself notes, place the form 'at an advantage over the novel . . . because it . . . is not weighed down (as the novel is bound to be) by facts, explanation, or analysis' – dictates that the majority of her narratives open and close *in media res*.[32] Mansfield's 'Marriage a la Mode' (1922), for example, opens as William makes his way to the station and closes as his wife Isabel runs down the stairs, into what we do not know. A more widely celebrated story, 'Prelude' (1920), begins midway through the loading of a buggy, and ends with Kezia tiptoeing away 'far too quickly and airily', to yet another undisclosed location. The same is true of Bowen's narratives – the first page of *The Hotel* sees a flustered Miss Fitzgerald hurrying 'out of the Hotel into the road' (*TH*, p. 7) following a quarrel with her close friend, Miss Pym, while 'The Storm' (1926) opens in the middle of a heated argument between a young husband and wife, foreshadowing, in its intensity, the drama of the meteorological storm that follows. Similarly, her novels and short stories tend to conclude 'in the middle of things'. 'The Contessina' (1924) closes on the eponymous heroine being rowed back to her hotel following Barlow's clumsy advances, boldly embarking on a new flirtation with his friend Harrison, while *Friends and Relations* ends on a busy scene in Cheltenham as Colonel Studdart takes his daughters out to tea. In each of these cases, the reader is left stranded, as it were, between events and denied resolution. Mansfield's short stories are themselves read as in-between by Bowen, who suggests that 'each stood to her as a milestone, passed, not as a destination arrived at'.[33] The concept of the in-between is also apparent in terms of narrative form and genre. The short story, employed by both writers, might well be regarded as a somewhat marginal form in modernist literature, existing somewhere between the more popular forms of the novel and poetry. While many other authors experimented with the form (such as James Joyce, Woolf and Bowen herself), Mansfield was one of the few (if not the only one) who used it exclusively, and Bowen notes that at the time of their publication 'there was a difficulty as to the placing of [Mansfield's] stories; individually, their reception was uncertain: no full recognition came till the volume *Bliss*.'[34] Similarly, while the lingering perception of Bowen as a middlebrow author has rightly been called into question due to the distinctly modernist traits evident throughout much of her writing, these categorisations have contributed to the 'in-between' critical placement of both Bowen and Mansfield.

It is in the topography of Bowen and Mansfield's fiction, however, that the impact of the in-between is most powerfully felt. There are (at least) three different, and crucially overlapping, types of in-between spaces that can be traced throughout their work: transition, suspension and the uncanny. 'Transition' encompasses those spaces that exist quite literally between one place and another, such as windows and balconies, doorways, gardens, stairs, hallways and/or corridors, train stations and platforms, docks, beaches and seaside towns. Modes of transport might also be placed in this category, being as they are a mode of getting from one destination to the next. It is within these spaces that moments of change, quite literally moments of transition, tend to occur in Bowen and Mansfield's narratives. In the category of 'Suspension' fall those spaces in which everyday reality is seemingly suspended: these include hotels, shops, cafes, restaurants, bars, parks and cinemas. The 'Uncanny' encompasses those in-between spaces which are unhomely, and which carry the threat of potential danger. These include vacant or deserted houses and ruins. These categories are by no means fixed or stable, and the spaces ascribed to them can, and inevitably do, exist in more than one or indeed all of them at any one time. A coastal town, in its location as a threshold between land and sea, may, for example, function as a space of transition, but it may also indicate a suspension of reality as well as of moral and social codes. Complex in nature, these spaces refuse to be easily pinned down to any one definition. Rather, this rough attempt at categorisation is intended to provide a framework through which the implications and potentialities of these spaces might be more fully understood.

Moments of transition occur frequently in the writings of Bowen and Mansfield, and form the very core of their narratives. The work of both writers deals heavily in exploring the often-dramatic turning points in the lives of their characters, and there is a discernible correlation between such pivotal moments in their texts and the spatiality of the in-between. Throughout their fictions, the crossing of – or proximity to – thresholds and boundaries, and the time spent in liminal spaces, are necessarily enmeshed with moments of significant personal change or development, whether for better or worse. Thresholds and boundaries are frequently the sites of romantic and/or sexual transgression for their female characters in particular. In the final section of Mansfield's 'At the Bay' (1922), as Beryl Fairfield – the young, unmarried sister of Lydia Burnell – sits on her window-seat dreaming of running away with a lover, she is suddenly confronted by the presence of the mysterious Harry Kember in the garden. He asks her to join him on a midnight stroll, and despite her initial refusal, she feels that 'already something stirred in her, something reared its head'.[35] Her desire, 'that weak thing within her', begins to 'uncoil, to grow suddenly tremendously strong', and in one sentence she has 'stepped over her low window, crossed the veranda, ran down the grass to the gate.'[36] While it may seem that it is her desire that drives or enables Beryl to cross these three thresholds – the window, the veranda, the garden – in such quick succession, it is the wider context of the bay as a coastal and thus liminal location, existing between land and sea and at a remove from moral codes, that encourages the growth of this desire. At the seaside, away from the restrictions of everyday existence, Beryl's inhibitions are shed and 'a quick, bold' feeling builds inside of her.[37]

Similarly, in Bowen's *The House in Paris* (1935), the illicit desire between Karen Michaelis and Max Ebhart develops in such in-between spaces as the garden of a vacant house, a railway carriage and the seaside towns of Boulogne and Hythe. In the latter town, described as a kind of 'no-place' which 'stayed like nowhere, near nowhere, cut off from everywhere else', a crucial turning point takes place for Karen, as it is here that she conceives their illegitimate son Leopold.[38] As 'no-places', such spaces figure as moments of suspension in the writing of both Mansfield and Bowen, so that characters seem somehow detached from reality. Their illusory nature is habitually reinforced by the way in which the two authors construct these spaces as a fantasy, often through an emphasis on the glamour and opulence found within them. In Mansfield's unfinished story 'Father and the Girls' (1923), a nomadic elderly father and his two single daughters arrive at another in a long line of hotels, and find themselves completely entranced by their room: they gaze in wonder at the intricate wood-patterned ceiling and floor, and at 'the doors that had lozenges and squares of green picked out in gold'.[39] Daughter Emily's realisation that the hotel was once 'an old château' alludes to the settings of the French fairy tales of Charles Perrault. Alongside the anthropomorphism of the room, signalled by a bed that 'looked as if it were breathing, softly, gently breathing' and 'the room itself that whispered joyfully, shyly' to its occupants, this reference further reinforces its dreamlike and fantastic quality.[40] Similarly, the 'vivid glitter of the lounge' (*TH*, p. 154) and the 'dark, thickly carpeted' corridors of Bowen's eponymous hotel (p. 26), together with the 'gold wicker settee' and 'shimmering' vestibule tiles of the Hôtel du Padoue in *To the North* (1932), convey a palpable sense of luxury and decadence that distances these spaces from those of day-to-day lived reality.[41] Removed from the banalities of everyday existence, characters lose their inhibitions and behave erratically, impulsively and uncharacteristically. In the Hôtel du Padoue, the seemingly reserved Emmeline Summers, in a 'passionless entirety of . . . surrender' finally succumbs to the advances of Mark Linkwater (p. 142). The engagement of Sydney Warren to James Milton, which takes place in the hotel of Bowen's first novel, seems similarly out of character to everyone, including herself, yet her realisation of the impossibility of their relationship continuing once they have left the hotel only takes place after their car nearly collides with another on a precarious hillside route. Dazed, Sydney breaks off her engagement, telling James that, 'I think we have been asleep here; you know in a dream how quickly and lightly shapes move, they have no weight, nothing offers them any resistance' (*TH*, p. 182), reinforcing the unreality of this space. While the behaviour of these female characters within these spaces could well be regarded as uncharacteristic – quite literally out of character – such incidents might also be seen as a more extreme form of catharsis triggered by the freedom found within the spaces of the in-between to explore their sexuality away from the 'resistance' posed by everyday reality.

These spaces thus offer the potential for liberation and emancipation from social codes and moral guidelines. As she settles into her train journey after initial feelings of fear and trepidation, the eponymous character of Mansfield's 'The Little Governess' begins to enjoy the ride and to find the speed of the train reassuring rather than terrifying: 'The train shattered on, baring its dark, flaming breast to the hill and to the valleys. It was warm in the carriage. She seemed to lean against the dark rushing and to be carried away and away.'[42] The governess finds comfort in the distance created between her and everything she knows, delighting in the unknown nature of the landscape rushing by her window: 'How pretty and how different! Even those pink clouds in the sky looked foreign. It was cold, but she pretended it was far colder . . . pulling at the collar of her coat because she was so happy.'[43] Not only does she find happiness and reassurance in the unrelenting speed and movement of the train, but the very experience of the journey and the solitary adventure engenders within her a growing sense of independence. Alone for a moment in the carriage, 'the little governess looked at herself again in the glass, shook and patted herself with the precise practical care of a girl who is old enough to travel by herself.'[44] This feeling of independence is echoed in Bowen's *To the North*, in the pleasure Emmeline takes in driving her car through

London: 'Leaving the hoarse dingy clamour, the cinema-posters of giant love, she turned into Regent's Park, swept round under lines of imposing houses and, out of the park again, steadily mounted to St John's Wood' (*TN*, p. 94). The 'imposing houses' of Regent's Park fail to intimidate Emmeline, who 'sweeps' past them with an assuredness, deftly negotiating the urban landscape and 'steadily' making her way to her destination; the passage reveals not only her accomplished control of new technologies such as the motor car, but also the confidence she feels in the uniquely liminal space of that vehicle. These spaces of transition allow Bowen and Mansfield's female characters to experience the independence they crave. Importantly, however, spaces such as the hotel room, railway carriage and motor car also offer women vital moments of reprieve away from the gendered roles of the private sphere and from the moral codes of the public sphere. They provide these characters with the privacy that Wendy Gan argues 'was becoming a key component of life for the modern woman, providing her with the space to affirm an alternative identity apart from a traditional domestic role or even the seemingly more progressive role of a wage slave. Privacy . . . was a means for a woman to process the upheavals of modernity.'[45] These in-between spaces afford these female characters the necessary distance from demands made of them elsewhere to reflect upon their own subjectivities, their changing position in the world.

It would be a mistake, however, to regard these spaces as engendering solely positive outcomes for these female characters and to read these only as moments of sexual freedom, catharsis and independence. To fail to recognise the complex twists of Bowen and Mansfield's narratives would be to overlook the insight that their writing provides into the experiences of women in the early twentieth century. Following these narratives through to their often-troubling conclusions, it becomes clear that the realisation of these desires and the glimpses of independence and/or privacy are not entirely unproblematic. The fiction of both writers reveals that they were alert to the fact that women's position in modernity, though clearly changing, was by no means one of complete liberation or freedom. In their narratives, moments of suspension from reality experienced by female characters within spaces such as the hotel merely serve to reinforce the fact that the freedom they experience there is just as illusory, just as transient, as the spaces themselves. Boundaries and other transitional spaces, too, do not always live up to the liberatory potential they initially seem to promise. Having crossed the thresholds to reach Harry Kember, Beryl Fairfax is suddenly filled with a dread that prevents her from going any further: '[N]ow she was here she was terrified and it seemed to her everything was different. The moonlight stared and glittered; the shadows were like bars of iron.'[46] The imagery of the bars evokes the sense of imprisonment Beryl feels with Harry, hinting at the entrapment she imagines would befall her in marriage, or else at the inevitability of the judgment that would be heaped upon her were she to be discovered in an illicit embrace. The sexual liberation and consummation of the affair between Karen and Max in Bowen's *The House in Paris* results in Karen's pregnancy and catalyses a tragic chain of events that lead, eventually, to Max's suicide. In Mansfield's 'The Little Governess', the inappropriate advances of the seemingly kind old man she meets in the train carriage sour the feelings of independence and joy felt by her protagonist, and in Bowen's *To the North*, the pleasure taken by Emmeline in her solitary car journeys climaxes in a fatal car crash at the end of the novel.

It is not only the eventual outcomes of these transitional moments that are problematic – in many cases, the very act of crossing thresholds and boundaries has an immediate and unsettling effect on the characters. In Mansfield's 'The Garden-Party' (1922), for example, Laura Sheridan reluctantly crosses the threshold of the house of the recently deceased carter to be led through a dark passage to the doorway of the bedroom: 'The door opened. She walked straight through into the bedroom, where the dead man was lying.'[47] In crossing the threshold of the bedroom, Laura comes face-to-face with mortality and is irrevocably changed by her experience. In a particularly dramatic passage from *The House in Paris*, doorways are again repeatedly foregrounded as Naomi informs Karen of Max's sudden and unexpected suicide. Events are related through the closing and opening of doors: Naomi 'heard the salon door open and Max go out through the hall', and then shortly after 'heard the street door open and strike the wall' (*HP*, p. 182). Doorways come to signify the seemingly unstoppable chain of events leading up to his death, and yet it is only when Naomi herself crosses the threshold of the salon that she is confronted with the grim reality: 'I saw his blood splashed on the marble, on the parquet where he had stood and in a trail to the door, smeared where I had trodden without knowing' (p. 183). The significance of the link made between the doorway and the trail of blood should not be underplayed – in crossing the threshold of the salon, Naomi's body is temporarily, and her memory permanently, stained with the blood of her fiancé. For both Mansfield's Laura Sheridan and Bowen's Naomi Fisher, these doorways are thresholds into what Homi K. Bhabha describes as the 'unknowable, unrepresentable', that which does not permit 'a return to the "present"'.[48] Once crossed, these boundaries deny these characters the possibility of returning to the safety and stability of their previous existence.

The unsettling atmosphere of foreboding that pervades the in-between spaces in Mansfield's and Bowen's narratives is often further intensified by their unhomely and uncanny nature, a powerful sense of which is exemplified in Mansfield's 'Prelude', in which Kezia, wandering round her empty house for the final time, is suddenly gripped by an irrational terror:

> The windows of the empty house shook, a creaking noise came from the walls and floors, a piece of loose iron on the roof banged forlornly. Kezia was suddenly quite, quite still, with wide open eyes and knees pressed together. She was frightened. She wanted to call Lottie and to go on calling all the while she ran downstairs and out of the house. But IT was just behind her, waiting at the door, at the head of the stair, at the bottom of the stairs, hiding in the passage, ready to dart out at the back door.[49]

With the unseen 'IT' lurking in the shadows, the deserted house recalls the haunted house that is, according to Anthony Vidler, the 'most popular topos' of classic ghost stories.[50] Emptied of her family's furniture and possessions, the house is at once familiar and unfamiliar to Kezia, and she finds herself displaced, somewhere between being at home and being distinctly not at home, thereby fulfilling James Rissner's argument that the 'uncanny space is . . . a place of displacement'.[51] Vacant houses and buildings are also scattered across Bowen's novels, often emanating the same sense of danger and portent. In *The Death of the Heart*, for example, Portia finds the vacant boarding-house at Seale on Sea 'threatening' and 'frightening', and a feeling of claustrophobia and entrapment dominates the space: 'the emptiness, the feeling of dissolution came upstairs behind one, blocking the way down.'[52] The foreboding nature of this ghostly abandoned building, inhabited only by 'sea noises, as though years of echoes of waves and sea sucking shingle lived in its chimneys, its half-open cupboards' (p. 195), is reified in the struggle between Portia and her young lover Eddie. It is here that they angrily reveal their true feelings for each other, and that the realisation of the impossibility of their relationship begins to dawn upon Portia, as 'with the resolution of sorrow, her eyes went round his face' (p. 201). Similarly, the deserted mill in *The Last September* possesses a 'sinister pathos', a fascination with which compels Lois to cross its crumbling threshold: 'Fear heightened her gratification; she welcomed its inrush, letting her look climb the scabby and livid walls to the frightful stare of the sky. Cracks ran down; she expected, now with detachment, to see them widen, to see the walls peel back from a cleft – like the House of Usher's.'[53] Through her explicit reference to Edgar Allan Poe's story, 'The Fall of the House of Usher' (1839), Bowen signals the impending crisis awaiting Lois and Marda inside the boundaries of the abandoned mill, a crisis which is realised in their discovery of a fugitive member of the Irish Republican Army whose gunshot grazes Marda's hand, providing one of the most shocking moments in the novel. The uncanny, threatening nature of these vacant and/or abandoned buildings stems from the strange, liminal zone in which they are located, situated somewhere between existence and oblivion, between life and death. The fear felt by Kezia, Portia and Lois, among others, is a fear that springs from an implicit awareness of the unpredictable, volatile nature of the in-between space.

Bowen and Mansfield do not offer a simplistic, idealised account of women's experiences of modernity but instead present a version that possesses all the nuances, shifts and complexities of its reality. For their female characters, in-between spaces provide an opportunity to explore their desires for sexual freedom, and to experience a wider sense of privacy and independence that was so vital to women in the early twentieth century. Yet, these two authors refuse to shy away from representing the dangerous and unsettling elements that ran alongside the triumphs and victories of the women's movement. While transitional spaces in their fiction possess the capacity to engender change, there is no guarantee that this change will be positive for their characters. As such, their narratives speak to the wider anxieties felt so acutely by women regarding the period of change in which they were living and the unknowable nature of their futures. Similarly, the suspension from reality afforded to their characters by the spaces of the in-between, which allows them the freedom to explore their desires, simultaneously reveals that freedom to be an illusion that is shattered the moment those characters return to the reality of the everyday. Finally, the threatening nature of the uncanny, deserted houses and buildings, and the dangers facing the characters who enter them, reflects the potential risks faced by women attempting to negotiate the shifting and unpredictable currents of society. Through the liminal spaces of the in-between, there emerges a clear and ongoing dialogue between Bowen and Mansfield, exiles drawn to such spaces in a key moment of transition in women's history.

Notes

1. Cited in Claire Tomalin, *Katherine Mansfield: A Secret Life* (London: Penguin, 1988), p. 23.
2. Elizabeth Bowen, 'Ireland Makes Irish', in *People, Places, Things: Essays by Elizabeth Bowen*, ed. Allan Hepburn (Edinburgh: Edinburgh University Press, 2008), pp. 155–61 (p. 155); Elizabeth Bowen, 'Ireland', in Hepburn, *People, Places, Things*, pp. 164–9 (p. 164).
3. Bowen, 'Ireland', p. 168.
4. Elizabeth Bowen, 'Pictures and Conversations' (1975), in *The Mulberry Tree: Writings of Elizabeth Bowen*, ed. Hermione Lee (London: Virago, 1986), pp. 265–98 (p. 274).
5. John Middleton Murry, 'Introduction' to *The Journal of Katherine Mansfield*, ed. John Middleton Murry (London: Persephone, 2006), p. vii.
6. Tomalin, *Katherine Mansfield*, p. 9.
7. Andrew Bennett, *Katherine Mansfield* (Tavistock: Northcote House, 2004), p. 3.
8. Elizabeth Bowen, 'A Living Writer: Katherine Mansfield', in *The Mulberry Tree: Writings of Elizabeth Bowen*, ed. Hermione Lee (London: Virago, 1986), pp. 69–85 (p. 80).
9. Anna Snaith, *Modernist Voyages: Colonial Women Writers in London, 1890–1945* (Cambridge: Cambridge University Press, 2014), p. 111.
10. Ibid.
11. Virginia Woolf, *The Letters of Virginia Woolf*, ed. Nigel Nicolson, vol. 5, 6 vols (London: Hogarth Press, 1979), pp. 299–300.
12. Bowen, 'Pictures and Conversations', p. 276.
13. Hermione Lee, *Elizabeth Bowen: An Estimation*, rev. edn (London: Vintage, 1999), p. 16.
14. Shannon Wells-Lassagne, '"He Believed in Empire": Colonial Concerns in Elizabeth Bowen's *The Last September*', *Irish Studies Review*, 15.4 (2007): 451–62 (p. 452).
15. Snaith, *Modernist Voyages*, p. 14.
16. Ibid. p. 11.
17. Elizabeth Bowen, *Early Stories* (New York: Alfred Knopf, 1951), p. viii.
18. Allan Hepburn, 'Introduction' to *The Bazaar and Other Stories*, by Elizabeth Bowen, ed. Allan Hepburn (Edinburgh: Edinburgh University Press, 2008), p. 6.

19. Bowen, 'Introduction' to *34 Short Stories*, by Katherine Mansfield (London: Collins, 1963), p. 20.
20. Ibid. p. 19.
21. Bowen, 'Pictures and Conversations', p. 282.
22. Ibid.
23. Ibid. p. 283.
24. Bowen, 'Introduction' to *34 Short Stories*, p. 19.
25. Elizabeth Bowen, *The Hotel* (London: Vintage, 2003), p. 145. Hereafter cited parenthetically as *TH*; Elizabeth Bowen, *Friends and Relations* (London: Penguin, 1943), p. 83.
26. Angela Smith, *Katherine Mansfield and Virginia Woolf: A Public of Two* (Oxford: Oxford University Press, 1999), p. 7.
27. Angela Smith, *Katherine Mansfield and Virginia Woolf: A Public of Two* (Oxford: Oxford University Press, 1999), p. 7.
28. Louisie Edensor, 'Me or I? The Search for the Self in the Early Writings of Katherine Mansfield', in *Katherine Mansfield and Psychology*, ed. Clare Hanson, Gerri Kimber and Todd Martin (Edinburgh: Edinburgh University Press, 2016), pp. 82–99 (p. 87); Antony Alpers, *The Life of Katherine Mansfield* (Harmondsworth: Penguin, 1982), p. 127.
29. Maud Ellmann, *Elizabeth Bowen: The Shadow Across the Page* (Edinburgh: Edinburgh University Press, 2004), p. 14; Edwina Keown, 'The Seaside Flâneuse in Elizabeth Bowen's *The Death of the Heart*', in *Modernism on Sea: Art and Culture at the British Seaside*, ed. Lara Feigel and Alexandra Harris (Witney: Peter Lang, 2009), p. 179.
30. Bowen, 'Introduction' to *34 Short Stories*, p. 20.
31. Bowen, 'Coming to London' (1956), in *The Mulberry Tree*, pp. 85–90 (p. 89).
32. Elizabeth Bowen, 'Preface' to *Stories by Elizabeth Bowen* 1959), in *The Mulberry Tree*, pp. 126–30 (p. 128).
33. Bowen, 'Introduction' to *34 Short Stories*, p. 14.
34. Ibid. p. 21.
35. Katherine Mansfield, *The Collected Stories of Katherine Mansfield* (London: Penguin, 2007), p. 244.
36. Ibid.
37. Ibid. p. 220.
38. Elizabeth Bowen, *The House in Paris* (London: Vintage, 1998), p. 148; hereafter cited parenthetically as *HP*.
39. Mansfield, *Collected Stories*, p. 470.
40. Ibid. pp. 470–1.
41. Elizabeth Bowen, *To the North* (London: Penguin, 1945), p. 142. Hereafter cited parenthetically as *TN*.
42. Mansfield, *Collected Stories*, p. 181.
43. Ibid. p. 182.
44. Ibid. p. 183.

45. Wendy Gan, *Privacy and Modernity in Early Twentieth-Century British Writing* (Basingstoke: Palgrave Macmillan, 2009), p. 3.
46. Mansfield, *Collected Stories*, p. 244.
47. Ibid. p. 260.
48. Homi K. Bhabha, *The Location of Culture* (Abingdon: Routledge, 2004), p. 6.
49. Mansfield, *Collected Stories*, p. 15; original emphasis.
50. Anthony Vidler, *The Architectural Uncanny: Essays in the Modern Unhomely* (Cambridge, MA: MIT Press, 1992), p. 17.
51. James Rissner, 'Siting Order at the Limits of Construction: Deconstructing Architectural Place', *Research in Phenomenology*, 22.1 (1992): 62–72 (p. 70).
52. Elizabeth Bowen, *The Death of the Heart* (London: Vintage, 1998), p. 196. Hereafter cited parenthetically as *DH*.
53. Elizabeth Bowen, *The Last September* (London: Vintage, 1998), pp. 123–4.

Chapter 7

'How Much of Nothing There Was': Trying (Not) to Understand Elizabeth Bowen

Damian Tarnopolsky

'Unmeaning'

Elizabeth Bowen's insistent interweaving of positive and negative elements in her novels of the 1930s and 1940s is unsettling, innovative and in many ways a key to her writing. In *The House in Paris* (1935), *The Death of the Heart* (1938) and *The Heat of the Day* (1948), Bowen relates the positive and negative stylistically, extends their connection thematically and elaborates upon the relation in historical terms. Examples range from sentences including double or triple negatives and words that cancel themselves out, to descriptions of parts of London destroyed by the Blitz, to scenes built around something missing. Her characters complain that they know nothing about each other or their own motives; her plots often resist final explanation, as if the novels are in some sense about 'nothing'. On every page, in sentences, in her characters' lives, in her sense of the world, Bowen's novels pursue a paradoxical task: charting the presence of lack, absence and negativity.[1]

This essay begins by exploring the textual connection between positive and negative elements through close reading, noting its workings on the level of word and sentence, plot and character and theme. Bowen's stylistic interest in the relation between what she often calls 'nothing' and more familiar novelistic 'somethings' is unusual and seems to call attention to itself, but it is much more than a surface tic or affectation. In closely examining the style in which Bowen relates something and nothing, my critical approach is aligned with the one described by Susan Osborn:

> Within the last decade, Bowen's readers have sought to recuperate her fiction by focusing their analyses precisely on those aspects of her work that produce the sense of interpretative strain early identified by [Jocelyn] Brooke and others, those problematic exchanges caused by the ungainly irregularities, the improprieties and 'thickened' stylistic effects that produce her works' uncustomary recalcitrance and that continue to challenge readers' interpretative abilities.[2]

Bowen's use of nothing and something is a difficulty, one that may prevent her fiction from being fully 'recuperated' even if it is focused upon, because writing the negative brings paradox with it from the start: how do you write (about) what is not there? Bowen's method adds to the challenge: explaining Bowen's exploration of nothing relies on interpreting the 'ungainly irregularities' of her style, but the irregularities, as Osborn notes in her study of Bowen's novel *The Last September* (1929), 'undermine the certainty upon which these readings rely for their force, and bar us from forming conclusive statements ... about [the text's] ultimate justification or meaning'.[3] Paradox is presented paradoxically, so one can never get to a final understanding of it; a 'final' understanding of Bowen's use of something and nothing would be somehow a misreading. But the lack of a final destination does not mean that one cannot fruitfully explore how Bowen's nothing is created in the text, and explore its startling effects and ambiguous ramifications.

To do so, this essay moves cautiously on to contexts: how Bowen's treatment of something and nothing is illuminated by her sense of life at mid-century and how it might align her with the work of her contemporaries. Exploring Bowen's 'nothings' is a way of understanding the fractured historical moment in which she wrote, and her response to it; it is also a way of placing her as a 'late modernist' novelist, responding both to world history and literary history, in particular the inheritance of 'high modernism'. To approach Bowen's difficulty this way is in part to follow Theodor Adorno's suggestions for such difficult works as those of Samuel Beckett, a contemporary of Bowen's with a famous 'taste for the negative'.[4] Adorno proposes an 'immanent criticism' that attempts to reconstruct and contextualise the meaning of a recalcitrant work's resistance to meaning rather than 'transcendentally' forcing it to have a single meaning.[5] His work offers a model for speculations on the challenging meanings of nothing in Bowen, a method that responds honestly to the difficulty that the interconnection of nothing and something poses. There is something about nothing that resists explanation, and that will always cause that sense of 'interpretative strain'. This essay seeks ways to understand Bowen's elaboration of 'something and nothing' as an ongoing relating of terms that deliberately resist finality. It examines what the text gains from its contact with nothing, and what the textual relating of something and nothing gives the reader. Moreover, it addresses the relation of 'nothing and something' in Bowen to larger questions about the positive and negative in life and literature. 'Nothing' is on every page an oddity. But taking it on and looking squarely at it, rather than rejecting it out of hand, is a way to shed new light on Bowen, on reading, on something and nothing. Looking this way at something and nothing is a way of trying to understand Bowen, with an emphasis on 'trying'.

Unwords

In her novels of the 1930s and 1940s, Bowen is stylistically obsessed with relating nothing and something. One sees this interest in her use of double and triple negatives, her coinages and use of rare or obsolete 'unwords', and her phrasings that appear deliberately to pursue a negative route when a positive one would seem more immediate and straightforward. These are some of the ways that Bowen lets nothing into her writing on a sentence-by-sentence level. Any particular example might not seem significant by itself, but taken together they form a pattern that at once calls for and challenges interpretation. In each case, negative and positive interact with puzzling, sometimes productive, sometimes disabling effects. The stylistic interactions are echoed in Bowen's larger structures: her longer descriptions, narrative technique, compositional methods and thematic interests. These structures are twisted and torqued by the effort to let nothing into something. The novels are built out of the relations between negative elements and positive ones, small and large.

'There used not to be nothing to say', Max says in *The House in Paris*, rather than, 'There used to be something to say.'[6] Some forty pages later Karen says, 'I haven't not thought of her' (p. 177), rather than 'I have thought of her.' Towards the end of *The Heat of the Day* comes the comment, 'Not that this is not a very nice room.'[7] One wonders why Bowen so often chooses the negative option; one also starts to wonder if the positive and negative formulations are synonymous, in fact, or what it is that the version which dwells on 'not' may paradoxically add. On occasion one finds triple negatives, as when Stella Rodney considers whether Harrison intends to take her out to dinner or not: 'His not having said so gave her no chance of saying she would on no account dine with him' (p. 21). Here, the text is describing something that is doubly not there: Stella is denied the chance to reject a dinner invitation that has not been made. In these sentences Bowen almost seems to pick at a more standard, positive statement with 'not' and 'no', allowing bleaker colourations to come through.[8] Madame Fisher 'used not to go to bed when there was nothing to say', Karen tells Max, describing his mentor. When he responds, '[t]here used not to be nothing to say' (*HP*, p. 137), the presence of absence is conjured up palpably, paradoxically, by the repeatedly negative phrasing.

Another way Bowen relates something and nothing in her sentences is through her frequent use of words beginning with the negative prefix *un-*. Words like 'unadmitted' or 'unreal', or a moment at which the countryside seems to be 'undoing the reality of the city' (*HD*, p. 138) for a returning traveller, are not especially strange by themselves. But, once again, when taken together they start to add up to a pattern in the text (or subtract a pattern from the text, perhaps), and as it becomes more extreme it calls for attention. In *The Heat of the Day*, Robert tells his niece 'what an un-clever, un-funny little girl' she is (p. 293), rather than calling her silly or dull. He himself displays 'a sort of provocative unindifference' (p. 205), a phrase that it takes some effort to understand. Sometimes the instances of 'unwords' occur in clumps one cannot miss, like symptoms or hauntings. On one page of *The House in Paris*, for example, Leopold's elbow 'undoubled' itself and his arm goes around Henrietta with 'unfeeling' tightness; he looks drowned, and it is as if the sea has washed over his 'unstruggling' face with eyes 'unchangingly open', though he and Henrietta remain 'unalarmed' (p. 200). The insistent use of *un-* is noticeable in itself, but one should also add that Bowen seeks out obsolete and rare 'unwords'. The *OED*'s only instance of 'undoubled' comes from 1598, for example, while 'unalarmed' and 'unstruggling' are nineteenth-century words. The words 'unexploring' (p. 118), 'unconcentratedly' (*HD*, p. 110) and 'unestablishable' (p. 154) are not in the *OED* at all. The only quotation it provides for 'unsalt' after 1598 is from *The House in Paris* (p. 151).

'Unmeaning' (*HD*, p. 154, p. 305) is a good word to describe what Bowen is after in her use of or invention of words that take something away, or render something strange, while adding something new. She is insistent: as well as curving her syntax in the ways described above in order to bring nothing into her writing, Bowen will also innovate on the level of the individual word itself. Something is about to be said, but as it is said it is being cancelled. When one encounters the sentence, '[h]ere the sea air was washed unsalt by the rain; you only smelled tamarisks and wet grass' (*HP*, p. 151), what matters is that one is guided along a negative road, told to look out for the absence of something rather than its presence. Or, perhaps, something absent becomes present in the form of a negative 'unword', so we are led to the presence of something that is at once absent. The meaning is there, but the opposite meaning is also there, and the result is neither nothing, nor quite something. Nothing and something are lexically intertwined. The negative is allowed entry and made to relate uneasily to the something we are used to, leaving us with both at once, facing each other. The relationship happens before us, within individual words.

Bowen's interest in connecting something and nothing moves beyond her choice of words and shaping of sentences into the kinds of situations she writes about, into her descriptions, plots and modes of characterisation. A room is described as having 'the look of no hour' in *The Heat of the Day* (p. 312); in *The House in Paris* a character 'did not even ask herself why *she* had said nothing' (p. 130; original emphasis). At one point in *The Death of the Heart*, Anna 'went on saying nothing'.[9] Sometimes nothing is brought into and undermines physical descriptions of something, as when in *The Heat of the Day* 'the unsubstantial darkness was quickened by a not quite wind' (p. 138). An 'unword' tells us that the darkness lacks substance; it is brought to life by a wind, but that wind is not all there. When Anna's friend St Quentin is described earlier as 'not noticing being not noticed' (*DH*, p. 33), the odd, deliberate phrasing somehow suggests that 'being not noticed' is something, and specifically something that the character ignores, rather than the absence of something.

In many cases the examples link to more complex, connected instances, some of them with great thematic significance. When Portia and Eddie awkwardly run into Major Brutt and Thomas Quayne in *The Death of the Heart*, for instance: 'They stood a foot apart but virtually hand in hand. Portia looked past Eddie liquidly, into nowhere, as though she did not exist because she might not look at him.' There are no 'unwords' here, nor any very special negative convolutions in the syntax, and yet versions of nothing are being described. Eddie and Portia are not physically touching and yet they 'virtually' are holding hands, announcing their attachment in front of Thomas 'in a way that showed complete indifference to the company . . . one more domestic fatigue' (p. 121). Portia looks 'into nowhere', another phrasing that is at once perfectly evocative of her willing her attention away from the social moment, and yet somehow suggests that nowhere is a place that one can see. Not being able to look at Eddie, not seeing him, somehow takes away Portia's being: if she cannot see him, it is 'as though' she is not there, and yet she is. There is a different kind of foreshadowing at work here, because when Eddie reveals himself to finally be indifferent to Portia, her world and that of the Quaynes will come crashing down.

Bowen often gives life to a scene by building it around something missing. As a matter of fictional technique, absence adds suspense and drama. For example, in *The Death of the Heart*, Eddie and Portia explore an empty lodging house, and '[t]here is nothing like exploring an empty house' (p. 255): what otherwise might be a scene of static description is torqued and enlivened by anchoring it in emptiness (as well as trespass). Other summonings of the negative are still more thorough, formal and enigmatic. Speaking of her absent son Leopold in a conversation that is itself unspoken dialogue and does not actually take place between the characters,[10] Karen's husband Ray says (or 'says'), '[w]e never are alone, while you're dreading him' (*HP*, p. 221). The fact that Leopold is not with them makes him loom large; he is the missing guest at every meal. By discussing Leopold's presence and absence in the form of an unsaid conversation, Bowen evokes the interplay of something and nothing in a form and style that mimics that interplay. The presence of nothing and absence in the characters' lives is evoked in a style that formally incorporates negatives and positives. The relation of something and nothing is part of the couple's being, and of the being of the text.

No Time, no place: history and late modernism

Encountering all these examples, one can start to feel like Louie Lewis in *The Heat of the Day*: unable to sleep, she 'clasped her hands under her head and stared up at nothing – it was oppressive though, how much of nothing there was' (p. 277). But certain aspects of something and nothing in Bowen's work suggest ways of interpreting it in terms of Bowen's sense of her historical moment, as well as ways of placing her alongside other late modernist writers. The historical approach to understanding Bowen's intertwining of something and nothing is suggested by examples such as a paragraph describing the living and the dead in London during the Blitz. In this description, the interplay of something and nothing becomes a theme with historical, real-world implications:

> Most of all the dead, from mortuaries, from under cataracts of rubble, made their anonymous presence – not as today's dead but as yesterday's living – felt through London. Uncounted, they continued to move in shoals through the city day, pervading everything to be seen or heard or felt with their torn-off senses, drawing on this tomorrow they had expected – for death cannot be so sudden as all that. Absent from the routine which had been life, they stamped upon that routine their absence – not knowing who the dead were, you could not know which might be the staircase somebody for the first time was not mounting this morning, or at which street corner the newsvendor missed a face, or which trains and buses in the homegoing rush were this evening lighter by at least one passenger. (p. 99)

These are significant details: the dead who make their presence felt are anonymous, but are felt as yesterday's absent living, not the present dead of today. One notes the appearance of another *un-* prefix in 'uncounted'. It is typical of Bowen to interrupt the commonplace phrase of making 'presence felt' with a comment in dashes, which both twists the writing away from cliché and also seems to serve as an instance of something getting in the way of the dead simply making their presence felt. Self-reflexively, these (un)dead 'pervade' everything they might see or hear with their 'torn-off senses'. More than one critic has noted that London was full of holes at the time Bowen describes, and part of the power of her writing is her success at capturing the presence of this very particular and present kind of nothingness. This is to say that there are ways in which Bowen's interest in nothing is an aspect of her realism, of her interest in the something-and-nothingness of the world and its effects on people. For all the stylistic innovation and strangeness of her writing, Bowen maintains a strong connection to realist modes.[11] This paragraph evokes a very particular historical moment: Clarence Terrace, where she lived, was 'blown hollow inside by a V1' in 1944.[12]

However, the subject matter does not explain or exhaust the stylistic choice or novelistic achievement – other writers described bomb craters in London without paradox, without seeking to create similar lacunae in their own texts, or exploring their much deeper and broader significance. So while it is important to note that while something and nothing might often seem a way to write the realities of wartime, the interplay is also part of Bowen's world well before the war. Bowen's novels of the 1930s underscore the suggestion that in considering positive and negative she is writing about something even larger than immediate crisis, something more widely political or even generational. In *The House in Paris*, Max has a grim sense of the impossibility of a tomorrow in a world which 'is no longer "history in the making," or keeps rules or falls in with nice ideas. Things will soon be much more than embarrassing' (p. 120). In *The Death of the Heart*, Thomas derides his generation as bland and aimless, epigones compared to the destructive generation of the First World War:

> We none of us seem to feel very well, and I don't think we want each other to know it ... But it took guts to be even the fools our fathers were. We're just a lousy pack of little Christopher Robins. Oh, we've got to live, but I doubt if we see the necessity. (p. 118)

In *The Heat of the Day*, Robert Kelway describes himself in obsessively negative terms as a member of 'a class without a middle, a race without a country. Unwhole. Never earthed in ... Not only nothing to hold, nothing to touch. No source of anything in anything' (p. 307). This is what Stella (placed as having been born around the same time as Bowen) in *The Heat of the Day* describes as being part of the generation which, '*as* a generation, was to come to be made to feel it had muffed the catch' (p. 24; original emphasis). If one follows the suggestions of the text, Bowen's intertwining of something and nothing can be seen as a way to represent a larger metaphysical gap: her characters have a sense of living in a hollow time, with no solid connection to the past or sense of a secure future.

To read in this manner is to take up the programme Adorno suggests for finding a respectful, accurate way of reading works that short circuit familiar ways of making meaning. Adorno's 'immanent critic' attempts to reconstruct the ways that challenging aesthetic gestures are not simply 'meaningless', but rather aim towards a 'determinate negation of meaning'.[13] Instead of attempting to consolidate or force the work's contradictions into a new and complete whole, the critical aim is to reconstruct the meaning of the work's meaninglessness. For Adorno, the meaning is ultimately social or political: Bowen, he might say, finds a way to express accurately, without rendering it aesthetically whole in a way that would falsify it, important news about the metaphysical gap in her times. The critic can see the shape of her gesture, but must respect the fact that its formal qualities – its integral lack of integrity – have as great an impact as its propositional meaning. One can adapt this point to see something new about Bowen's aesthetic context: that is the meaning of the work's resistance to meaning has aesthetic contexts as well as historical ones. The relation of something and nothing in Bowen speaks to what Virginia Woolf, discussing the writers who succeeded her own generation, called their lack of 'knowledge of a settled civilisation'.[14] Woolf argued that a nostalgic strain even within her peers' innovative writing could be attributed to a memory of a past, before the First World War, that was felt to make sense; later modernist authors lacked such anchoring.[15] In these terms, Bowen's use of nothingness is one of her innovations in prose, but it is an innovation governed by doubt as much as certainty, in a more 'late modernist' fashion. 'Nothing' helps make the novel something new, sentence by sentence; it also has realistic qualities, but at the same time, and this is Bowen's difference, it resists any effort to wrap the chaos of the world or the novel into a new and final order.

Necessary and impossible: working with nothing

Bowen's baroque double and triple negatives, her characters' absence from themselves and from each other, her ambiguous plots – the ways that nothing relates to something in Bowen's writing is unusual and affecting, disabling and exciting. Bowen's interest in nothing illuminates her sense of and place in her period, through her descriptions of time and place, her sense of her generation's metaphysical crisis and her links to other similar writers. But textually, nothing in Bowen has continuing, disturbing, extensive, destabilising effects. One cannot limit the effects of her investigation of something and nothingness to being 'about' something, even indirectly. The relation of something and nothing in Bowen is an element that invites interpretation but resists confirmation. It is one of those aspects that, as Osborn puts it, makes it impossible to produce a competent reading of Bowen's work.[16] In which case, how is one to respond to the continuing challenge posed by something and nothing in Bowen's writing?[17] The psychoanalyst Adam Phillips comments in a different context that perhaps we worry too much about understanding: perhaps we try too hard to understand, and do not think enough about what understanding things stops us from seeing and thinking about.[18] If one takes a slightly different critical approach, one can focus not on understanding a desired 'end result' (an interpretation of a paradox), but instead on observing the process of relating something and nothing that Bowen performs sentence-by-sentence within her work. The key is that it is a process, an ongoing relating that happens contradiction-by-contradiction – to settle it by giving it a positive or negative name or a meaning is to misread its aesthetic effects within the text and its effects on the reader.

One can start by tracking the textual effects of this ongoing relation. Bowen's use of nothing and something, on every level (as a tool in sentences, as a theme, as a mode of characterisation), helps her generate a radical mode of writing that (again, looking for analogies) stays on the move, that suggests meanings but steps back from them, that is itself both something and nothing at once. This is one important way 'she makes a difference', as Neil Corcoran aptly puts it: as well as being significant to our lives, to the canon, to literature, her work strangely makes of itself something one might call 'a difference'.[19] When one deliberately lets nothing in one formally makes a text that cannot be explained. This is what the text is given by 'nothing'. This is something like a formalist response to nothing and something, one that tracks and charts: not to explain, but to chart and follow, is to stay true to the bewildering textual effects of something and nothing.[20] As critics we want to decide; Bowen makes us look differently at this urge, step back from it and look again at the wonder of the text.

One can also make this point in reader-response terms. By writing in this way, Bowen may be giving us something, the experience of the pleasure and terror of not being able to understand. She places the reader within the experience she describes: a London reduced to holes, a generational time that does not make sense. Like Stella walking between craters in London, like Anna and Thomas living in such a way that 'something edited life in the Quaynes' house' (*DH*, p. 221), like Leopold waiting to meet a mother of whom he has no memory, we have to find ways to deal with gaps, incompleteness, the dislocating presence of shadows and voids in our lives. Reading Bowen, we may have to accept understanding less than we are used to; our experience, like that of her characters, may be partial, painful, puzzling and dissatisfying, as well as containing bliss and laughter. When one deliberately lets nothing in one makes a text that gives the reader the experience of something and nothing. Plot holes are left gapingly unfilled. Gestures go noticeably unnoticed. In *The Heat of the Day*, Stella's relationship with Robert Kelway starts with, and is given force by, words they do not say because a bomb hits (p. 103); Rodney Roderick is puzzled by the commas that are missing from his Cousin Francis's will (pp. 95–6); before leaving, Kelway counsels Stella to 'live most in the hour we never had' (p. 324). On the last page of *The House in Paris* we are told that when Ray and Leopold leave the train station, 'no taxi came immediately' (p. 245). Rather than indicating that they have to wait for something to happen, the phrasing seems almost to suggest that something *is* happening: a 'no taxi' is what comes. Nothing comes into something. These are the kind of moments that stay with the reader of Bowen's nothings, and what Ray and Leopold must do is what any reader of Bowen has to do: face an absence made into words. At the close of *The Death of the Heart*, the servant, Matchett, is sent to pick up Portia from Major Brutt's hotel. We do not know what will happen to Portia or how she will fare, though the fingers playing the piano that Matchett hears do finally find their way to a chord – a reminder that, again, one has to stress the interplay of the positive and the negative in Bowen's work (p. 417).

Artistic creation is sometimes spoken of as making something out of nothing. But in Bowen the radical and strange effort is to make nothing out of something too. Whether one focuses on the text or its effects on the reader, one is still inevitably left struggling to find words for the extraordinary ways Bowen does and undoes, makes and unmakes. Seeing the text as working in both directions at once helps us admire the complexity with which Bowen relates nothing and something. Reading for something and nothing together may transform our approach to her sense of her time as well as to the meanings of her style. Reading the text as an ongoing process that constantly relates something and nothing suggests new ways to savour what is recalcitrant or difficult more generally. It may help us resist the reflex to say that the difficult, ungainly or straining text is something other than what it is, to look again at what is there. Looking this way at something and nothing is a way of trying to understand Bowen, with an emphasis on 'not'.

Notes

1. The concept of the negative in literature has a long history; for some important contemporary theorisations see Maurice Blanchot, *The Space of Literature*, trans. Ann Smock (Omaha: University of Nebraska Press, 1989); Jacques Derrida, 'How to Avoid Speaking: Denials', in *Languages of the Unsayable: The Play of Negativity in Literature and Theory*, ed. Sandford Budick and Wolfgang Iser (New York: Columbia University Press, 1987); and Simon Critchley, *Very Little,*

Almost Nothing: Death, Philosophy, Literature (London: Routledge, 1997). Focused studies of nothingness examine everything from the adulterous female body in medieval literature (Peggy McCracken, 'The Body Politic and the Queen's Adulterous Body in French Romance', in *Feminist Approaches to the Body in Medieval Literature*, ed. Linda Lomperis and Sarah Stanbury (Philadelphia: University of Pennsylvania Press, 1993)) to the meanings of absence in Gogol (Natascha Drubek-Meyer, *Gogol: Exploring Absence: Negativity in Nineteenth-Century Russian Literature* (Bloomington: Slavica, 1999)). 'Nothing' can be approached linguistically, psychologically, existentially and in many other ways. This essay resists applying a particular pre-existing framework in favour of looking at the relations of negative and positive as Bowen's work explores it, and the ways that this relationship works to resist categorisation.
2. Susan Osborn, 'Introduction' to *Elizabeth Bowen: New Critical Perspectives*, ed. Susan Osborn (Cork: Cork University Press, 2009), pp. 1–12 (p. 5).
3. Susan Osborn, '"How to Measure this Unaccountable Darkness Between the Trees": The Strange Relation of Style and Meaning in *The Last September*', in Osborn, *New Critical Perspectives*, pp. 34–60 (p. 36).
4. The title of Shane Weller's study of Beckett (*A Taste for the Negative: Beckett and Nihilism* (London: Legenda, 2005)). The use of Beckett's engagement with nothing for readers of Bowen has been suggested by Maud Ellmann, whose introduction includes section headings with such Beckettian titles as 'Company' (*The Shadow Across the Page* (Edinburgh: Edinburgh University Press, 2003)). Sinéad Mooney compares Bowen's 'suspended characters' in *Eva Trout* (1968) to those in Beckett's early novels *Watt* (1953) and *Murphy* (1938) ('Unstable Compounds: Bowen's Beckettian Affinities', in Osborn, *New Critical Perspectives*, pp. 13–33). Also, Harold Pinter connected the two authors in adapting *The Heat of the Day* for the screen: in the final scene, Stella and Harrison wait at a window for an air raid to end. They finally hear the All Clear, but in words that repeat the last stage direction of each act of *Waiting for Godot* (1953), 'They do not move' (see Harold Pinter, 'The Heat of the Day', in *Collected Screenplays*, vol. 3 (London: Faber & Faber, 2000), p. 242; Samuel Beckett, 'Waiting for Godot', in *Samuel Beckett: The Grove Centenary Edition*, vol. 3, ed. Paul Auster (New York: Grove, 2006), p. 88). The connection is also noted by Neil Corcoran in *Elizabeth Bowen: The Enforced Return* (Oxford: Oxford University Press, 2004), p. 200; and Phyllis R. Randall in 'Pinter and Bowen: *The Heat of the Day*', in *Pinter at Sixty*, ed. Katherine H. Burkman and John L. Kundert-Gibbs (Bloomington: Indiana University Press, 1993), pp. 173–82 (p. 181).

5. Theodor Adorno, 'Commitment', in *Aesthetics and Politics*, ed. Ronald Taylor, trans. Francis McDonagh (London: NLB, 1977). For Adorno's reading of Beckett see 'Trying to Understand *Endgame*', in *Notes to Literature*, ed. Rolf Tiedemann, trans. Shierry Weber Nicholsen, vol. 1 (New York: Columbia University Press, 1991).
6. Elizabeth Bowen, *The House in Paris* (New York: Vintage, 1957), p. 137. Hereafter cited parenthetically as *HP*.
7. Elizabeth Bowen, *The Heat of the Day* (New York: Anchor, 2002), p. 349. Hereafter cited parenthetically as *HD*.
8. Alain Badiou describes Beckett's minimalism as a way of picking at the surface of contemporary knowledge to reveal what is beneath (*On Beckett*, ed. Alberto Toscano and Nina Power (Manchester: Clinamen, 2003)).
9. Elizabeth Bowen, *The Death of the Heart* (New York: Anchor, 2000), p. 130. Hereafter cited parenthetically as *DH*.
10. Though of course Bowen's inclusion of this conversation undermines the force of this 'actually'.
11. See Rod Mengham 'Broken Glass', in *The Fiction of the 1940s: Stories of Survival*, ed. Rod Mengham and N. H. Reeve (London: Palgrave, 2001), pp. 124–33; and John Mepham, 'Varieties of Modernism, Varieties of Incomprehension: Patrick Hamilton and Elizabeth Bowen', in *British Fiction After Modernism: The Novel at Mid-Century*, ed. Marina MacKay and Lyndsey Stonebridge (London: Palgrave, 2007), pp. 59–76.
12. Hermione Lee, *Elizabeth Bowen: An Estimation* (London: Vision, 1981), p. 166.
13. Adorno, 'Commitment', p. 191.
14. Virginia Woolf, 'The Leaning Tower', in *Collected Essays*, vol. 2 (London: Hogarth, 1981), p. 170; Michael Gorra, *The English Novel at Mid-Century: From the Leaning Tower* (Basingstoke: Macmillan, 1990), p. 6.
15. Michael Gorra's elaboration of Woolf's point guides my discussion here.
16. Osborn, 'How To Measure this Unaccountable Darkness Between the Trees', p. 36.
17. The most significant studies to examine Bowen's use of nothing are by Ellmann, Neil Corcoran, and Andrew Bennett and Nicholas Royle. Ellmann's is particularly relevant: she notes that, like Beckett, Bowen 'seems to feel obliged to express the resistance of nothing to expression' (*The Shadow Across the Page*, p. 12), and points to a 'shadowy third' element in Bowen's writing between the positive and the negative. Bennett and Royle illuminate the dissolving effects of Bowen's writing in greater depth and with more theoretical complexity, drawing on such concepts as psychoanalytic encryptment and literary telepathy (*Elizabeth Bowen and the Dissolution of the Novel* (New York:

St. Martin's Press, 1995)). Corcoran offers the salutary reminder that Bowen is highly tonally varied: 'Though she is drawn to fracture and disintegration, this is more inflected with affirmation – since she often is primarily a comic writer – than some recent criticism has made it seem' (*The Enforced Return*, pp. 12–13).

18. Adam Phillips, *Missing Out: In Praise of the Unlived Life* (New York: Farrar, Straus & Giroux, 2012), p. 63.
19. Corcoran, *The Enforced Return*, p. 15.
20. This essay has repeatedly, if implicitly, returned to the comparison between Bowen's use of nothing and Beckett's, and drawn on critical responses to Beckett's use of nothing in trying to understand Bowen's. But what makes Bowen perhaps the more radical writer, from one perspective, is that her work retains so much of the conventional furniture of the novel (recognisable characters, settings, plots) that Beckett discards, and yet allows in the disabling and disconcerting being of the negative as fully as Beckett's.

Chapter 8

Bowen's Recesses: From Realism to Inter-Objectivity

Laurie Johnson

He might have been stepping into a picture postcard.[1]

From realism . . .

A significant current in the renewed critical interest in Elizabeth Bowen's work has focused on the question of what Maud Ellmann calls 'the narrative business of the realist'.[2] While Bowen shared Virginia Woolf's exasperation with this business, Ellmann continues, she nevertheless relished what realism offers: 'it releases her from the stifling rose-house of inner life into the world of cars and cocktail-shakers, typewriters and telephones – in short, into the modern world, which claims her attention just as much as the archaic phantasms of the mind.'[3] Whereas Woolf's objects 'serve as springboards for flights of consciousness', for Bowen, 'things behave like thoughts and thoughts behave like things, impugning the supremacy of consciousness', thus creating the sense that 'every object has a psyche; in fact, her objects even have neuroses – every house, for instance, has a watchful face; every car a gamut of anxieties.'[4] Ellmann's readings recuperate in Bowen this sense of the *business* of realism – the insistence in realism of overlaying character and dialogue with the trappings of everyday life – but as Julie Anne Stevens astutely observes, these readings reflect the critic's own desire to read Bowen through a psychoanalytically inflected feminist lens, leading from the object's neuroses inevitably back toward the positively charged libidinal economy of the female protagonists.[5]

Bowen was mindful of, and cautious about, the label of realism being applied to her novels: writing in 1959, she avers, '[a]t no time, even in the novel, do I consider realism to be my forte'.[6] Neil Corcoran declares, by contrast, that it is not until after this time, in the novels of the 1960s, that Bowen 'loses touch with classical realism and its customary methods'.[7] Corcoran's Bowen is until 1959 in thrall to Charles Dickens, Gustave Flaubert and Henry James, among many other exponents of the realist form, and their influence is seen at every turn in her work, but he also maintains that we should reread these forebears in the wake of Bowen's homage: 'it is radically insufficient, for instance, for critics of Bowen to notice an indebtedness to, say, Henry James, without noticing also how we may read James differently in Bowen's later light', even to the point where we may 'find fault' in the work of her progenitors.[8] Realism in Bowen is, for Corcoran, ultimately irreducible to the 'endlessly death-inflected, dissolved, haunted, cryptic' impulses he sees modulating Ellmann's work, for example.[9]

If these two approaches might seem intractable, Phyllis Lassner's examination of the earlier critical work on Bowen's shorter fiction may help us to navigate the impasse. Lassner critiques readings that characterise Bowen's short fiction as psychological realism, as social comedy and as moral realism.[10] Readings akin to the last of these categories, such as can be found in the criticism of James M. Haule, run the risk of positing a reality 'that remains so abstract it discredits his sympathy for the plight of Bowen's female characters'.[11] Not that the opposite end of the spectrum, psychological realism, offers an antidote: Lassner observes, following Daniel V. Fraustino's work, that 'psychological interpretation appeals to readers as a way of ameliorating the story's disturbing effects, but its ambiguities and ambivalences warn us that such a reading may be interpolation rather than textually valid.'[12] The point to be drawn from Lassner's critiques is that this spectrum of realist readings is just that – a spectrum *of readings* – tending to find in the text the very thing that the critic was seeking to find. Stevens suggests this is somewhat true of Ellmann's approach as well, and Sarah Savitt points out in her reading of Corcoran's book that the influence of the great writers is potentially also a product of the critic's meticulous unpicking of the many literary allusions, a feature even of his readings of the novels that follow Bowen's rejection of realism. Of Corcoran's analysis of *Eva Trout* (1968), Savitt notes 'a comprehensive untangling of the various biblical and literary allusions (primarily Shakespeare, Dickens, James) which saturate the work'.[13] Yet Savitt adds that Corcoran's modus operandi is to contextualise by situating Bowen's stories within her Anglo-Irish heritage, her memories of childhood and ultimately her experience of war – his search for the classical realist Bowen seems, as a result, to be at times a distraction. Lassner attends to literary allusions when the text demands, such as when Bowen makes an explicit reference to Miranda from Shakespeare's *The Tempest* in 'Sunday Afternoon' (1941), but she does not hunt down such allusions assiduously.[14] In contrast to Corcoran, Lassner is most interested in pursuing context, especially when it is demanded by the text itself, and the question of realism is therefore secondary.

In what follows, I seek to reorient considerations of the realist elements in Bowen's writing by concentrating in the main, like Lassner, on her short stories, and particularly those written during the tumult of the Blitz and in the aftermath of the Second World War. I frame my readings of the wartime short fiction according to a series of 'recesses': the first of these is the 'recess' as a building feature, which I shall use to frame a discussion of the status of 'things' in these narratives and the techniques through which 'setting' was abandoned as a narrative component to enable buildings, spaces and things to be foregrounded; the second is 'recess' as a cue for the notion of receding – against claims about consistency in the narrative voice in Bowen, and claims about the use of character as the perfect foil for this voice (in free indirect discourse, for example), I argue that Bowen's 'voice' can be shown, increasingly, to recede, leaving the speaking subject-position in such doubt as to compel the willing reader to complete the point of view in lieu; and finally, 'recess' is used in the sense of a suspension or adjournment, as I argue that as narrative agency in Bowen's narratives becomes suspended, any sense of 'subjectivity' is untenable. The term I will use to describe the coming together of people and things in Bowen's short fiction – in her writings about the world of the Blitz – will be 'inter-objectivity'.

Foregrounding

Jessica Gildersleeve points out the particular immediacy and intensity with which the war insinuates itself into the short fiction on which Bowen concentrated her writing energies in that period: 'Just as Londoners were each night during the Blitz forced underground for protection, in these stories retreat into psychical recesses is necessary for survival.'[15] This is not to say that such a retreat is reserved exclusively for the stories written during this war; indeed,

Gildersleeve devotes an entire chapter of *Elizabeth Bowen and the Writing of Trauma* to a reading of *The Little Girls* (1963), Bowen's penultimate novel, as 'crypt' – inspired, perhaps, by Ellmann's brief invocation of this concept in relation to the same novel.[16] The notion of the crypt derives from the work of psychoanalysts Nicolas Abraham and Maria Torok, who revised Sigmund Freud's topography of the human psyche to explain that traumatic loss can cause a person to fail to acknowledge (and thus not properly mourn) loss by preserving the lost object intact within their own ego – the splitting of the ego is, as Freud had explained, a normal aspect of psychical growth, but this capacity for splitting also makes possible the formation of a 'crypt' or psychical enclave in which the loss can be kept secret and the object can be retained.[17] While Corcoran expresses disdain for deconstructive-psychoanalytic readings that rely on 'cryptic' formulations of this kind, I am inclined to think that he might be persuaded by Gildersleeve's reading of the 'box theme' in *The Little Girls* as the 'hole' of it, 'the cryptic silence around which the novel is built'.[18] His own readings of the late novels *Eva Trout* and *A World of Love* (1958) hinge on claims that after Bowen finally abandoned the customary methods of classical realism, her writing begins to resemble the late prose of Samuel Beckett – this is more than a mere stylistic predilection: it filters into her late novels through an approach that is 'so underminingly severe as to make the novel's modes of characterisation congruent with radical postmodern conceptions of the hollowing out of subjectivity'.[19] The severe hollowness at the core of *The Little Girls*, as described by Gildersleeve, is entirely congruent with this analysis.

Suggestions by Gildersleeve that a similar cryptic hollowness underscores the wartime short stories might not be so persuasive to Corcoran nor, for that matter, to Ellmann, for whom the 'wartime fiction, with its meticulous inventories of household objects, each depicted with surreal intensity, strives to rescue treasures from destruction'.[20] As we have noticed, Ellmann associates Bowen's surreal depictions of objects with presentations of psychological phenomena that are bestowed upon the objects themselves – the result is, Ellmann points out, a 'fragmentary artform' for a world in which the trappings of civilisation have been blasted by war. In this artform, the objects are inventoried and given life to save them from destruction. In Gildersleeve's reading of the same artform, the psychological detachment of the characters 'figures a kind of psychical defence . . . The psychic savings enable the characters of these stories to except themselves, and to be kept safe, from the traumatic reality of war.'[21] To boil this down to a point of difference, then, it seems to me that while Ellmann's reading focuses on psychical plenitude in objects to save objects from the reality of war, Gildersleeve's reading focuses on psychical detachment in characters to save characters from the reality of war. I contend that a difference of this kind is not intractable; rather, the two readings focus on different aspects of the same process that I will identify at work in Bowen's wartime short fiction – there is in the wartime short fiction a constant shifting of the terms of the subject-object relations, leading to moments in which the relationship is directly reversed.

In the words of renée c. hoogland, Bowen's writing had become recognisable by 1949 for its 'disruptive techniques . . . double negatives, inversions, broken syntactic order, and unconventional passive constructions'.[22] I shall show that these techniques are not quite as disruptive as they are generally taken to be, nor perhaps are they so 'underminingly severe' as Corcoran suggests. In the wartime fiction, in particular, we see these techniques in abundance, freed as the short fiction is from the constraints of the novel such as the extended development of character or theme. It is tempting to read unconventional constructions as the absolute lack of structure, the fragmentary artform needed to mirror the fragmentation caused by the Blitz, for example; yet, these negatives and inversions in Bowen's writing – which are consistently apparent in the wartime short fiction – create disruptions only at the level of the hierarchy of subject over object in grammar. Where the rule of character pertains in narrative, grammatical subject (or person) determines the primary position and the object is secondary. When this hierarchy is disrupted, the primacy of character is also undermined. Yet this effect will only be deemed 'severe', as in Corcoran's assessment, where a loss of character is seen as a terminal flaw in a narrative, whether or not the reader is even aware that he or she clings to character as a fundamental point of connection to a narrative. I argue here that character *as such* – and not just characters, individually – retreats, as Gildersleeve puts it, into 'psychical recesses' constructed through these techniques of inversion, yet as a product of this inversion that which is nominally present as a recess in conventional grammatical constructions comes instead to the foreground to occupy the primary position. In simpler terms, where the subject recedes in Bowen's wartime short fiction, the object is moved into its place.

First recess

In 1938, the year before the Second World War began, Bowen wrote in *The Death of the Heart* that '[a]fter inside upheavals, it is important to fix on imperturbable *things*.'[23] The quite free and rather all-too-direct narrator of this novel highlights the importance of the stability of things but also, perhaps more importantly, the key role of perception to 'fix on' things when faced with upheaval. The narrator then explains that these things 'are what we mean when we speak of civilisation: they remind us how exceedingly seldom the unseemly or unforeseeable raises its head', and declares emphatically, and somewhat prophetically, that the 'destruction of buildings and furniture is more palpably dreadful to the spirit than the destruction of human life' (pp. 207–8). As hoogland points out, this statement might seem painfully prophetic, but it also demonstrates, in advance of the war, how 'Bowen's conscious acknowledgement of the material inscription of subjectivity' equipped her to deal with the destructiveness of the Blitz when it was unleashed on London.[24] Yet hoogland quotes what Bowen herself adds in her 1945 commentary on the wartime stories in *The Demon Lover and Other Stories*: that the destruction of the war threatened to splinter people from the things that had symbolically connected them to their histories and identities, and that the role of fiction at such times is to construct the 'small worlds-within-worlds of hallucination' to enable safe storage of some sense of the 'I' until such later time as it can be reconnected to the real.[25]

In the wartime story 'Unwelcome Idea' (1941), there is more than a page of description of the landscape along Dublin bay through which the tram on the Dalkey line is proceeding, before the character of Mrs Kearney is introduced. Even then, when she boards, the reader is offered the sense that it could have been otherwise: 'All the time it approaches the Ballsbridge stop Mrs Kearney looks undecided, but when it does pull up she steps aboard because she has seen no bus' (CS, p. 574). Perhaps more importantly, we have also already seen the description of the landscape through which the tram will proceed following this stop: 'After Ballsbridge, the ozone smell of the bay sifts more and more through the smell of chimneys and pollen and the July-darkened garden trees as the bay and line converge. Then at a point you see the whole bay open' (p. 573). The 'potential' shift in narrative point of view – is this a move to second-person or is it simply a case of the indefinite personal pronoun being used in the third-person? – at the beginning of this second sentence is perhaps more disruptive than if an intended shift was made clearer by the lexical context, but I suggest that the anchor of the 'ozone smell' in the first sentence already locks the narrator's relationship to the reader into an intersubjective mode. The appeal to olfactory knowledge removes this passage from the mode of visual description and locates it within a broader sensory field, relying on the reader to do more than just complete the picture of Dublin bay.

In narrative terms, then, the opening page of 'Unwelcome Idea' is not merely creating the setting for the story of Mrs Kearney and Miss Kevin on the Dalkey tram; the tram and its regular journey is presented to us as *scenario* instead of *scene*, in which the reader takes the journey to completion before we are introduced to a character who only takes the tram on this occasion as an *incidental* decision – that is to say, the encounter between the two women becomes one incident in an otherwise much broader range of narrative possibilities. It is also worth noting that their encounter is fixed on the *objets d'art* with which they surround themselves and which provide the objective for their journey. In 'Oh! Madam . . .' (1941), the descriptive mode is removed altogether as the entire narrative is delivered as one half of a dialogue in which a maid attempts to put her lady's mind at ease following damage to their home from a bombing. According to Anne Besnault-Levita, the implied structure of dialogue invites the reader 'to fill in the gaps, complete characterisation and assess values'.[26] Besnault-Levita refers specifically to the gaps created by the absent interlocutor, so we are dealing here with gaps in speech and, therefore, an implied exchange between speaking subjects. While it is true that the maid addresses her words to the lady whose entrance and exit bookends the maid's 'obsequious monologue', the house is her constant point of reference, which means that the gaps the reader might fill and the values assessed remain at all times oriented toward the house. As soon as the maid locates her interlocutor, her words are turned toward the house and its furnishings: 'I dusted this chair for you. Yes, the hall's all right really; you don't see so much at first – only, our beautiful fanlight gone' (CS, p. 578). Much of the maid's speech thereafter is directed toward mounting a defence of the state of the house, seeking to dissuade her lady from departing: '*But you couldn't ever, not this beautiful house!* You couldn't ever . . . I know many ladies *are* . . . But, madam, this seemed so much your home' (p. 581). What is key to the presentation of the bombed house here is that it is never given to us as the setting or backdrop to implied dialogue between speaking subjects; rather, the maid's monologic discourse denies the reader a moment of narrative scene so that the house and its interior can be foregrounded and the maid's words can 'fix' upon it with ever more insistence.

In 'Careless Talk' (1941), Mary Dash cannot enjoy the conversation with a circle of friends at a restaurant without fearing for the fate of the three eggs gifted to her upon Joanna's arrival. While there is some description of setting and of waiters melting to get past the backs of chairs, a broader set of circumstances is insinuated throughout: Eric, we are told, is 'at the War Office', even as he is present at the conversation – the phrase was a common enough reference to where somebody worked, but it reminds the reader here that no matter where else he might be, Eric is also always 'at' the War Office and his constant checks of his watch reinforce the point. The group's regular session at the restaurant is clearly an opportune moment to attempt to forget the war and to talk without care, yet the fragility of the three eggs becomes a reminder of the inability of *things* to be imperturbable. Indeed, Céline Magot points out, there is a persistent refusal by the interlocutors in 'Careless Talk' to talk *about* any-*thing* in particular, as indefinite phrases abound throughout and any questions are followed immediately by polite retractions.[27] Lassner notes that the casual name dropping in which the interlocutors engage here creates a tension between the 'hope it didn't matter my having told you that' and 'the anxiety that it does matter, both politically and personally'.[28] Magot adds that the 'Careless Talk Costs Lives' poster series – from which Bowen took the name of the story, having originally published it in the *New Yorker* of October 1941 under the name 'Everything's Frightfully Interesting' – emphasised just how much the talk about nothing in particular *mattered*. By the time we get to 'Mysterious Kôr' (1944), 'setting' as such has given way altogether to the 'worlds-within-worlds of hallucination' – as John Bayley notes, the mention of the name of the mythical Kôr is enough for Pepita to summon in place of the London she beholds at that same moment with Arthur, 'the image of an abandoned city, its towers, walls, and stone steps lit up by the moon, empty and unchanged throughout centuries'.[29] Unlike the lady in 'Oh! Madam . . .' who abandons her home, Pepita and Arthur are in search of a home with which to begin their story and they conjure one from Rider Haggard's *She* (1887). What Pepita invokes, I would add, is an always empty locale, a cityscape defined as a no-place and so therefore impossible to populate. Their invocation of Kôr creates potential for the infinite recession of Pepita and Arthur as characters in relation to each other – they have *nowhere to be*, let alone to be with each other – signalling the ultimate void toward which Pepita turns at the story's end. Without hope of a reconnection to the real, the 'I' is not stored safely here; it recedes totally.

Second recess

The last of Bowen's stories to be published before the end of the Second World War, 'Mysterious Kôr' signals the void into which Bowen would leap with her postwar novels. Elizabeth C. Inglesby reminds us that by 1951 Bowen had made a significant reassessment of her approach to the material world based on her experiences of wartime London and that this new view was discussed in radio interviews and incorporated into her novels.[30] *The Little Girls* reveals 'in almost parodic form the author's incompletely resolved approach to material reality by deliberately downplaying and even obfuscating the inner life of characters and making the contents of caves, coffers, and houses a major focus of the novel'. The narrator 'takes on the task of recognising this unseen world, despite the short-sightedness of those who actually live in it in embodied fashion.'[31] What I take this to mean is that the characters in *The Little Girls* are superfluous to the narrative – they exist in this narrative world purely to fail to see the caves, coffers and houses on which the story focuses. It is as if this world results from a decision to populate Kôr: spaces remain empty despite characters being patently there in the space; they are as invisible to it as it is to them. In a reading of *The Hotel* (1927), Patrick W. Moran claims that Bowen's work, 'while remaining more involved with its realist business, is almost equally invested in staging a drama of lifelessness: her obsessive interest in manners and the elaborate artifice of her fictive societies signals an anxiety that her characters risk being consumed by the vacancy that surrounds them.'[32] Characters 'being consumed by the vacancy that surrounds them' might also seem like a perfectly apt description of the fate of character in 'Mysterious Kôr' and *The Little Girls*, published seventeen and thirty-seven years after *The Hotel*, respectively. In addition, though, the senses of 'anxiety' and 'risk' that are attached to the prospect of the consumption of characters by vacancy is not entirely present in the world of Kôr – not, that is, until the final fateful sentence – and not at all a feature of *The Little Girls*.

What I suggest, then, is that the wartime fiction hinges on the necessity of consuming character per se, and it does this by absolving the material world of any risk of putting itself before the characters for whom it might more conventionally be deemed correlative. This paves the way for the failure of vision suffered by the characters in the longer postwar work like *The Little Girls*. In Inglesby's description of the later novel, there does remain a strong unifying force at work throughout: 'The narrative voice Bowen adopts in *The Little Girls* allows her to speak about setting and atmosphere from a multilayered perspective that includes both the palpable sense that objects and scenes live and the skepticism and irony with which her jaded characters regard such a disturbing intuition.'[33] While I am sympathetic toward Inglesby's desire to account for the fundamental separation of character from object in the later fiction, the description of the double vision in the narrative voice carries with it the potential to collapse the two into a single structure of narration: the narrator's multilayered perspective contains the vision that sees objects as entities, but it also conveys what a character would think about that vision. Thus the narrator takes on the role of character where everything about its vision suggests character is irrelevant and even obstructive to this vision.

In a similar vein, Lis Christensen identifies throughout all of the later novels a tendency to construct a narrator who adopts a role such that 'what may seem at first glance to be neutral exposition often proves to reflect the viewpoint and style of a character'.[34] If Christensen's descriptions of this drift from neutral exposition to character-oriented narration in the form of 'free indirect thought or speech allusion' are indeed true of all of the later fiction – and it is beyond the scope of the present work to explore this prospect further – it may be a consequence of the sustained demand for character that one expects to find in a novel: a feature of the form, no matter how much the author may seek to undermine it.[35] In the shorter wartime fiction, however, the same demand is diminished. I have already shown here that there is a marked transition in Bowen's approach to presenting descriptions of scene through the wartime fiction – the same is true, I will argue, for her use of narrative voice. In the case of 'Oh! Madam . . .', of course, the narration is ostensibly only conveyed in the voice of a character, but this strategy enabled Bowen to slip the shackles of scene that dominated the opening passages of 'Unwelcome Idea'. 'Summer Night' begins in similar fashion to 'Unwelcome Idea', with a prolonged description of the view from the road down which the 'small woman drove with her chin up' (*CS*, p. 583), but the presentation of the description does not lead us automatically to a space outside the only incidental encounter to which we are invited to bear witness in the earlier story. In 'Summer Night', the perspective seems ostensibly limited to that offered by the driver, but the content of the descriptions comes from outside of her experience and contains her within it: 'The big shabby family car was empty but for its small driver – its emptiness seemed to levitate it – on its back seat a coat slithered about, and a dressing case bumped against the seat' (p. 583). Here the woman who would be a focal character is merely the first in the series of objects, occupying a vehicle that at first 'was empty'.

The woman, whose name we learn to be Emma only from the snippet of the telephone conversation she eventually initiates from the hotel lobby, has left her family to rendezvous with her lover, Robinson, but the story then unfolds through a series of vignettes in which the story-worlds inhabited by the other characters – including Robinson – stubbornly refuse to be drawn toward Emma. As Gildersleeve argues in a detailed reading of this story, the prevailing reading in which the character relations and their shattered illusions are paramount does not fully capture the 'wartime pressure' that remains constant throughout.[36] Characters cling here to memories in order to avoid the traumatic present. To this I would add that the narrative voice drifts from character to character, incapable of finding one suitably locked in the present to enable a third-person limited perspective to develop fully. Perhaps the closest the narrator comes to adopting the voice of a character occurs when Aunt Fran retreats to her bedroom to reflect and lament on her family's undertakings: 'Who shall be their judge? Not I. The blood of the world is poisoned, feels Aunt Fran, with her forehead over the eiderdown' (*CS*, p. 599). Even at this moment, the narrative voice is destabilised: the 'I' that seems to speak as Fran gives way immediately to the limited perspective that describes in third person what she 'feels'; the shift in tense is palpable, continuing for the remainder of the passage, until a shift in vignette restores us to past tense which, perhaps appropriately, shifts the focus of the narrative to living death: 'Queenie understood that the third child, the girl, was dead' (p. 600). It is as though Aunt Fran, who comes closest to capturing the narrative voice for her own, is also Bowen's reminder that at this time, presence, being in the here and now of 'wartime pressure', is death.

By the time we arrive at the ghost stories, such as 'The Demon Lover' (1941) and 'Ivy Gripped the Steps' (1945), the narrative voice – such as it is in the wartime fiction anything resembling a consistent voice – drifts closer to the realisation of this prospect that present tense is death. In 'Ivy Gripped the Steps', for example, the ivy that 'gripped and sucked at the flight of steps' prompts the narrator to immediately reveal only a limited sense of the material world: 'One was left to guess at the size and the number of windows hidden by looking at those in the other side' (*CS*, p. 686). Not for this narrator is there to be the kind of insight into material things that will accrue in the later novels – if ivy blocks the view, then 'one' is left to guess what it conceals. After the encounter with the ivy affords the narrator a chance to introduce us to the protagonist-of-sorts, Gavin Doddington, there is a shift in the story which is marked in the most literal fashion: 'The story originated in a friendship between two young girls in their Dresden finishing year' (p. 689). Gavin's perceptions, such as they are, are locked into two dimensions: 'Not that afternoon, not indeed, until some way on into this first visit did Gavin distinguish at all sharply between Mrs Nicholson and her life. Not till the knife of love gained sufficient edge could he cut out her figure from its surroundings' (p. 690). And as 'his senses began to be haunted by the anticipation of going back' (p. 692), experiencing new information only in an anterior mode, he is described in terms that are reminiscent of the ivy with which the reader's perspective was initially obscured: 'gripping the handrail, bracing his spine against it . . . in the hopes of intercepting her line of view' (p. 694), 'he gripped his way, flight by flight, up the polished banister rail, on which his palms left patches of mist; pulling himself up away from her on the staircase as he had pulled himself towards her up the face of the cliff' (p. 702).

Similarly, for the fated Mrs Drover in 'The Demon Lover', there is no consolation in a fixed narrative perspective – the foreboding letter from her long-forgotten soldier appears out of nowhere, prompting a collapse of past and present that does not register as wholeness: the house and its hollowness 'cancelled years on years of voices, habits and steps' (p. 664). There is no sense, either, that the reader enjoys being present in a position from which to look upon events, as the taxi from which she screams at the last 'made off with her into the hinterland of deserted streets' (p. 666). In order to fix upon character here, Bowen removes all other people from the extended location of the story, and the effect is ultimately fatal for the individual upon whom the narrative settles. Sinéad Mooney has pointed out that Bowen's ghost stories 'force her reader to accommodate a fictional universe entirely *au fait* with the innovations of modernity – what "Look at All Those Roses" [1941] sums up as "the typewriter, the cocktail shaker, the telephone . . . the car" . . . but which is a world where ghosts, nonetheless, walk.'[37] In Bowen's ghost stories, these technical innovations provide a sense of a material world entirely familiar to a reader, but in these inventions that have enabled people to collapse the distances between them, the familiar also jars with the reality of the Blitz, in which 'the world' is too much with the hinterland and the houses. In such a world, where the narrative voice might be expected to cling to character – to fix upon persons more perhaps than things – the result is instead a splintering of voice from anything like a speaking subject, shouting instead into an abyss from which life does not speak back.

Third recess: . . . to inter-objectivity

Referring to *Bowen's Court* (1942), Bowen's wartime memoir of her family home, Derek Hand observes that the descriptive mode used to convey impressions of the house is like 'the time-lapse technique made use of primarily in wildlife and nature documentaries', which on replay means that 'changes that to the naked eye "in real time" would be almost imperceptible are clearly observable'.[38] Importantly, as Hand notes further, the backdrop against which this subtle surface movement unfolds remains unwaveringly constant and still – 'the countryside, the demesne, and the house are the calm points around which these changes happen' – and the place is devoid of human activity.[39] Referring to two of Bowen's novels from the interwar period, *The Last September* (1929) and *The House in Paris* (1935), Lassner and Paula Derdiger demonstrate that the homes in Bowen's narratives always exceed their objective status as the backdrop for domestic drama: 'regardless of how insular or stable, domestic space in Bowen's writing is never merely private, but rather always generative of and invaded by the history and politics constituting the public sphere'.[40] I suggest that the tumult of the Blitz hammered home this point about the invasion of the private sphere by the public sphere to Bowen's own lived experience of house and home during her time in London, but that *The Last September* had already provided occasion for her to link the inherited family home to the politics of rupture. By the time she reflects on Bowen's Court during the war, then, it is a space already invaded, so to speak. The time-lapse technique described by Hand could be seen on the basis of this history as an attempt by Bowen to divest the location of its link to the public sphere – to divest it of its history. Of course, in *Bowen's Court*, this is only a temporary measure, as the pressures of family chronicle weigh too heavily on the text and, as Lassner notes, Bowen's inherited home provided the model for the idea that houses – especially those that change hands – 'are haunted by the wishes and fears its original owners invested in them'.[41]

If the time-lapse technique proved only temporary in the case of *Bowen's Court*, it may be that we can see it operating more thoroughly in the opening of 'Unwelcome Idea' and the developing narrative mode as I have explained it in other wartime short stories. Keri Walsh has suggested that the stories written during the Blitz are not divorced from the Anglo-Irish Gothic tradition, but that this tradition is merged with Surrealist techniques to create specific haunting effects.[42] Whereas Bowen had experimented with Surrealism in her work of the 1930s, her use of detailed descriptions in the wartime short stories, Walsh explains, mirrors Salvador Dali's veristic Surrealism, based on the discovery that 'realism, pressed to an extreme of detail, could subvert one's sense of reality'.[43] This technique is particularly well suited to the ghost stories as the subversion of a reader's sense of reality generates the kind of haunting effects to which Walsh refers. I would go further here to suggest that this description of Bowen's version of veristic Surrealism provides us with the necessary tipping point we require to get us to where we need to move, beyond realism, to a fuller sense of the technique employed in Bowen's wartime fiction: it is not that realism has been abandoned altogether in this work; it is rather that realism is pressed 'to an extreme of detail' in order to subvert the real *for the reader*. One of the difficulties for any writer attempting this version of veristic Surrealism is surely that a technique made most perfect on a painted canvas will struggle to translate to a medium that lends itself to character and plot, to the unfolding of events in time. For Bowen, even in the incidental encounter upon which we focus momentarily in 'Unwelcome Idea', a sense of the encounter is nonetheless vital to hold the story together.

In the drift toward the extremes of detail that more clearly define the later stories of the war years, though, we see that Bowen's technique more insistently removes from characters their role as narrative agents. A return to the first-person perspective, such as in 'The Dolt's Tale' (1944), is by that time no longer able to be categorised as the tale of a character: it becomes, instead, the tale told by an idiot, as the saying goes – full of sound and fury, signifying nothing. The story could be a dream, although the narrator assures that it is not, and the lack of detail and faulty memory about what has actually happened is stultifying. Even here, then, in the midst of a first-person narrative, the reader is no longer able to *relate to* a speaking subject. The intersubjective relationship that a reader may otherwise normally expect to be able to form in the engagement with a narration is stumped by Bowen's technique in these stories. The result is a reversal of subject–object relations that amounts to what might be called instead an *inter-objectivity*, which may explain in part the disconcerting effect they can have on the reader. It is, in other words, as if the reader is addressed not as interlocutor but as another of the objects through which the story is always in the process of *being told* – a process that remains unfinished even at the ends of the tales in question.

Within the experience of the Blitz, it may be fair to say that nobody could know if the war would ever end. The lack of closure in the shorter fiction carries with it the resonance of this uncertainty. There is, after all, no absolute present from which the tale of the Blitz can hope to have spoken of the events as if they are in the past tense. For this reason, the wartime short stories remain constantly in suspension, collapsing past and present time, confusing the temporal location from which any statement can be made. Beyond the war, when Bowen was to turn her hand once more to the novel form, the will to write about the war in the same terms remained intact. In *The Heat of the Day* (1949), a good many of the same techniques are extrapolated at length, and even characters – the lifeblood of the novel form – struggle throughout to learn some truth about each other unless it comes from the material world of objects and photographs. Stella's confusion is at one point contrasted to the list of instructions left behind by Cousin Francis, from '*Clocks*, when and how to wind . . .', to '*Hysteria, Puppies*, in case of . . .', to 'In case of *My Death* . . .', and 'In case of *Emergency Message from Lady C.*' Stella, who has not thought quite so much ahead is instead forever grappling with a past from which it seems she emerged only as a spectral residue of worldly possessions: 'Oh to stay here for ever, playing this ghostly part! Unwillingly she looked behind her – her gloves, shaped by her hands, her bag, containing every damning proof of her identity, were still, always, there on the centre table where she had put them down.'[44] Even her lover, Robert, can be easily imagined as dead by the simple act of turning his photograph to the wall, 'in order to try to picture life without him', although, ironically, it is this attempt at erasure that brings the power of his impact on her home with fuller force: 'she had to hold on to the chimneypiece while she steadied her body against the beating of her heart . . . She tried to say "Robert!" but had no voice' (p. 277). In the postwar novel about the war, then, Bowen continues the work that had taken shape under the pressure of the Blitz: the work of being done with the business of realism, of the receding of character and plot, and the foregrounding of detail without ever giving over solely to the demands of scene. Where Gavin Doddington had more than once to grip the steps, Stella now grips onto the chimneypiece – the trappings of their houses remain the only stable aspect of their lives – and in so doing, they find they have no voice.

Notes

1. Elizabeth Bowen, *The Collected Stories of Elizabeth Bowen*, ed. Angus Wilson (London: Vintage, 1999), p. 759. Hereafter cited parenthetically as *CS*.
2. Maud Ellmann, *Elizabeth Bowen: The Shadow Across the Page* (Edinburgh: Edinburgh University Press, 2003), p. 5.
3. Ibid.
4. Ibid. pp. 5–6.
5. Julie Anne Stevens, 'Bowen: The Critical Response', in *Elizabeth Bowen*, ed. Eibhear Walshe (Dublin: Irish Academic Press, 2009), pp. 179–92 (p. 185).
6. Elizabeth Bowen, 'Preface' to *Stories by Elizabeth Bowen* (1959), in *The Mulberry Tree: Writings of Elizabeth Bowen*, ed. Hermione Lee (San Diego: Harcourt Brace Jovanovich, 1986), pp. 126–30 (p. 130).
7. Neil Corcoran, *Elizabeth Bowen: The Enforced Return* (Oxford: Oxford University Press, 2004), p. 4.
8. Ibid. p. 6.
9. Ibid. p. 11.
10. Phyllis Lassner, *Elizabeth Bowen: A Study of the Short Fiction* (New York: Twayne, 1991), pp. 159–63.
11. Ibid. p. 163.
12. Ibid. p. 160.
13. Sarah Savitt, 'Bowen Redux,' *Cambridge Quarterly*, 34.2 (2005): 188–92 (p. 191).
14. Lassner, *A Study of the Short Fiction*, p. 78.
15. Jessica Gildersleeve, *Elizabeth Bowen and the Writing of Trauma: The Ethics of Survival* (Amsterdam and New York: Rodopi, 2014), p. 88.
16. Ibid. pp. 147–67; Ellmann, *The Shadow Across the Page*, p. 199.
17. Abraham and Torok's revisions of the Freudian model are demonstrated practically in *The Wolf Man's Magic Word: A Cryptonymy* (Minneapolis: University of Minnesota Press, 1986) and explained most cogently, I suggest, in their *The Shell and the Kernel: Renewals of Psychoanalysis* (Chicago: University of Chicago Press, 1994). For my own analysis of the theory of the crypt and its origins within psychoanalysis, see *The Wolf Man's Burden* (Ithaca: Cornell University Press, 2001), and 'Cryptonymic Secretion: On the Kind-ness of Strangers,' in *Re-Reading Derrida: Perspectives on Mourning and Its Hospitalities*,

ed. Tony Thwaites and Judith Seaboyer (Lanham, MD: Lexington, 2013), pp. 117–30.
18. Gildersleeve, *Elizabeth Bowen and the Writing of Trauma*, p. 149.
19. Corcoran, *The Enforced Return*, p. 8, p. 128.
20. Ellmann, *The Shadow Across the Page*, pp. 146–7.
21. Gildersleeve, *Elizabeth Bowen and the Writing of Trauma*, p. 88.
22. renée c. hoogland, *Elizabeth Bowen: A Reputation in Writing* (New York: New York University Press, 1994), p. 119.
23. Elizabeth Bowen, *The Death of the Heart* (Harmondsworth: Penguin, 1984), p. 207. Hereafter cited parenthetically as *DH*.
24. hoogland, *A Reputation in Writing*, p. 112.
25. Ibid. p. 114. To my way of thinking, hoogland's account of the shift in Bowen's writing is accurate, certainly to the extent that the techniques and concerns evident in the wartime fiction did not spring from nowhere. Unfortunately, the account is disbursed in three short pages as a brief explanatory interlude covering the changes that transpired in Bowen's life and writing from *The Death of the Heart* in 1938 to *The Heat of the Day* in 1949, albeit without specific examples from the short stories in question. I would like here to provide more detail to the map of this transition.
26. Anne Besnault-Levita, 'The Dramaturgy of Voice in Five Modernist Short Fictions: Katherine Mansfield's "The Canary," "The Lady's Maid" and "Late at Night," Elizabeth Bowen's "Oh! Madam . . ." and Virginia Woolf's "The Evening Party"', *Journal of the Short Story in English*, 51 (2008): n.p.
27. Céline Magot, '"Careless Talk": Word Shortage in Elizabeth Bowen's Wartime Writing', *Miranda*, 2 (2010): n.p.
28. Lassner, *A Study of the Short Fiction*, p. 39.
29. John Bayley, *The Short Story: Henry James to Elizabeth Bowen* (Hemel Hempstead: Harvester Wheatsheaf, 1988), p. 169.
30. Elizabeth C. Inglesby, '"Expressive Objects": Elizabeth Bowen's Narrative Materialises', *Modern Fiction Studies*, 53.2 (2007): 306–33 (pp. 306–7).
31. Ibid. p. 307.
32. Patrick W. Moran, 'Eizabeth Bowen's Toys and the Imperative of Play', *Éire-Ireland*, 46.1/2 (2011): 152–76 (p. 160).
33. Inglesby, 'Expressive Objects', pp. 307–8.
34. Lis Christensen, *Elizabeth Bowen: The Later Fiction* (Copenhagen: Museum Tusculanum, 2001), p. 102.
35. Ibid. p. 101.
36. Gildersleeve, *Elizabeth Bowen and the Writing of Trauma*, p. 94.
37. Sinéad Mooney, 'Bowen and the Modern Ghost', in *Elizabeth Bowen*, ed. Eibhear Walshe (Dublin: Irish Academic Press, 2009), p. 78.
38. Derek Hand, 'Ghosts from Our Future: Bowen and the Unfinished Business of Living', in Walshe, *Elizabeth Bowen*, pp. 65–76 (p. 74).

39. Ibid.
40. Phyllis Lassner and Paula Derdiger, 'Domestic Gothic, the Global Primitive, and Gender Relations in Elizabeth Bowen's *The Last September* and *The House in Paris*', in *Irish Modernism and the Global Primitive*, ed. Maria McGarrity and Claire A. Culleton (New York: Palgrave Macmillan, 2009), pp. 195–214 (p. 195).
41. Lassner, *A Study of the Short Fiction*, p. 5.
42. Keri Walsh, 'Elizabeth Bowen: Surrealist'. See chapter 2.
43. Robert Hughes, cited in Walsh 'Elizabeth Bowen: Surrealist', p. 40.
44. Elizabeth Bowen, *The Heat of the Day* (London: Random House, 1998), p. 164. Hereafter cited parenthetically as *HD*.

Chapter 9

'Some Really Raging Peculiarity': Female Fetishism in *The Little Girls*

Patricia Juliana Smith

> You know, a person's only a person when they have some really raging peculiarity.[1]
>
> These fragments I have shored against my ruins.[2]
>
> The term 'fetishism' almost has a life of its own. Instead of functioning as a metalanguage for the magical thinking of others, it turns against those who use it, and surreptitiously exposes their own magical thinking.[3]

Elizabeth Bowen had an eye for things. Throughout her fictional works she provides sustained descriptions of objects as well as individual characters' relationships to them. At times her female characters' interactions with objects appear fetishistic, as they attain an undue level of interest or power in their lives that goes well beyond mere functionality or metaphorical value. To discuss these objects and their often-overdetermined significance as fetishistic, though, is problematic in terms of traditional scholarly discourse, which generally defines fetishism through three different and potentially conflicting disciplinary or ideological perspectives, those of psychology, Marxist theory and anthropology.

Freudian psychology views fetishism primarily in erotic terms, as a means of phallic surrogation to alleviate castration anxiety; thus fetishism is thought to be an exclusively male indulgence. Marxist theory holds fetishism as a sign of decadent consumerism in capitalist culture and, as such, constitutes a social ill. Finally, anthropology situates the origins of fetishism outside of Western culture, the term itself deriving from the Portuguese *feitiço*, denoting the various beads, trinkets and other insignificant objects that European colonisers and merchants exchanged with indigenous peoples in Africa, Asia and the Americas, usually for something of much greater value. Accordingly, Eurocentric thought considered the indigenous attraction to these objects as indicative of idolatry, and thus un-Christian, backwards, savage and perverted.[4] Filtered through these lenses, any discussion of fetishism must inevitably define these human relationships with objects as negative or pathological.

None of these discourses adequately delineate Bowen's characters' often intense and at times irrational connection to certain objects. Elements of eroticism, consumerism and, by means of what might best be described as 'magical thinking', some sort of superstitious investment of power are undoubtedly present, yet their functions do not strictly conform to any of these discourses. They primarily involve female rather than male characters and are hardly represented as perverted or problematic; indeed, Bowen expresses little in terms of value judgement regarding these attachments. Moreover, virtually everything in Bowen's output is situated entirely within the realm of Western culture; there is no attempt to exoticise the objects or their possessors' behaviours. Accordingly, given the predominance of these three typical means of analysing fetishism, there has been little critical discussion of what Bowen's characters are doing with objects, to the extent that these unusual actions become nearly invisible in plain sight. Recent scholarship questioning conventional thinking about fetishism, however, can provide a means for understanding fetishism in Bowen's work. In his exhaustive study, *Fetishism and Culture: A Different Theory of Modernity* (2014), Harmut Böhme not only challenges the assumption that fetishism is a product of non-European culture but also maintains that it is an integral part of modern life. E. L. McCallum's queer feminist critique, *Object Lessons: How to Do Things with Fetishism* (1999), challenges the male-only construction of fetishism, suggesting that fetishism, which she sees as related to melancholia, must be approached in a manner that departs from culturally inscribed binary thinking.

Traditional interpretations of Freud's thoughts on fetishism – indeed, Freud's own understanding of it – suggest that it results from a male child's castration anxiety upon realising that his mother lacks a phallus. It would follow, then, that the female child would be immune from this particular fear (although she could, within the parameters of Freudian theory, be afflicted with penis envy), making female fetishism impossible. McCallum questions this assumption, positing that fetishism is not so much the result of *lack* as it is of *loss*:

The shift from lack to loss which brings fetishism into view with melancholia also puts pressure on the binary interpretation of gender, which is premised on both heterosexuality and the literal presence or absence of a penis and is thus intimately associated with lack. This framework serves to deny the possibility of women being fetishists, since it is their purported lack of a penis that provides the very reason for women's exclusion from fetishism. Shifting the grounds of fetishism to loss would seem to render fetishism accessible to all humans without regard to gender, since we all have experienced primordial loss in individuation from our mothers.[5]

McCallum's position adheres closely to Bowen's female characters and the manner in which they ascribe symbolic meaning to particular objects. Without exception, they are responding, directly or indirectly, to traumatic losses, either past or recent but nonetheless unresolved.[6] Similarly, Emily Apter's understanding of female fetishism is equally apt when applied to Bowen's novels:

> Using [the] language of a gynotextual desire that recognises the feminine relic as symbolising something both more than and less than a simple compensatory object, we might better understand the polysemic character of female fetishism. Whether standing in for lover, parent, child, or female double, the female fetish belongs to an erotic economy of severance and disappropriation, itself less fixed on a fiction of castration anxiety. In interpreting Freud's statement that the 'horror of castration sets up a sort of permanent memorial to itself by creating this (fetish) substitute', I am tempted to retain his concept of a memorial or marker to which the female subject 'clings' but would want to question the preeminence of a 'castrated' site within the female fetishist's Imaginary.[7]

Apter also suggests that such use of fetish objects is understood between and among women through a linguistic or semiotic 'gynotext' to which she refers. Citing Luce Irigaray's *Speculum of the Other Woman* (1985), she observes that '[w]omen . . . discover in . . . each other a "language of their own"'.[8] This shared language/semiotic might well explain why a specifically female form of fetishism is generally unremarked – or even invisible to – Freud and other male theorists.

Bowen's female characters, most of whom interact primarily with others of their sex, rarely evince behaviours that could be legitimately construed as castration anxiety or penis envy; rather, they are almost always commemorating a loss or severance. Bowen understood that such markers are frequent among women and begin in pre-adolescence. A curious passage in 'The Mulberry Tree' (1934), a memoir of Bowen's life at Downe House, the girls' school she attended during the First World War (and upon which the school in *The Little Girls* is based) suggests that she was able to comprehend a degree of female fetishism intuitively early in life:

> [Among the] features of . . . the house [was] a modern addition . . . in the form of a chalet, from whose balcony I played Jezebel with a friend's teddy bear.
>
> The survival of such childish inanimate pets was encouraged by fashion; several dormitory beds with their glacial white quilts were encumbered all day and shared nightly with rubbed threadbare teddy bears, monkeys or in one case a blue plush elephant. Possibly this seemed a good way to travesty sentiment: we cannot really have been idiotic girls. A friend of mine wore a carved ivory Chinese dog round her neck on a gold cord for some days, then she was asked to wear this inside her djibbah. A good deal of innocent fetishism came to surround these animals; the mistress of the blue elephant used to walk the passages saying: 'You must kiss my elephant' . . . The ever difficult business of getting oneself across was most pressing of all at this age: restricted possessions, a uniform dictated down to the last detail and a self-imposed but rigid emotional snobbishness shutting the more direct means of self-expression away. Foibles, mannerisms we therefore exaggerated most diligently.[9]

Beginning with a note of the vaguely kinky but 'innocent' play frequent among pre-adolescent girls, Bowen sees these activities as an expression of individuality while outwardly mocking sentiment. Obviously these actions in the homosocial context of a girls' school are not about enactments of lacking a phallus. The sense of 'travesty[ing] sentiment' – or at least the disavowal thereof – nonetheless suggests an underlying element of loss such as that which McCallum and Apter describe. The girls are separated from home and, accordingly their mothers. They cling to childish things even as they attempt to individuate themselves among their peers, yet use these objects ironically as if to suggest they are beyond these things.

Inanimate objects exert a powerful influence over characters in many, if not most of Bowen's fictions, but nowhere else to the extent that informs *The Little Girls*, which can easily be deemed a novel about objects. As Andrew Bennett and Nicholas Royce observe, '[o]bjects in Bowen's novels function in shifting and unstable ways. In *The Little Girls*, they function, above all, as displaced simulacra of life: they live on for us in posterity, representing our idiosyncrasies, idiosyncrasies which constitute our identities, but in some sense they are those identities.'[10]

Dinah Delacroix (née Diana Piggott, also known by her childhood nickname, 'Dicey') is, in the narrative present, a sixtyish widow and grandmother of means, living comfortably in a well-appointed country house in Somerset. She lacks occupation, and the empty cave on her property that she seeks to fill with the familiar objects of her neighbours, 'things (a dozen from each) which they couldn't have normally borne to part with', can be understood as symbolic of the emptiness of what would seem a pleasant and easy life (*LG*, p. 11). Her quixotic, manic notion of creating a sort of time capsule 'for someone or other to come upon in the far future ... hundreds or perhaps thousands of years hence' is, moreover, a sublimation and repetition of a historical trauma, one that she has banished from her conscious mind until a familiar sight triggers its recollection (p. 10). As the plot unfolds, it becomes increasingly clear that Dinah's obsession and identification with buried objects – or 'incubed' ones, as both Maud Ellmann and Jessica Gildersleeve deem them – signify the extent to which she is trapped in an endless childhood that leaves her as isolated, solipsistic and traumatised as any of Bowen's adolescent *naïfs*.[11] If *The Little Girls* is the least appreciated – or possibly most maligned – of Bowen's late works, it might well be that some critics and readers have failed to grasp this most crucial aspect of the novel.[12] Yet this is not the only reason that this novel is baffling to so many readers. Lis Christensen notes that in *The Little Girls* 'we now find the actions and words of her characters, and the comments of their friends, replacing psychological analysis – and much narrative report – on the part of their creator.'[13] Bowen's friend Spencer Curtis Brown recalls that while writing the novel, 'she for the first time deliberately tried ... to present characters entirely from the outside. She'd determined never to tell the reader what her characters were thinking or feeling.'[14] Accordingly, one is left to interpret character motivation through conversations and actions, making any critique of the work highly subjective. Even so, Bowen provides an abundance of clues from which one can draw valid and insightful conclusions.

Laura Mulvey posits that '[t]he fetish object ... commemorates ... [It] fixes and freezes the historic event outside rational memory and individual chronology. But the fetish still stays in touch with its original traumatic real and retains a potential access to its own historical story.'[15] For Dinah, if only subconsciously, the collecting and burying of objects links two traumatic historical events, the first of which comprises the anxiety-filled days of July 1914, leading to the commencement of the First World War and the loss and bereavement that ensued. The second, set in the late 1950s or early 1960s as the novel begins, is linked to an apprehension so horrifying that Dinah can barely articulate it. When Mrs Coral, her prosaic neighbour, asks who will seal the cave, Diana experiences momentary dissociation:

> Showing frantic estrangement from all surroundings, she beat one fist, irregularly and slowly, on the palm of the other hand. She seemed by turns to be seeking. Listening, or dazedly simply waiting for some answer . . . [H]er face looked white – not . . . from distress: here, rather, was some consuming excitement . . . [She] said nothing.

Her eventual response, 'Oh, whoever's the last!' leads her companion, Major Frank Wilkins, to add, '[w]e may all go out with the same bang' (*LG*, p. 13). That the novel was written when the threat of nuclear annihilation was at its peak and published in the year of the Cuban Missile Crisis, the historical moment in which the United States and the Soviet Union came closest to mutual destruction is hardly coincidental.

By getting her neighbours to participate, Dinah attempts to transform her personal angst into a communal one. While there is little doubt that the fear of death by atomic bomb was widespread, those around her remain unconvinced of the merits of her enterprise. Her attempt to explain the importance of the objects to future generations, as illogical as it might seem on the surface, reveals much about her own relationship to fetishism:

> Clues to reconstruct us from. Expressive objects. What really expresses people? The things – I'm sure – that they have obsessions about: keep on wearing or using, or fuss when they lose, or can't go to sleep without. You know, a person's only a person when they have some really raging peculiarity – don't you notice that . . . with all your friends? (p. 11)

Her linking of objects and obsessions is a garden-variety description of fetishism, which she further connects with personal peculiarity. In effect, she suggests that fetishism is a condition of identity itself, without which a person is not a person. The unfolding of the novel's plot demonstrates the extent to which Dinah defines her own identity by means of objects, perhaps without clearly understanding her reasons for doing so.

The question of sealing the cave, combined with a glance at a crooked swing that Mrs Coral imagines to be unsafe, evokes a Proustian moment for Dinah, in which she 'remembered something all in a flash, so completely that it's not "then" but "now"' (p. 20). At that moment, the cave becomes for her 'really only a repetition . . . a going back, again, to something begun'; that is, to a school at which a similar swing existed and where she and two other girls buried a coffer full of objects at the beginning of another war (p. 21). In a manic burst of energy, she composes and sends off personal notices to newspapers throughout England. Their vague and urgent wording suggests something scandalous, possibly criminal:

> Sheikie and Mumbo, where are you? Your former confederate Dicey seeks you earnestly, in connection with a matter known so far only to us. Whole affair now looks like coming to light. Essential we meet before too late. You or anyone knowing the present whereabouts of Sheila *née* Beaker and Clare *née* Burkin-Jones, who in 1914 were at St Agatha's, Southstone, should at once write to Box xxxx. (p. 28)

Dinah, whom Frank accuses of being 'fey', demonstrates a solipsistic disregard for the perspectives of others and a certain lack of maturity, in plotting this scheme, a seemingly disproportionate reaction to a recollection of a childhood prank. The notices' intended recipients, alarmed not only by the public nature of these messages but also their sheer perversity, see it as such. Sheila and Clare meet to discuss the meaning of this escapade, but after nearly fifty years, they are strangers as much to each other as they are to Dinah.

Dinah's behaviour, though confused and even silly, is more complex than either Sheila or Clare – or even Dinah herself – can imagine. The wording of the offending notices indicates that Dinah, both in the past and in the present, has invested much more meaning into the ritual burial of the objects than either of her friends, so much that she feels compelled to recreate and revisit the event, and believes that her erstwhile companions share her feelings while blissfully unaware that she could be causing them embarrassment or discomfort. Child psychologist Jean Piaget's comments on infantile solipsism might well describe Dinah:

> The true solipsist projects his states of mind onto things ... [and] is entirely alone in the world, that is, he has no notion of anything exterior to himself. In other words, the true solipsist has no idea of self. There is no self: there is the world. It is in this that it is reasonable to call a baby a solipsist: the feelings and desires of a baby know no limits since they are a part of everything he sees, touches, and perceives ...
>
> [E]gocentrism in children clearly appears to be a simple continuation of solipsism in infants. Egocentrism ... is not an intentional or even a conscious process. A child has no idea that he is egocentric. He believes everybody thinks the way he does, and this false universality is due simply to an absence of the sense of limits on his individuality. In this light, egocentrism and solipsism are quite comparable: both stem from the absence or the weakness of the sense of the self.[16]

In effect, a significant part of Dinah's psyche has never completely grown up. Her fuzzy thinking throughout the novel along with her relationship to objects show 'an absence of the sense of limits' as well a distinct 'weakness of the sense of the self'.

That Dinah has managed to survive for nearly six decades in this infantilised state is the result of several factors. As Clare points out several times, both in the past and present, Dinah was never a very clear thinker. On the day of her parting with Clare, a day coinciding with the assassination of Archduke Franz Ferdinand, the event that precipitated the First World War, she asks Clare in bewilderment, '[w]ho did kill that Australian duke?' Clare, irritated, corrects her: 'Austrian ... Archduke. Get that into your head' (*LG*, p. 162, p. 163). Later that day, she fails to comprehend the meaning of the poignant farewell between Major Birkin-Jones, Clare's father, and Mrs Piggott, her mother, marking the end of their affair. Throughout her life, Dinah has been taken care of by one protector after another. After her mother's death, the affluent and responsible Cousin Roland sees to her education and provides her needs. Although her husband died while her sons were still children, she was left financially secure and her sons, despite their age, saw to her well-being: 'Had they guided her, rather than she them, throughout the problems of their fatherless childhood and then youth? If she had made a good mother (to the surprise of many) it was owing to them' (p. 259). With her sons grown and married, she manages to get away with her fey eccentricities as she lives in a remote village, enabled by two relatively feckless men, her neighbour Frank Wilkins and her houseboy Francis.[17] Frank is obviously smitten with Dinah, yet constantly irritated by her capricious ways. Their relationship is in some ways overly familiar – he enters and leaves her house at will – yet curiously lacking in passion. Despite his military rank, he is touchy, even neurotic, in his fear of children and masks, and he displays various negative traits – nagging, pouting, manipulating – that are stereotypically ascribed to women. Dinah's sons, observing his anti-social behaviour, remark that 'poor old Frank' has 'always acted up' (*LG*, p. 278, p. 279). Once Dinah reconnects with her childhood friends, he becomes jealous, telling Clare, towards whom he bears a considerable animosity and blames for Dinah's eventual breakdown, that '[y]ou mean more to [Dinah] than you know': possibly more to Dinah than he does (p. 285).

Francis, on the other hand, is an orphan from Malta, convinced of his own intellectual superiority and afflicted with strabismus which has prevented him from pursuing his occupation of choice, that of a secret agent. He compensates by reading Dinah's mail and perusing her personal effects while she is out, gossiping whenever he has the opportunity, and responding with high-handed disdain to household orders that he regards as impositions. Like Frank, he is petulant and unable to function in any real emergency. In a variety of ways, they are both more whimsical than Dinah, and thus unable to provide her with an example of rationality.

Finally, Dinah lacks a clear sense of her own identity or, as Piaget would observe, she has a weak sense of self. This becomes clearer when she reunites with Clare and Sheila (whom she persists in calling by their childhood nicknames). Sheila continues to live in Southstone, where she is married to Trevor Artworth, a childhood friend whom the girls manipulated and bullied, now an influential estate agent. Once a self-centred local child star who failed to succeed on a professional level, she has nonetheless achieved a respectable place in her community and is careful to protect it – for reasons that become clear only much later. Clare, although once briefly married, is a successful businesswoman who owns and operates her own company, Mopsie Pye, a chain of upscale gift shops. Her occupation is an ironic comment on Dinah's predilections. While Dinah is attracted to arcane objects, Clare makes her living selling objects that have little practical value. Although differing substantially from one another, both Sheila and Clare have well-defined identities; they have responsibilities towards others and obligations that keep them occupied, unlike Dinah who lacks both. Yet, in spite of their misgivings, Sheila and Clare agree to meet with Dinah, who promptly attempts to coerce them into a scheme to return to the original time and place to dig up the coffer filled with the items they buried a half-century before.

Part II of *The Little Girls* is an extended flashback to July 1914, detailing the girls' life at school and home and revealing their individual and collective relationships with objects as well as the secrets and traumas the objects signify. Dicey lives with her widowed mother at Feverel Cottage, a place crammed with objects that betoken a previous, much more affluent life, including an abundance of china, 'reputed to be or have been priceless' (p. 92).[18] The size of the collection indicates that it was once housed in a larger abode: 'Having no special cabinet, the china overflowed from the chimney piece on to two and a half tables and a three-tiered whatnot, and ... rambled along the top of a low bookcase' (p. 92). Dicey's father committed suicide, throwing himself under a train, shortly before her birth. Her mother is apparently from a respectable family; one cousin is a bishop and another, Cousin Roland, quietly supports her, keeping her supplied with flowers and novels, the only things she really cares about. Her indolence and the obliviousness she experiences while reading – to the point that she cannot tell her own child from Mumbo – suggest a permanent state of mourning and melancholia. If Dicey is an 'idiot baa lamb' who often fails to see the obvious, an inattentive mother would be a likely cause. If Dicey shows little interest in the china, she is aware of other interesting objects in the cottage: a pistol concealed under 'many pairs of long, long gloves, folded up and beautifully put away'. Although she has no knowledge of its provenance, she assumes it was 'one of the things [her mother] inherited that she didn't exactly know what to do with' (p. 248). That Dicey takes the gun, a phallic object, probably her father's, and makes it the secret object she places in the coffer evokes the typical Freudian concept of fetishism – except that the fetishist is, in this case, a female child. Nonetheless, it remains a cross-gendered variation on McCallum's hypothesis of female fetishism inasmuch as it signifies the loss of a parent, albeit her father rather than her mother (who also dies not long afterwards), in a house filled with melancholy. This attraction to phallic objects is evinced years later by her overwhelming desire for a butter knife with a 'handle huge (quite out of proportion), gnarled and dark and with a knuckle bend in the middle' that she sees in one of Clare's shops: 'The more I think about it, the more I want it.' She knowingly adds, '[a]nd you need not worry if it is a symbol, as practically everything is, as we now know' (p. 193). That the very sight of the knife, which she calls a 'sailor's thumb', makes both Frank and Francis cringe leaves little doubt of the object's phallic appearance (p. 238).[19] That the object is a knife also suggests their respective castration anxieties.

Mumbo and Sheikie have their own peculiar relationships with objects. For Clare, it is the china collection in Feverel Cottage. While not her own objects, she invests in them an uncharacteristically romantic fantasy – something she will later disdain:

> [T]he scenery motifs spoke in particular to Clare. Their miniature vastness was of a size for her; their look of eternity could be taken in in less than a minute. She had lived within them. That she knew each landscape, to her a planet, to be linked in destructibility with the cup, bowl, or plate upon which it was, added peril to love. One saw here, how china could break. One foresaw also how, one day or another, it must do so beyond repair. (*LG*, p. 93)

The china had already seen numerous repairs. Mumbo notes the

> . . . tiny alloy claws [that] enabled handles to keep their grip on cups; cemented cracks formed networks cradling fine bowls, and where hatted and curled heads of shepherdesses or braceleted forearms of court ladies had been fitted back again on to throats of elbows, healed wounds were to be pointed out . . . These ingenuities had for the children more merit than had the pieces themselves. Still 'perfect' pieces seemed deficient – of those, however, the Piggott collection contained few. (p. 92)

Thus for Mumbo, these damaged, fragile yet fascinating objects symbolise Mrs Piggott, with whom her father is romantically involved and with whom she, too, is enamoured to the extent that an eleven-year-old can be. That the china is held together with 'claws' also indicates the potential of harm to those who become too deeply enthralled with it. Social scientist Sherry Turkle, paraphrasing Claude Levi-Strauss, suggests that '[m]aterial things . . . [are] goods-to-think-with and . . . good-to-think-with as well.' Drawing on Levi-Strauss's concept of *bricolage*, she explains how this notion works by 'combining and recombining a closed set of materials to come up with new ideas'.[20] These damaged pretty things with images that she knows cannot exist in reality, 'freak intellectual child' that she is, enable her to sort out her perceptions of adult romance that she is only beginning to comprehend (*LG*, p. 99).

Years later, Clare will observe the china again in Dinah's home and feel a pang of loss. It is possible that she continues to experience some lingering feeling of mourning and melancholia, like Dinah's, from the loss of her father, who died in combat soon after the beginning of hostilities and not long after she and Dicey parted company at Southstone. Clare once again examines the images on the china: 'She looked with longing at the everlasting sea shores, mountain peaks, bays and lakes, even at the castles on the frail rounded sides of the cups and bowls . . . She loved them because they were not for her' (*LG*, p. 306). After childhood trauma, a brief and unsuccessful marriage, and, it would seem, a lifetime of struggling with her own sexuality, she chooses a life of rational detachment, understanding that the realm of romance was not her own.

It is noteworthy that Clare, once fascinated by Mrs Piggott and her china, begins her rejection of romanticism early on. Her contribution to the coffer, unknown to the others, was the poems of Shelley: 'I thought he was WRONG' (p. 242; original emphasis). Wrong about what she does not specify, but one can assume that she found him wrong in his Romantic philosophy of life, something she realises is a fiction even at a young age. In adult life, Clare earns a living selling objects of whimsy, some of which will undoubtedly be fetishised by their purchasers, while no longer needing fetishes herself.

Sheikie, the materialistic would-be star dancer, has a relation to objects that more closely resembles the Marxist/consumerist model. Her bedroom – 'surely the prettiest in Southstone? – probably England, possibly the world' – in effect a shrine to herself and her own small-scale celebrity, is filled with significant objects celebrating the eternal feminine:

> Enamelled furniture shed an ivory gleam. From within the cupboard, tissue-wrapped dancing dresses (accordion-pleated), block-toed dancing sandals (satin of every colour), and rainbow dancing scarves made their existences felt. Vestments. That these should cohabit with her St Agatha's winter reefer, serge kilts, game boots, hockey pads – such as any girl has – made the room not less of a little temple . . . Her castanets, on a ribbon, hung over a knob of the little bed: on the pillow, the teddy bear wore a bow to match. Her tambourine had the rather more restless air of an object constantly shifted from place to place. (p. 135)

Bowen goes on to describe various photographs on the chimneypiece, those of a popular actress, a child tennis star and photos of herself in a variety of theatrical costumes and poses, suggesting that she put her talent and celebrity on a par with theirs. Her room not only speaks of her fantasy-driven vanity and aspiration to fame but it also situates her as the self-indulged child of the bourgeoisie, which

Female Fetishism 157

is what she is in reality. Another collection on display betokens the conspicuous consumerism of her home environment as well as her sense of entitlement:

> She also was a collector of Free Samples, sending for any the makers offered ... Patent foods packeted in miniature, tiny but strong-scented cakes of soap, creams in jars the circumference of a shilling, unguents or dentifrices or anything else squeezable out of baby tubes, condiments or lotions in bottles small enough to be swallowed. (p. 135)

These items, designed for use, are instead for show. She does not need them, but she feels entitled to them because they are free, regardless of the intent for which they were manufactured. Sheikie's fetishism in this regard is not so much a matter of investing power in an object; it is almost as if her collections exist to pay homage to her and thus empower her.

Even so, Sheikie has a darker, secret fetish that she confesses only late in the novel. The would-be dancer was born with a sixth toe on one of her feet. Readily amputated, it was preserved in a spirit-filled jar in her mother's possession: 'When the day came when I thought I should have a mascot, I asked her if she would give it me back. "What a strange idea," she said, but didn't say no. So there I was with a mascot' (p. 304). The choice of the word 'mascot' is provocative. Coming from the French *mascotte*, its original meaning, which Sheila apparently uses, is a good luck charm, hence a superstitious type of fetish object. An analogy might be drawn between a rabbit's foot, a common mascot, and an infant toe – or even a 'pilot's thumb'. She soon realised that for a mascot to be effective it would need to be carried about with her, even as she would need to keep it hidden from prying eyes. Faced with the difficulty and unwilling to show others her 'deformity', as she calls it, she places it as her secret contribution in the buried coffer. Although Sheikie seems the most superficial of the triad as well as the most 'normal' (according to social standards), hers is the object most clearly fetishistic. As an aspiring dancer, she lives almost entirely in the body with little exertion of the intellect. The objects in her room indicate the extent to which she is preoccupied with physical beauty, thus anything deemed a deformity would denote imperfection, a secret she would not want her admirers to know. Yet her dreams of fame fell short. Rejected by a respected London dance school – her mannerisms were 'vulgar' and she had 'too much to unlearn' – she enters into a scandalous affair that ends with her lover's death on the day she walked out on him (p. 220). Her family connections and eventual marriage to Trevor, who had become a partner in her father's business, redeemed her in the eyes of her social peers, an ironic twist for one who looked down upon Mrs Piggott's supposed vulgarity and immorality.[21] Years later, she is a perfectly groomed society wife, financially and socially secure, yet fearful of scandal and full of hidden disappointment.

The idea of burying some sort of artefact began with Dicey, the trio's fantasist. Entrapped in an encounter with a classmate's eccentric aunt, she finds herself unable to carry on a cogent conversation. Shocked that Dicey is unsure about the history of the Roman settlement of the Channel coast, she piques the child's curiosity about archaeology while questioning the efficacy of her education and poking fun at her naive ignorance:

> 'There are interesting, fine Roman things in museums. There should be many in the museum here. It a little surprises me . . . that all you girls shouldn't have been shown them!'
> 'Oh, we've been shown them; but all those things have been found. Would there still be anything there, anywhere?'
> 'You could always go with your little spade and see! . . . You never know, you know – one can never tell!' the woman continued.
> 'Did Romans live underground?'
> 'No, dear – my goodness, what *do* they teach you here? But the Romans, I'm sorry to say, have been long gone, and as time goes on things bury themselves.'
> 'Oh. Doesn't anyone bury them? . . . Have *you* found anything, ever?' she by now deeply wanted to know. (pp. 111–12; original emphases)

Thus, as the result of the aunt's sarcasm aimed at an unknowing but highly imaginative child, the seeds of the escapade were planted. Unlikely to dig up anything, the girls to decide instead to bury something to be discovered in the future. Their concept is more that of pirates secreting their loot than anything to do with antiquity as they search the town for 'fetters' (in reality a chain for a large dog), animal bones and a 'coffer' (a wooden chest that Sheikie wheedles out of her readily compliant father). Mumbo inscribes a curse, written in blood, in a language she invents. Finally, they converge in a thicket overlooking the school, dig a hole, perform a ritual and entomb the box that, they imagine, some future generation will exhume and marvel over.

Most individuals tend to put away childish things, forgetting them, particularly when none of the original participants are around to remind them. Dinah's own forgetfulness of the event, even as she engages in a madcap scheme that replicates it, would suggest that it was either not terribly important to her or that it was of such traumatic importance that she needed, consciously or otherwise, to repress it. So overwhelming is the recovered memory that she seeks to exhume the buried objects – literally – and can only do so in the presence of her original companions. Despite their initial misgivings and repeated refusals, Clare and Sheila eventually go along with the plan. The quest is not without difficulty. Dinah does not realise that places change over time and that Southstone is not what it was fifty years before. She is shocked to learn that St Agatha's was bombed 'into thin air' during a German bombing raid in the Second World War (p. 76). The thicket where they buried the coffer is now in sight of the villas built after the war, and to access it would be to trespass on private property. Nevertheless, they persist. The tersely rendered result would, on the surface, seem anti-climactic:

> It was there.
> It was empty.
> It had been found. (p. 201)

A quest narrative demands that something be found, if not necessarily that which is sought. The novel could end at this point with the characters laughing at their own absurdity, including their interactions with the property's owner moments after the discovery. Clare and Sheila would be content to do just that and let the whole episode fade into memory, just as the original burial had done. Dinah, however, cannot accept that her quest has gone unfulfilled and falls into a profound psychological crisis immediately thereafter: 'Nothing's real any more' (p. 208). Bennett and Royle suggest that 'Dinah has unknowingly built her life on the possibility of an ultimate return . . . to the past or an ultimate return of the past . . . as ghost or revenant, and this discovery of a void in the past results, eventually, in her collapse.'[22] It is as if the contents of the box represented her entire personal ontology, as if her very sanity and well-being depended upon their intact existence.

Following Christensen's argument that one can only look for clues within the narrative and not in the characters' minds, one must grasp at fragments to analyse Dinah's bizarre overreaction. If, as previously posited, Dinah has never really grown up psychologically, then the whole business of the burial – or, more precisely in this sense, the incubing – must play a significant role in whatever arrested her maturity. The objects were buried just days before their lives – indeed, most of the Western world – was forever changed. As a result, the three girls never saw or communicated with each other until Dinah put out notices in the hope of finding the other two. The Birkin-Jones family left Southstone, as military families do, leaving both Piggotts bereft of their respective love objects, then their planned holiday in Cumberland turned in to a permanent move, culminating in Mrs Piggott's death during the influenza epidemic that followed the war. In effect, her childhood attachments ended abruptly without having reached their logical conclusions. One might speculate that the pain of these accumulated losses was such that she repressed the memory for five decades. Once the memory came to the surface with her cave venture, she needed to go back to that moment in time; but more than that, she wanted to resurrect her friendships with Clare and Sheila (or, rather, Mumbo and Sheikie). The objects in the coffer represented her closest connection with them; that the objects had vanished likely ignited her fears that her erstwhile friends would vanish from her life as well.

In the days and weeks after the discovery of the empty box, she goes to great lengths to keep in touch with Sheila and especially Clare. Clare's reluctance to pursue a further relationship drives Dinah to the breaking point. Nicola Darwood posits that 'Clare has poured all her energies into her chain of shops and, in so doing, constructed an identity that does not rely on relationships or friendships and thus becomes a barrier which protects her from emotional upheaval, a barrier that she attempts to maintain even against Dinah.'[23] Various critics have suggested that Dinah realises a desire for Clare.[24] Clare, for her part, says that she is 'not exactly' a lesbian when Dinah asks her if she is, adding '[s]hall we leave this at that?' (*LG*, p. 254). To be 'not exactly' a lesbian is not to say she is heterosexual. The ambiguity of this phrase leaves it open to interpretation, but the most likely would be that she has spent most of her life suppressing her same-sex desires and leading a celibate life in order not to jeopardise her business at a time of strong prejudices against homosexuality. Her ensuing hostility towards Dinah would suggest not only her recollection of the liaison between their respective parents but also her fear of the temptation Dinah might offer.

Immediately after this encounter, Dinah plunges further into a psychological collapse and somehow incurs a head injury. Concern for her brings all three protagonists together again. Sheila arrives and takes it upon herself to act as Dinah's nurse. Her doing so makes, in a sense, an atonement for walking out on her previous 'patient', her long ago paramour, on the day he died. Seeing Clare as the alienator of Dinah's affections, Frank blames Clare for her collapse and warns her away, yet she lurks about guiltily, until an opportunity arises for her to slip into Dinah's room, hoping to say goodbye in order to repent not doing so on that last day at Southstone: 'And now, nothing. There being nothing was what you were frightened of all the time, eh? Yes. Yes, it was terrible looking down into that empty box. I did not comfort you. Never have I comforted you. Forgive me' (pp. 306–7). Dinah then wakes to Clare saying, 'Goodbye, Dicey', possibly intending never again to return. The lines ending the novel bring a kind of closure to it, albeit not a complete one, while opening the story up to new possibilities:

> 'Who's there?'
> 'Mumbo.'
> 'Not Mumbo. Clare. Clare, where have you been?' (p. 307)

By refusing the name 'Mumbo' and at last calling Clare by her adult name, Dinah acknowledges she is ready to interact with Clare and Sheila on an adult basis, without fetishised objects as a means of connection. As McCallum notes, '[c]laims about fetish objects . . . need to be interpreted through the dynamic of fetishism, knowing that the object is not particularly or necessarily special, but believing nonetheless that it is':

> [I]t is . . . necessary to think through fetishism, rather than about it . . . Through its particularity, a fetish provides an anchor against relativism, while at the same time its meaning does not require mediation through some transcendent Truth or in reference to some absolute standard. Fetishes provide grounds for sympathy and cooperation among subjects without requiring assimilation.[25]

The confessions Dinah, Clare and Sheila make during the closing chapters not only resolve past mysteries but also make it clear that their quest was not in vain. They did not recover the fetishised objects, but instead all found a means of coming to terms with the past, thus attaining self-knowledge. Having arrived at this, the vanished items cease to matter.

Notes

1. Elizabeth Bowen, *The Little Girls* (1963) (New York: Anchor, 2004), p. 11. Hereafter cited parenthetically as *LG*.
2. T. S. Eliot, 'The Waste Land' (1922), in *The Waste Land and Other Poems* (New York: Faber & Faber, 1995), line 430.
3. Jean Baudrillard, *For a Critique of the Political Economy of the Sign*, trans. Charles Levin (St Louis: Telos, 1981), p. 90.
4. See Hartmut Böhme, *Fetishism and Culture: A Different Theory of Modernity*, trans. Anna Galt (Berlin and Boston, MA: De Gruyter, 2014), pp. 140–6.
5. E. L. McCallum, *Object Lessons: How to Do Things with Fetishism* (Albany, NY: State University of New York Press, 1999), p. 113.
6. Jessica Gildersleeve's *Elizabeth Bowen and the Writing of Trauma: The Ethics of Survival* (Amsterdam and New York: Brill/Rodopi, 2014) focuses on the extent to which a history of trauma informs the actions and decisions of characters in most – if not virtually all – of Bowen's fictions. Much of the fetishism displayed by Bowen's female characters stems from some sort of loss, often of a traumatic nature.
7. Emily Apter, *Feminising the Fetish: Psychoanalysis and Narrative Obsession in Turn-of-the-Century France* (Ithaca: Cornell University Press, 1991), pp. 121–2.
8. Ibid. p. 121.
9. Elizabeth Bowen, 'The Mulberry Tree' (1934), in *The Mulberry Tree: Writings of Elizabeth Bowen*, ed. Hermione Lee (San Diego: Harcourt Brace Jovanovich, 1986), pp. 13–21 (p. 14).
10. Andrew Bennett and Nicholas Royle, *Elizabeth Bowen and the Dissolution of the Novel* (New York: St. Martin's, 1995), p. 132.
11. Ellmann notes that '[t]o "incube," an obsolete nonce-word, is to infix like a cube, to box in'. She likens incubing with Nicolas Abraham and Maria Torok's concept of encryptment, 'in which the lost object is boxed into the ego, entombed alive'. She further notes that *The Little Girls* 'explore[s] the psychic consequences of "incubing," as opposed to burying, the dead: a process that results in an inability to come to terms with loss'. See Maud Ellmann, *Elizabeth Bowen: The Shadow Across the Page* (Edinburgh: Edinburgh University Press, 2003), p. 177. See also Gildersleeve, *Elizabeth Bowen and the Writing of Trauma*, pp. 154–61.
12. For example, in her harshly critical reading Hermione Lee argues 'That Elizabeth Bowen's highly charged, contrived and controlled style should have been reduced to the clumsy procedure of *The Little Girls* can be attributed to more than obvious reasons of old age and dissatisfaction with out-dated formulae,' seemingly suggesting the possibility of dementia as a cause for what she sees as 'failures of assurance' (*Elizabeth Bowen: An Estimation* (London: Vision, 1981), pp. 205–6).

Neil Corcoran, on the other hand, tersely dismisses *The Little Girls* as a 'deeply flawed book' about which he has 'nothing of interest to say'; consequently, he completely elides any discussion of it in his monograph surveying Bowen's novels (*Elizabeth Bowen: The Enforced Return* (Oxford: Oxford University Press, 2004), pp. 7–8). For an apt response to Lee's enumeration of the novel's alleged failures, see Bennett and Royle, *Elizabeth Bowen and the Dissolution of the Novel*, pp. 122–4.

13. Lis Christensen, *Elizabeth Bowen: The Later Fiction* (Copenhagen: Museum Tusculanum, 2001), p. 113.
14. Spencer Curtis Brown, 'Foreword', in Elizabeth Bowen, *Pictures and Conversations* (New York: Knopf, 1975), p. xxxviii.
15. Laura Mulvey, *Fetishism and Curiosity* (London: British Film Institute, 1996), p. 5.
16. Jean Piaget, 'The Mind of the Baby: From Action to Thought', in *The Essential Piaget*, ed. and trans. Howard E. Gruber, and J. Jacques Vonèche (New York: Basic, 1977), p. 201.
17. The doubling of the men's names is curious, similar in a sense to the two Roberts, Stella's lover Robert Kelway (who is in reality a spy) and the spy Robert Harrison (who aspires to be her lover) in Bowen's *The Heat of the Day* (1949). Frank and Francis, despite their differences of age and ethnicity, are in many ways similar, particularly in their passive-aggressive behaviour and their emotionality. See Bennett and Royle, *Elizabeth Bowen and the Dissolution of the Novel*, pp. 133–4.
18. In keeping with the temporal settings of the novel, I am using the protagonists' nicknames for the sections set in their childhood and their adult names in the narrative present. Feverel Cottage is probably an allusion to George Meredith's *The Ordeal of Richard Feverel* (1859), a novel admired by many novelists including E. M. Forster (who alludes to it in *Howards End* (1910)) and Virginia Woolf, for its honest treatment of sexual issues, including adultery, which is suggested here in the implied affair between Major Birkin-Jones, Mumbo's father, and Mrs Piggott, Dicey's mother. In this regard, it is worth noting that novels are one of Mrs Piggott's few interests in life in her widowhood.
19. An allusion to the witches' chant in *Macbeth*: 'A pilot's thumb, wreck'd as homeward he did come' (1:3:28–9). The three protagonists are likened to the three witches in *Macbeth*, particularly in the curse that they pronounce as they bury the coffer. See Christensen, *The Later Fiction*, pp. 116–17.
20. Sherry Turkle, 'Introduction', in *Evocative Objects: Things We Think Through*, ed. Sherry Turkle (Cambridge, MA: MIT Press, 2007), pp. 3–10 (p. 4). In a manner similar to McCallum, Turkle links fetishism with melancholia and loss, clarifying in a footnote that 'fetish objects . . . are stand-ins for thoughts that cannot be expressed; they take the place of what cannot be spoken' (p. 329, n. 9).

21. Christensen, examining some of the double entendres in Bowen's representation of Mrs Piggott, suggests these are clues insinuating her sexually 'easy-going ways' that are never explicitly defined (139).
22. Bennett and Royle, *Elizabeth Bowen and the Dissolution of the Novel*, pp. 124–5.
23. Nicola Darwood, *A World of Lost Innocence: The Fiction of Elizabeth Bowen* (Newcastle upon Tyne: Cambridge Scholars, 2012), p. 182.
24. On Dinah's desire for Clare, see Jane Rule, *Lesbian Images* (Trumansburg, NY: Crossing Press, 1982), pp. 119–21; Christensen, *The Later Fiction*, pp. 55–7; and Patricia Juliana Smith, *Lesbian Panic: Homoeroticism in Modern British Women's Fiction* (New York: Columbia University Press, 1997), pp. 102–13. On lesbian self-fashioning and sexual identity, see Laura Doan, *Fashioning Sapphism: The Origins of a Modern English Lesbian Culture* (New York: Columbia University Press, 2001), pp. 125–96.
25. McCallum, *Object Lessons*, p. 162.

Chapter 10

Housekeeping and the Fiction of Subjectivity in *Eva Trout*

Jasmin Kelaita

Houses and domestic spaces are a mainstay of Elizabeth Bowen's writing, central not only to her novels but also, as Elke D'hoker notes, to her short fiction.[1] In *Elizabeth Bowen: The Shadow Across the Page* (2003), too, Maud Ellmann recognises the materialist drive of Bowen's fiction: '[f]ascinated by the gadgetry of modernity, Bowen's writing documents the changes to personal and social life wrought by innovations in technology throughout the century.'[2] By pointing to her interest in the personal and social as they were impacted by the technologies of modernity, Ellmann highlights Bowen's abiding desire to account for the material situation of people, places and things, to borrow Allan Hepburn's recent description.[3] Bowen was 'always mindful', she writes, 'of the furniture of life, the objects that hold the subject in position'.[4] In what Ellmann calls Bowen's 'addiction to personification' we can begin to understand the telling potency of space in Bowen's fiction and its uncanny ability to capture the subject, sustain and challenge it. The subject becomes entangled with and informed by the practices and the histories of spaces as well as the spatial relations inherent to these histories.

'In Bowen, things behave like thoughts and thoughts like things', suggests Ellmann.[5] Similarly, many Bowen critics are attuned to Bowen's focus on space as a means of styling her narratives. Ashley Maher contends that Bowen 'examined interior and architectural design as a means of expressing [her] apprehension about her own style and its political implications in years when form became newly politicised'.[6] Elizabeth Inglesby offers an account of Bowen's representation of space and objects as one which 'elucidated not only the human condition but also the hidden current of vitality that she sensed was coursing through the physical world'.[7] Bowen's novels thus imagine 'the possibility that furniture, houses, and even such thoroughly domesticated natural items as cut flowers in vases can register opinions and have relationships with one another'.[8] The seemingly embodied material objects of Bowen's fictional worlds betray an important aspect of her literary importance – that of the inverted hierarchy of subject and object worlds. The animated architectures of Bowen's writing thus offer an important avenue of discovery when attempting to understand the ways in which subjectivity may be formed at the nexus of the personal and material worlds found in fiction.

The issue of domestic spaces and the 'things' that make up the interior worlds of the homes in Bowen's fiction are an ongoing fascination. In 'The Idea of Home' (1953), Bowen lays out her thinking on home and homemaking, not simply as the maintenance of material shelter, but as a conceptual arrangement producing identity. While her study mainly critiques the American suburbanisation of the home, it also displays Bowen's explicit views on the home as engendering the moral and ethical practices enshrined by the domestic in modernity: '"Home" connotes to people an institution which has a practical-economic base, but which tapers up towards a moral ideal: there is involved, when one speaks of "home," at least some notion of the ethics and the aesthetics of living.'[9]

For Bowen, the subject is so dependent on the home that it is the only requirement for subjectivity in modernity: 'the dependence on home is one of the few dependences which are not weakening: on the contrary, this is an origin of strength. We not only require, we are as human completed, by what the home gives us – location. Identity would be nothing without its frame.'[10] To be a subject, in Bowen's world, one must have a home. This basis for identity is significant when we consider that so much of Bowen's fiction traces the lives of homeless women.[11] Rather than being a formal oversight, this choice to follow the narratives of the homeless offers a testing ground for Bowen to evaluate the strengthening capacity of domestic space. My reading of *Eva Trout, or Changing Scenes* (1968) reveals the chaos that encumbers a homeless adult life and the troubling effect this chaos has on narrative, especially given that Bowen's narratives are typically dedicated to the material urgency of domestic space and its importance for plot and character development.

As such, Bowen's final novel, *Eva Trout*, amplifies the issue of the domestic and the 'things' that build subjective containment and betray non-normative, unstable and difficult narrative subjects, by claiming that Eva Trout is such a subject: difficult and utterly indeterminate.

In order to draw on the value-laden potency of 'home' for women in fiction calls upon Bowen's contemporary, one who might be described as the quintessential author of homelessness, Jean Rhys. Rhys's novel *Good Morning, Midnight* (1939) shows how the issue of domestic space becomes paramount to the workings of narrative for women writers and their female protagonists. Unlike Rhys's protagonist Sasha Jensen, who does not attempt to make any specific space her home but rather moves between rented rooms in a hope for nominal protection, Eva Trout repeatedly attempts to make herself in relation to domestic spaces. As I will show, Eva is not very good at 'keeping house' or homemaking.[12] She is unable to establish a stable domestic existence in accordance with conventional gender expectations. The way that women make homes and, in very material and embodied ways, occupy space is significant in Bowen's fiction, where objects, ephemera and domestic stability are crucial to the development of character and narrative. Housekeeping is an explicit theme in *Eva Trout* and is commented upon both positively and negatively by various characters in the novel. Eva is contrasted with more stable and identifiably normative subjects, and the tensions generated through this differentiation allow Bowen to throw Eva's problematic existence into relief. I will show how this is directly linked to her inability to develop what Iris Marion Young calls a 'material mirror' in relation to her surroundings, precisely because they have always been 'changing scenes'.[13]

Eva and homelessness

Eva's living situation – homeless and transient – is at odds with the marker of permanence for feminine subjectivity: the stable home. The novel opens with Eva on a day trip with the Dancey family, Eva's temporary neighbours. Despite being a regular feature of the Dancey home 'she did not live with them: her base, not too far from the vicarage, was the home of friends with whom she looked like making an indefinite stay. She was a paying guest' (*ET*, p. 16). The home reported here is Larkins, the abandoned fruit farm where Iseult and Eric Arble reside. Larkins is a markedly uncomfortable domestic space, dominated by out-of-date and out-of-style decor: 'The full-blooded, late-Victorian furniture had been Eric's people's. The carpet had been bought to last, and was lasting. The armchairs and settee to match had been borne home by Eric from an hotel auction during the trauma preceding marriage' (p. 19). Because Iseult Arble is a thoughtless homemaker the furnishings suggest her broader failure to meet feminine ideals. As such, Iseult's 'own touches had been less fortunate: thought-out bookcases, now in place, for all their content looked cramped and petty; block-printed linen curtain, skimped by economy, had between them strips of vacuous darkness – as also the room, in the main was . . . spectral (p. 19). Questionable homemaking is thus linked to transgressive feminine subjectivity in *Eva Trout*. The Arble home is one example of the ways in which a failed home aesthetic is linked to the failed feminine. The Arbles eventually divorce and Iseult, formerly a brilliant teacher, attempts to rekindle her hopes as a writer. This too fails, or rather, in the state of this aborted text, is never realised. Like Iseult, Eva's own attempt at housekeeping and homemaking illustrates the relationship between bad housekeeping and perverse femininity in Bowen's novels.

Iris Marion Young has explored the ways in which decor and the material possessions that make up the house and home are involved in the production of subjectivity and, relatedly, its destabilisation. For Young, as for Bowen, the home is more than a container for the self but functions as an embodied measure of the practices and acts that define the processes of subjectification. Young sees the house as a support system for the practices of selfhood: '[t]he home displays the things among which a person lives, that support his or her life activities and reflect in matter the events and values of his or her life.'[14] There are two 'levels' in this process of 'the materialisation of identity in the home'.[15] First, 'my belongings are arranged in spaces as an extension of my bodily habits and support for my routine.'[16] The material elements making up the home are significant as they shape the embodied and ritualised connections the subject has with their surroundings. The second level connects these material things to the practices that shape the subject and, importantly, the transformation of this interconnection into meaning: 'many of the things in the home, as well as the space itself, carry sedimented personal meaning as retainers of personal narrative.'[17] Significantly, one's 'personal narrative' is directly tied to one's capacity to build embodied routines within the home; to form subjectivity in an embodied and continuous way is to shape a domestic space accordingly.

As the novel progresses, we are given glimpses of several domestic spaces, all of which are characterised by Bowen's attention to material detail, and all of which are shaped by a pervasive uneasiness. *Eva Trout* is decidedly a postwar novel, staged within the muddled times of mid-to-late-twentieth-century modernity where the constancy of home is all but lost amid the proliferation of gadgetry, confused relations and bungled communication. An early example of the uncanny nature of domestic space in *Eva Trout* occurs on a day trip Eva takes with the Danceys to a local castle. This is, Eva claims, the site of a marriage proposal from her former fiancé (who is never seen or met by any other character and considered to be a figment of her imagination), and also, incidentally, the place where she went to school as a child. The forgery of experience detailed by Eva is represented by 'the inhospitable castle' that 'receded, already, into its ink-like woods, taking on a look of the immaterial – its reflection, even, fainted out of the lake, over which was forming a frozen vapour. No pathos invested the scene. There was no afterglow – there had been no sun. And the swans were gone' (*ET*, p. 15). The reader never enters this castle and therefore cannot attest to its suitability as a domestic space. It is represented only in its 'immaterial' exterior which fades into the background of a vacuous scene, bereft of 'pathos' or feeling or of a palpably felt reality. In this way, the castle becomes emblematic of the novel's own immaterial and unreal presentation of plot and character – their dreamlike or 'unbelievable' quality, as Ellmann puts it.

The Dancy house equips Eva and the reader with an idea of home which is necessary to manifest the self.

> The room behind them showed signs of exhaustion, like Mrs Dancey; but also bespoke, by its very scars – tracks trodden like field-paths across the carpet, veneer chipped from furniture and the hard-used look of the cabinet wireless in the window – the inexhaustible energy of her brood. Mental avidity showed in cascades of books on the general table and tattered mountains of periodicals on chairs. It was a saying of Mrs Dancey's that she liked a room to look lived in, and this did. It also was unmistakably one of those homes there is no place like. (*ET*, p. 70)

In this passage, the Dancey family home is characterised as a space defined by the constant and continued habits of family life. These conjure a constancy of character and familial belonging. The room's 'inexhaustible energy' suffuses the material existence of its objects and the traces of corporeal life that have left identifiable marks. Therefore the physicality of the body marks the spaces of the Dancey home, which in turn shapes the subjects that inhabit it: the material object of the house is worn and used while also facilitating the containment for familial routine. The scuffed flooring suggests the repeated acts of domestic life, and the narrator correlates the 'cascades of books' and the 'mental avidity' of the inhabitants. Again, Young's insights on home-life and identity are useful in capturing the importance of lived space for the development of the subject:

> The process of sedimentation through which physical surroundings become home as an extension and reflection of routines also deposits meaning onto things. Material things and spaces themselves become layered with meaning and personal value as the material markers of events and relationships that make the narrative of a person or group. The meaningful things in my home often have stories, or they are characters or props in my stories.[18]

The Dancey home is layered with the material accumulated over years of familial interaction. According to Young, this accumulation initiates the narratives vital to the fully formed subject. An example of such a subject is Henry Dancey, who is characterised as a particularly well-rounded and comfortable individual, and who becomes a guide for Eva, even though she is twelve years his senior. In the short account of the Dancey home in the novel, Bowen is unwavering in binding the domestic and architectural specificity of the vicarage with the lives of the family, indicating that the construction of subjects represented in fiction require this sedimentation of domestic space, material presence and constancy.

Possibly inspired by the homeliness and subjective sedimentation of the Dancey house, Eva's attempts to build routine and normality are tied to her attempts to situate herself spatially within her own domestic setting. As such, on gaining her immense inheritance on her twenty-fifth birthday, Eva attempts to organise a domestic life in a structurally precarious house, Cathay, that she rents in Kent: although Cathay is 'spacious, as promised, it was not yet falling down' (*ET*, p. 70). While Eva is 'eager to take up residence' (p. 77) at Cathay, she fails to make any impact on its material state. This is made evident when she is introduced to the house by Mr Denge, who only just manages to keep his cool as Eva questions him on simple household requirements and procedures:

> 'I take it you have brought with you your plates and linen?'
>   'No. What are they?'
>   'Ha-ha – sheets, and so on. Spoons and, ha-ha, forks.'
>   'How should I possess those?' asked Eva moodily. 'Must I buy them? Are they very expensive?' (p. 77)

Following several similar exchanges, one of which sees Eva impatiently quieten and attempt to contain Mr Denge – 'you make too many noises in my house' (p. 77) – she finally agonises: 'Stop! – One thing you must show me! How is a kettle boiled?' (p. 81) The procedures of domestic life remain alien to her. The objects which make up the home are not recognised as useful tools but rather as encumbrances.

Much like the Dancey home, Cathay reflects the lives of its previous, unnamed owners: 'you could see that everything had its history: chair-backs wore grease-darkened circles where heads had rested, and chair-arms, tables and flooring not only were mapped by wandering stains but abounded in small charred troughs burned by cigarettes' (p. 80). The furniture that fills Cathay is marked by spectral lives and reflects the residual effects of their homemaking and housekeeping and not Eva's own. These effects are bodily contextualised by the movements of the inhabitants and structured by a memory of events situated outside the narrative. These traces of the lives of others reinforce the reader's sense of Eva's surfacial existence. As Young suggests, 'homemaking consists in the activities of endowing things with living meaning, arranging them in space in order to facilitate the life activities of those to whom they belong, and preserving them, along with their meaning.'[19] The fact that Cathay bears the imprint of its previous residents in this way casts Eva's failure to make herself at home as all the more telling: the house offers the capacity for sedimentation and constancy of the routines of living exhibited in the Dancey house. Eva, however, for the short time that she inhabits Cathay, never succeeds in compelling it to coincide with her own desires. The objects she adds to the house simply gather dust. If 'dwelling in the world means we are located among objects, artefacts, rituals, and practices that configure who we are in our particularity', as Young argues, then Eva is never rendered as particular and ultimately remains unknowable.[20]

The established way in which the Dancey family inhabits domestic space presents a stark contrast with Eva's homelessness. This contrast highlights not only the fact that she is alone in the world without family, but more importantly, that she lacks any domestic support – does not occupy and is not preoccupied by any space in particular. Eva remembers the acts and practices engendered in the Dancey house eight years later when she visits the house and somehow finds her 'vicarage voice' (*ET*, p. 149). Evidently, the space revives the traces of embodied habits: 'Back again in the drawing-room, Eva settled into her former place, at her particular end of the long lean sofa' (p. 149). '"You find us where we were," he reminded her, "at any rate. Why we still are and whether we always shall be, I can't tell you"' (p. 151). The 'lived-in' subjects of the Dancey house, who are defined by the practices of their domestic spaces, contrast sharply with Eva's own failed or unhoused subjectivity.

When the living spaces of Cathay and the Dancey vicarage are compared, it is clear that the 'lived-in' space of the Dancey home cannot be recreated at Cathay. Eva's inability to create a home within the material parameters of her house reflects her incongruence with established ideas of rootedness and fixity. Eva buys Cathay without issue because of her abundance of financial means. It is because her history is speckled with familial loss, dislocation and disappointment that Patricia Juliana Smith suggests that 'despite all her material privilege, [Eva] is not only homeless but also an alien in whatever environment she enters.'[21] Eva is not only incongruent with the spaces she visits – the Dancey home – but also the ones she attempts to live in. Perhaps what she was after is best specified by Constantine later in the novel when he begs Eva to '"Get him a father – wouldn't you," asked he – referring to their surroundings, this enclave – "like any of this? There is much to be said for it"' (*ET*, p. 172). The 'it' to which Constantine refers is the neat suburban road, in which 'nice-looking cars were parked all along the kerbs under the balconied stucco houses, spotlessly painted white, cream, pearl. "The soul," he said, admiring the facades, "of normality"' (p. 169). The normal life Eva tries to achieve at Cathay is linked to this subjective stability traditionally garnered to domestic space. However, as Constantine paradoxically informs her: 'we are outsiders Eva' (p. 169). Though Constantine and Eva recognise the stability and subjective containment the neat houses and their accompanying material arrangements present, neither one of them can properly facilitate them to stabilise their identity.

The problem of Eva's inconstancy, of her incongruence with the practices of domestic space, is demonstrated in a particularly revealing moment at Cathay. Eric Arble mysteriously arrives soon after Eva moves in and finds the house lacking domestic warmth; Eva is awkward and unable to remedy this absence: 'Eric took in the drawing room, saying nothing. Its disreputability was what chiefly struck him. On top of that, the whole place was filmed with dust and, if not cold yet, made stale by used up sunshine' (p. 70). While Eric's response to Cathay occurs at a moment when Eva has not inhabited the space for long, it is clear that Eva's failure to play the role of homemaker is more than a transitional condition. Noticing that 'round the bay window were copious strewings of crumbs', Eric cannot 'restrain himself' from passing comment: 'you'll be bringing mice in' (p. 85). The cause-effect logic of simple domestic upkeep is lost on Eva. The confused way in which she approaches domestic life betrays her inability to function within a space traditionally connected to stable subjectivity. Eva's way of being here denies singularity; she lacks the personal specificity that close relations to the objects and ephemera of home-life would give her. As Young suggests, she has been unable to construct a 'particular identity', and her character remains accordingly vague and ill-defined. In fact, rather than instilling order in the 'things' that fill her living space, Eva propagates mess and domestic chaos without worrying or even noticing. Her form of subjectivity is fundamentally not that of a homemaker; she does not configure the material world she occupies in line with her 'particular identity'; rather, she is overwhelmed by the sheer volume of objects available to her because of her wealth.

The stable subject, then, requires a house and a stable feminine subject is required to, more or less, be a housekeeper. Constantine nominates Eva as an outsider and a pariah not only because she cannot manage to make a home for herself, but also because she remains single. He advises her to 'take root' and find her son a father – and by association, a husband for herself. For Constantine, this would resolve 'the problem of Eva' by placing her in a heteronormative domestic setting. However, as Smith states, Eva remains a 'homeless alien' and her existence as a single, unhoused woman likens her to other composite figures in twentieth-century women's writing.

Jean Rhys and the homeless woman

In Rhys's treatment of the unhoused single woman, hotel space replaces the house as the space where the feminine subject must take shape. Unlike the home, however, the hotel room does not allow one to 'take root' but rather proliferates the subjective 'things' – objects and spaces that accrue meaning over time – that are normatively associated with the containment of feminine subjectivity. Thus, for Rhys's protagonists, the hotel room is not domestic or protective: it is momentary, transitory and marked by hypermobility. Sasha Jensen, the protagonist of *Good Morning, Midnight*, has a relationship to hotel rooms that reflects her marginal position within the wider social milieu of the modern metropolis. Kathy Mezei and Chiara Briganti have noted that Rhys's 'boarding houses [are] a structural representation of the decline of great houses and the upper classes and of a more urban, mobile society', and in them 'shelter figures on the margins of society, single, impoverished, and genteel who must work for a living and live "in digs".'[22] Rented spaces offer 'shelter', but they do not offer substitutes for the 'great houses' that fix subjects and focus novels. Indeed, in her study of boarding houses and apartments in nineteenth-century British and French fiction, Sharon Marcus identifies the comprehensive association of 'the very word home' with 'the middle ground of domesticity. An interior first and foremost, this home's many rooms abound in the furniture, decorations, and material goods that make it a self-contained world.'[23] For Marcus, the interior of the home is duly separated from 'the competitive marketplace that funds the domestic oasis'.[24] As such, 'this home is hard to situate in the larger spaces of street, city, village, or region, because it is by definition abstracted from external influences; it is enclosed, built to hold only one family and to stand freely on its own plot of land.'[25] 'Enclosed' and separate, the domestic interior holds itself apart from the wider spaces of modernity: streets, cafes and other sites of public interaction.

Good Morning, Midnight begins in London but is set primarily in Paris, with excursions to Brussels and Amsterdam. This distinctly European geographical scale, however, does not produce a cosmopolitan exploration of a woman travelling, finding romance or finding herself. Instead, the novel charts the long exposure of a woman moving through, making do and barely surviving. Sasha's existence is mapped across daily disasters, emotional instability and precarious encounters with strangers and near-strangers. The novel's scope is largely confined to the prosaic record of the routines involved in this process: '[u]sually, in the interval between my afternoon sleep and my night sleep I went for a walk, turned up the Boulevard Arago, walked to a certain spot and turned back.'[26] Sasha's survival is not measured in relation to epic adventures or even the mundane progress of a career, but rather in repetitive, day-to-day negotiations of urban space. Her life emphatically does not follow the trajectory of a conventional *Bildungsroman*: she passes no milestone, does not attain knowledge through difficult experience. Rather, her life is a project of risk aversion, relayed with black humour and self-deprecation.

> My life, which seems so simple and monotonous, is really a complicated affair of cafés where they like me and cafés where they don't, streets that are friendly, streets that aren't, rooms where I might be happy, rooms where I never shall be, looking glasses I look nice in, looking glasses I don't, dresses that will be lucky, dresses that won't, and so on. (*GMM*, p. 40)

Through her first-person narration, Sasha directly tells the reader how 'complicated' her life really is, how difficult it is to measure your existence by the ever-changing yet heavily charged spaces of urban modernity – the cafe, the hotel room, the street. These spaces are not blank and lifeless for Sasha, but reflect the gaze and conspiring eyes of the world at large. Sasha's ability to represent herself or be represented – in the looking glass, in a lucky dress – is dependent on her relations with these spaces, thus situating her at the mercy of the exterior, of surfaces. In other words, her subjectivity is an effect of these surfaces.

For Sasha, whose habitat is the rented room, there is little refuge from the public pressures of urban life. Unlike the house or the apartment, which are typically occupied by their owners or long-term tenants, the rented room is not a stable space; rather, it is precarious and subject to change. The opening of the novel describes Sasha's search for a room to live in during her extended stay in Paris. After looking through several options in various hotels, Sasha concludes that the reality of her situation is that the particular room does not matter: a room is simply a place to hide.

> A beautiful room with a bath? A room with bath? A nice room? A room? . . . But never tell the truth about this business of rooms, because it would bust the roof off everything and undermine the whole social system. All rooms are the same. All rooms have four walls, a door, a window or two, a bed, a chair. A room is a place where you hide from the wolves outside and that's all any room is. (p. 33)

Rather than occupying a domestic space that she can intuitively build around her with objects relevant to her identity, Sasha has resigned herself to a borrowed space where she can momentarily evade the pressures of her hyper-public life. Consequently, the 'things' that would normally be required for the homemaking subject are rendered useless for the life of a woman like Sasha who only wants respite from the urban milieu she otherwise inhabits.

Sasha's existence is an effort of survival. Patricia Moran argues that '[t]he Rhysian protagonist's preoccupation with fashion, clothing, hair, and make-up' functions as 'a defensive mechanism ... providing her with the necessary armour she needs to blend in with other people and thereby forestall their critical and contemptuous staring'.[27] Eating a meal in a public space, a daily occurrence for Sasha, results in crippling paranoia, and she repeatedly indicts her own choices. This also suggests, however, that Sasha does not simply see herself as a victim of those around her, but as an agent with small daily choices available. Jessica Gildersleeve has linked Sasha's choice to live in this momentary, transitory, unstable way as a strategy for avoiding the conventional and stable way of life for women, arguing that it suggests 'women's increasing resistance to traditional concepts of femininity' so that 'Sasha "chooses" internal and external drowning – alcoholism and suicide – rather than succumb to patriarchal expectation.'[28] Because we only see the world through Sasha's eyes we can never be sure if her paranoia is warranted, but the discomfort and exclusion she *feels* is everywhere present in the text. The paranoia Sasha exhibits reveals the extent to which her homelessness affects the way in which she occupies spaces. This is also the case with Eva. Her relations with the realtor, with Eric Arble and with Constantine all exhibit her seeming inexperience with communication but, as this comparison with Rhys's novel shows, are also more broadly symptomatic or emblematic of Eva's homelessness.

Eva's hypermobility is demonstrated by the ease with which she is able to fly to America and live across various hotel spaces. This period of the novel is only narrated in a small section and exists as an aporia in the text, infusing the narrative with a mysterious temporal distance that results in Eva returning to England with a son. Contrastingly, Sasha's experience as a homeless woman is written onto the streets of Paris and expressed in the mobile 'homes' she purchases as temporary spaces for protection. Sasha, as the anti-domestic subject, finds temporary sanctuary in the hotel. In one particularly poignant scene, Sasha sits in the bath and listens as other anti-domestic characters arrange their own entry to the space.

> The bathroom here is on the ground floor. I lie in the bath, listening to the patronne talking to a client. He says he wants a room for a young lady-friend of his. Not at once, he is just looking around.
> 'A room? A nice room?'
> I watch cockroaches crawling from underneath the carpet and crawling back again. (*GMM*, p. 29)

The juxtaposition between the request for a 'nice room' and the cockroaches crawling from underneath the carpet plays out for Sasha's eyes and ears alone; in this instance, only she can see the paradoxical nature of the cheap hotel. Yet the man's request is not for himself to stay in such scrappy digs but rather for his 'young lady-friend' – his mistress. The contrast between the nice room and the cockroach infestation suggests that the space for the mistress is strictly not a home. This anti-domestic space creates a parallel between Sasha's identity and that of the mistress who, being absent, does not herself have any say in her placement for the purposes of her 'benefactor'. The hotel space in *Good Morning, Midnight* is thus not only anti-domestic in the sense of being shabby, cheap and dirty, but it expressly houses subjects that cannot be otherwise housed. Moreover, the power relations in this scene, and in the novel more broadly, are represented in a conversation heard because of the porosity of hotel space – Sasha overhears this conversation and reports back. The apparently private space is made public and is infiltrated by the gender politics of urban modernity – the mistress has a place to stay, but she does not have a home.

The 'Rhys Woman' indicates an important movement in the modernist novel because it centralises the experience of unstable, unmarried, lowly and vulnerable feminine subjects.[29] The Rhys Woman's narration is flecked with inconsistencies, blank spots and fatigue, offering plotlines and interactions that seem unfinished and unreliable. Yet, this is perhaps her greatest strength: the ability to, as Lauren Elkin has noted, 'ventriloquise the dominant culture in order to challenge it'.[30] Rhys's novels depart from the norms of modernist women's writing, not simply because they omit the use of stable domestic space, but because her focus is on the unrelenting tribulations of 'life (for women) on the street', as it were.

The temporary spaces that punctuate *Good Morning, Midnight* afford narrative primacy to a non-normative feminine subject, unconnected with housekeeping and homemaking. Sasha is formed between the competing tensions of fleeting private interiors and ever-present public streets. This condition produces a self that is not easily tracked – one that lacks the fullness of a more conventional kind of fictional character. Indeed, she seems to see her life as a succession of rooms, which become difficult to separate from each other: 'This damned room – it's saturated with the past . . . It's all the rooms I've ever slept in, all the streets I've ever walked in. Now the whole thing moves in an ordered, undulating procession past my eyes. Rooms, streets, streets, rooms' (*GMM*, p. 91). The way that the rooms are untethered from chronology means that Sasha's narrating subjectivity is similarly fluid. My reading of Rhys's novel allows us to recognise the ways in which homeless subjectivity for women in fiction is formed at the nexus of public and private space. Sasha exists as an ever-moving figure between public spaces where she must eat and move, and the more private, yet not entirely sequestered, space of the hotel room. This existence makes Sasha marginal to the programmes of domesticity for women and likens her more to a street urchin than a wife whose domestic containment would preclude her from having to experience such street-life.

The (non)-subject and narrative

Eva is also a non-normative subject – so disruptive, in fact, that she disturbs the narrative progress of the novel named for her. She speaks with 'a hint of evasion' (*ET*, p. 155), and this can be said for the novel's plot as well. The narrative is split between 'Part One: Genesis' and 'Part Two: Eight Years Later', but no specific time period is given to these sections and the reader is left to ascertain a broadly postwar period by the modern gadgets that clutter the text. In the absence of clear temporal markers, plot and character are both made uncertain. Hermione Lee's comments express the shock of *Eva Trout* after Bowen's comparatively more conventional earlier works: 'the novel's haphazard plot and sketchy relationships', she argues, 'make it startlingly different from Bowen's other work. There are patchy attempts at depth of character . . . but clearly this isn't what interests Bowen now.'[31] Bowen's critics cannot fail to note the novel's difficulty in providing fullness of plot and character. Ellmann's assessment is that 'the details of the plot are scarcely plausible', while Jessica Gildersleeve notes that the 'changing stills, screens, and scenes of *Eva Trout*' do not compose a coherent narrative space in which Eva can become a fully-formed character.[32] The 'startlingly different' novel constitutes, as renée c. hoogland suggests, 'the evacuation of representation'.[33] It is precisely this evacuated form which allows the depiction of the fractured feminine subject as she attempts to find meaning. Ultimately, however, Bowen offers up the novel as a dissolute form unable to express the complexities of homeless and houseless feminine subjectivity.

Nevertheless, Eva journeys through the haphazardly located spaces – a few houses and a litany of hotels – with the aim of solidifying her subjectivity. Eva's homelessness begins in her childhood when, after her mother's desertion (and death two months later), she lives with her father, Willy Trout, and Constantine. Not only does this relationship disrupt normative conventions of the family, the group also travels constantly; despite her father's wealth and mobility, Eva is homeless. As John Coates points out, then, 'her aimless wanderings from one expensive hotel or rented home to another, with a father who has little interest in her, have left her with no faculty to make sense of her life.'[34] Coates further claims that this is why Eva 'is repeatedly shown trying to construct some order, place or routine'.[35] Eva's continual movement from one domestic space to another negates the stability she both desires and requires to generate a cohered self. This disruption continues throughout her life. Before attempting to organise her own home, Eva is in close association with two other domestic spaces – Larkins and the Dancey vicarage nearby. Her presence at Larkins, with Eric and Iseult Arble, is described as 'the Larkins solution' (*ET*, p. 33): a means of getting her out of Constantine's way following her father's death. 'The Larkins solution' also points to a novelistic attempt to 'place' Eva, a subject who is yet to be recognisably formed. Placing her in a home is akin to placing her within the traditional and recognisable bounds of subjectivity, especially for women. Her presence in this home, however, is problematic: Eva is so destabilising to this domestic space that she breaks up the Iseults' marriage. Eva's disruption of the lives of those around her is perhaps best described by Henry Dancey, who first appears as an astute twelve-year-old boy and ends the novel (eight years later), as Eva's mock-husband. As he quips, 'ethically perhaps you're a Typhoid Mary. You plunge people's ideas into deep confusion' (p. 179). Eva is an unsignifiable character and subject, and this status becomes troubling to others, even infectious. 'Oversized, inept and fabulously wealthy', Eva exists as an aberration that disturbs the rational, familial and domestic.[36] She is not able to generate a consistent identity in the novel because she is unable to establish a connection with domestic spaces, including her own. Ultimately, Eva is an unreadable figure and a failed feminine subject.

Eva Trout is the story of a problematic, homeless and indefinable character. Eva displays no interiority or self-narration and the novel refuses to fill the gaps left by such a shapeless and unreadable protagonist. This leaves a novel of material things – of shapes made by spaces and set pieces that, without the mutually constitutive relation between subject and space, are left to exist in their inauthentic condition. Cathay and Larkins are unliveable shells. Bowen's final novel removes all sense of materialist and embodied vitality. Without the mutual constitution of domestic space and subject, *Eva Trout* emblematises the failed form that accompanies the failed feminine subject.

Notes

1. 'Houses feature in her ghost stories and war stories as much as in her satirical comedies, childhood stories and Irish stories,' making the house 'an intriguing image . . . that deserves further consideration' (Elke D'hoker, 'The Poetics of House and Home in the Short Stories of Elizabeth Bowen', *Orbis Litterarum*, 67.4 (2012): 267–89 (p. 268)).
2. Maud Ellmann, *Elizabeth Bowen: The Shadow Across the Page* (Edinburgh: Edinburgh University Press, 2004), p. 5.
3. Allan Hepburn (ed.), *People, Places, Things* (Edinburgh: Edinburgh University Press, 2008).
4. Ellmann, *The Shadow Across the Page*, p. 5.
5. Ibid.
6. Ashley Maher, '"Swastika Arms of Passage Leading to Nothing": Late Modernism and the New Britain', *ELH*, 80.1 (2013): 251–85 (p. 256).
7. Elizabeth Inglesby, 'Expressive Objects: Elizabeth Bowen's Narrative Materialises', *Modern Fiction Studies*, 52.2 (2007): 306–33 (p. 306).
8. Ibid. p. 307.
9. For Bowen, American homes were created by 'the instinct to imitate in a new land the way of life to be conducted in better circumstances' ('The Idea of Home', in *Listening In: Broadcasts, Speeches, and Interviews*, ed. Allan Hepburn (Edinburgh: Edinburgh University Press, 2010), pp. 162–5 (p. 165, p. 162).
10. Ibid. pp. 162–3.
11. Bowen's two masterpieces *The Death of the Heart* (1938) and *The Heat of the Day* (1949) both featured homeless protagonists: Portia Quayne and Stella Rodney.
12. Elizabeth Bowen, *Eva Trout or Changing Scenes* (London: Random House, 1968), p. 154. Hereafter cited parenthetically as *ET*. Bowen consistently uses the phrase 'kept house' in *Eva Trout*; for example, when, late in the novel, Eva and Jeremy take up residence at a Parisian hotel: 'they had in a way kept house, established themselves – their surrounding accumulation of heaps of objects, and still more, imponderables, had quieted, assuaged him and reassured him' (p. 205).
13. Iris Marion Young, *On Female Body Experience: 'Throwing Like a Girl' and Other Essays* (Oxford: Oxford University Press, 2005), p. 152.
14. Ibid. p. 139.
15. Ibid. p. 156.
16. Ibid. p. 139.
17. Ibid. pp. 149–50.

18. Ibid. p. 141.
19. Ibid. p. 143.
20. Ibid. p. 143.
21. Patricia Juliana Smith, '"Everything to Dread from the Dispossessed": Changing Scenes and the End of the Modernist Heroine in Elizabeth Bowen's *Eva Trout*', *Hecate*, 35.1 (2009): 228–49 (p. 229).
22. Kathy Mezei and Chiara Briganti, 'Reading the House: A Literary Perspective', *Signs*, 27.3 (2002): 837–46 (p. 841).
23. Sharon Marcus, *Apartment Stories: City and Home in Nineteenth-Century Paris and London* (Berkeley: University of California Press, 1999), p. 1.
24. Ibid.
25. Ibid. p. 2.
26. Jean Rhys, *Good Morning, Midnight* (London: Penguin, 1939), p. 72. Hereafter cited parenthetically as *GMM*.
27. Patricia Moran, 'Shame, Subjectivity, and Self-Expression in Cora Sandel and Jean Rhys', *Modernism/Modernity*, 22.4 (2015): 713–34 (p. 718).
28. Jessica Gildersleeve, 'Muddy Death: Fate, Femininity and Mourning in Jean Rhys's *Good Morning, Midnight*', in *Rites of Passage in Postcolonial Women's Writing*, ed. Pauline Dodgson-Katiyo and Gina Wisker (Amsterdam: Rodopi, 2010), pp. 227–44 (p. 230).
29. Sue Thomas first used the term the 'Rhys Woman' to conjure the consistent tropes connecting the protagonists of Rhys's interwar novels (*The Worlding of Jean Rhys* (Westport, CT: Greenwood Press, 1999), p. 3). I use the term to draw a wider net of female experience, with the aim of confronting traditional and conventional boundaries of feminine subjectivity in fiction.
30. Lauren Elkin, 'Getting the Story Across: Jean Rhys's Paranoid Narrative', *Journal of Narrative Theory*, 46.1 (2016): 70–96 (p. 72).
31. Hermione Lee, *Elizabeth Bowen: An Estimation*, rev. edn (London: Vintage, 1999), p. 172.
32. Ellmann, *The Shadow Across the Page*, p. 207; Jessica Gildersleeve, *Elizabeth Bowen and the Writing of Trauma: The Ethics of Survival* (Amsterdam and New York: Rodopi, 2014), p. 170.
33. renée c. hoogland, '"Nothing but a Pack of Cards": Semi-Fictitious Persons and Flopping Jellyfish in Elizabeth Bowen', *Women: A Cultural Review*, 22.1 (2011): 1–14 (p. 1).
34. John Coates, 'The Misfortunes of Eva Trout', *Essays in Criticism*, 48.1 (1998): 59–79 (p. 66).
35. Ibid.
36. Tessa Hadley, 'Introduction' to *ET*, p. x.

Chapter 11

Elizabeth Bowen on the Telephone

Andrew Bennett

In her biography of Elizabeth Bowen, Victoria Glendinning records the writer's considerable telephonic proficiency. Noting her prodigious mid-career energy and productivity, Glendinning records that in the 1950s Bowen would 'descend' on London, New York or Rome and plan her visit by having a 'session on the telephone': 'Mornings were for writing', Glendinning comments, 'telephoning could only be begun after noon.' 'Before that hour', Glendinning continues, 'the telephone paralysed her; after it, she became tremendous in her telephoning.'[1] By contrast, in a diary entry for January 1955, Charles Ritchie, Bowen's long-term and mostly long-distance lover, noted the strangeness of speaking to Bowen on the telephone: 'Rang up E today', he writes, noting that it was like 'talking to someone on another planet or trying to communicate with the spirit world.'[2] The marked sense of distance that Ritchie registers allows us a glimpse of the other side of Bowen's telephoning, one that is related to the paralysis that Glendinning mentions, and to the sense that one gets from reading her work that however proficient Bowen could be at telephoning, the telephone was for her an unnerving apparatus, a machine that could generate absence and unfulfilled desire, misunderstanding and non-communication.[3]

Like telegrams and like letters, telephones are critical in the plotting of many of Bowen's novels, as well as in several of her stories.[4] In this essay, I will argue that Bowen's novels are often plotted around the (mis-)communicative possibilities of the telephone and that, as such, the modernist technology of telephony plays an important part in her thinking about communication, language and personal identity more generally.[5] Indeed, only three of her novels do not prominently feature telephones: in her first novel, *The Hotel* (1927), none of the guests in the Italian Riviera hotel in the early 1920s use the telephone, while *The Last September* (1929) and *A World of Love*

(1955) are set in Irish Big Houses that – like Mount Morris in *The Heat of the Day* (1949) and Bowen's Court until 1939 – remain unconnected to the telephone network.⁶ In all three, telephones are mentioned, but only to mark their absence.

Bowen's novels of the 1930s reflect the dramatic increase in telephone ownership and usage that marks that decade.⁷ *Friends and Relations* (1931) is the first of Bowen's novels to be fully plugged into the telephone network, featuring as it does the singularly disconcerting character Theodora Thirdman, who finds the telephone 'at once her distraction and torture'.⁸ The adolescent Theodora develops a habit of pseudonymously telephoning famous people, often pretending to be the fictitious 'Lady Hunter Jervois': 'Passionately passing along the wire', Theodora becomes 'for those moments the very nerve of some unseen house', we learn (*FR*, p. 28). But Theodora's thirdness, her condition of being an extraneous third-party in other people's relationships, is not allayed by the supplement or prosthesis of the telephone, even if it can momentarily make her seem to be the very nerve-centre of another's home. In this context, it is notable that telephones play a central role in the novel's two crises: although it is instigated by a letter from Theodora to Laurel (pp. 92–3), Edward's hysterical journey to remove his children from the interdicted presence of Lady Elfrida and Constantine at Batts is signalled by Janet's telephone call to Lady Elfrida at the chemist in Market Keaton (pp. 83–4), while the subsequent barely repressed panic at Batts is interrupted and yet also exacerbated by a call from Lewis Gibson (p. 108). Back in London three weeks later, the frantic hours of Edward's early-morning disappearance after his final meeting with his almost-lover Janet are marked by the making of, the thought or suggestion or lie about, or the failure to make, a total of twelve telephone calls.⁹

While *To the North* is organised around travel and transport, it is also notable for the transmission of messages via the networks of the telegraph and the telephone: fired up by the telephone, characters in *To the North* are, as Maud Ellmann puts it, '"wired" in every sense'.¹⁰ The novel seems almost phone-addicted, like Cecilia, who feels compelled to make calls even when she wishes she wouldn't and who feels herself 'crystallise over the wire'.¹¹ The plot finally hinges on the telephone, indeed, as Emmeline's calls to her unreliable and frankly unsuitable lover, Markie, go unanswered. It takes three late-night calls finally to convince Emmeline that Markie has rejected her. The first is to his empty flat, where she hears the telephone 'tingle and dot out its double note' like a desperate Morse code message. Although no one answers, Emmeline continues to listen to the telephone's call, feeling, pathetically, that 'the repetitive bell made her in some way present.' Bowen's prose produces a telling telephonic pun at this point: 'Having wrung from that silence so stamped with his absence no stir or answer, she hung up at last' (*TN*, p. 214). Next, Emmeline telephones Markie's sister, Mrs Dolman, who is unhelpfully and distantly amused, particularly by Emmeline's attempt to disguise her identity. Finally, Emmeline reluctantly telephones Markie's former or other lover, Daisy. When she asks Daisy if Markie is with her, Daisy 'bound[s] audibly': 'I – I don't know', she replies unconvincingly about a man who is in the same room as her, as Bowen explores the full tragicomic potential of the telephone call: 'I'll see', she says (pp. 215–16). Although Daisy puts her hand over the receiver to speak to Markie, 'small chinks of sound' come through to Emmeline who, mortified, is finally confronted with her lover's treachery: '*Fool*', she hears him say to Daisy in a preposterous and telephone-specific lie, 'I'm not here' (p. 216). Perhaps unsurprisingly, as Emmeline subsequently wanders 'blindly' through the noisy streets of London, she continues to hear above the 'hollow thunder' of traffic 'the whirr of unanswered telephones' (p. 225). And almost the last word of the novel goes to the telephone as, after Emmeline and Markie leave Oudenarde Road to drive north to their deaths in a car crash, Cecilia notices 'by the telephone Markie's white scarf that he had forgotten' and 'Emmeline's gloves that she would not wear' (p. 247).

The plot of Bowen's next novel, *The House in Paris* (1935), is organised around telephone calls in three specific ways. First, the secret affair between Karen Michaelis, who is betrothed to Ray Forrestier, and Max Ebhart, who is Naomi Fisher's fiancé, is instigated by a phone call from Max to Karen. This telephone call leads to and indeed makes possible every significant event of the novel: the affair itself, the birth of the illegitimate Leopold, and Max's suicide. Second, writing and telephoning – ancient and modern forms of communication at a distance – are strikingly enmeshed when Karen chances upon the indented trace of a discarded written message from a telephone call that reveals that her mother knows about her clandestine meeting with Max.[12] Third, the telephone features disruptively at the novel's end: having decided to 'steal' Leopold from his adoptive parents and return him to Karen, Ray asserts more than once that he must telephone Karen to tell her what he has done, but fails to do so. The novel ends on a marked sense of uplift outside the Gare du Nord as Leopold is promised a future with his birth-mother. But it also ends on a prospective telephone call that remains unaccountably unmade – and therefore on the possibility that the call will never be made, that it is simply not possible, that what must be said on the telephone (that Ray has 'stolen' Leopold, that he has unilaterally decided to compensate for Karen's unaccountable failure to come to her son by taking him to her) cannot be communicated, telephonically or otherwise.[13]

Bowen's 1938 novel *The Death of the Heart* is also decisively if undecidably governed by the strangeness of the telephone. The lives and conversations of the inhabitants of 2 Windsor Terrace are punctuated, repeatedly interrupted, by telephones, including by a 'room-to-room' or 'house' telephone which, 'instead of ringing, lets out a piercing buzz'.[14] Windsor Terrace is presented as a house that is organised around the telephone.[15] For Thomas and Anna Quayne, the telephone operates as a way of controlling access to their home. Major Brutt seriously errs in presuming to call at the house without phoning first: it is an unwritten rule that the Quaynes are 'surrounded by an electric fence' and that 'friends who did not first telephone did not come' (*DH*, p. 87). The fact that everyone at Windsor Terrace lives 'impaled upon a private obsession' means that '[t]he telephone, the door bell, the postman's knock' are seen as 'threatening intimations' of the outside world (p. 171). But the telephone is even used internally in *The Death of the Heart*, where the 'house telephone' is employed to police the boundaries between people: Anna and Thomas use the internal telephone to communicate between the gendered locales of Thomas's lair, his study, and Anna's drawing room. Communicating *between* these rooms implicitly allows for the absence of communication *within* them: by linking people with each other, the telephone at the same time *dis*connects them. As in *To the North*, where Markie lives both 'completely cut off, at the top of his sister's house', and connected to his sister by an internal telephone (*TN*, p. 66, p. 193), Bowen suggests that people can be cut off by the telephone link, by what Avital Ronnell refers to as the telephone's 'disconnecting force'.[16] But the centrality of telephones in *The Death of the Heart* is emphasised by the fact that the unravelling of things, which begins almost one hundred pages before the novel's end, is effected largely by means of telephone calls, prompted by a 'telephone crisis' (*DH*, p. 271) in which the adolescent Portia is caught making an unauthorised call from Miss Paullie's telephone at school to Eddie, her boyfriend, at work (p. 267, p. 273). Eddie's character has already been established as somewhat dissolute and untrustworthy, in part by references to his over-use (amounting to professional misuse) of the office telephone (pp. 265–6, p. 272).[17]

His subsequent call to Anna to inform her of the crisis leads, characteristically, to talk and no action at Windsor Terrace, until eventually Major Brutt is forced to telephone from his hotel to say that Portia has turned up there unannounced. Anna promises to call back once she and Thomas have decided what to do, but after a lengthy and difficult discussion they resolve not to call back since they cannot decide what to say: 'This is a *coup* or nothing', Thomas declares. 'We don't talk; we do the obvious thing' (p. 313). The 'obvious thing' is to send the housekeeper, Matchett, to sort things out instead of using the telephone to communicate. The novel ends, therefore, in the decision not to telephone as, in effect, a final avoidance or suspension of decision and indeed of responsibility.

In 1944, Bowen commented that modern lives seem to be 'telephone ridden', and in her Second World War novel *The Heat of the Day* the telephone is both prominent and ominous, bound up as it is in the discourses of war and espionage.[18] The novel includes a minor character, Connie, whose role as an Air Raid Precautions warden autobiographically registers one of Bowen's own roles in the war – a function that, for Connie at least, mainly seems to involve sitting or sleeping by the telephone (*HD*, p. 148, p. 158). But it is one of Bowen's other wartime roles – as an informer, a kind of 'spy', in Ireland for the British government – that is most clearly reflected in a novel that, as Adam Piette puts it, 'transpos[es] the secret story of Bowen's spying on her country into Stella's spying on her lover'.[19] The conflation of telephoning and spying is marked most explicitly by the ringing of a telephone which, despite not being answered, somehow alerts Robert Kelway to the fact that he has been revealed as a Nazi spy (*HD*, p. 278). But it is to the sheer uncanny communicative coding and uncoding, the sense of the potential complicity and treachery at work in any telephone call, that the novel decisively responds. Most notable, perhaps, is the telephone call that interrupts a highly fraught conversation between Harrison, the secret-service agent, and Stella, a woman romantically involved with the fascist sympathiser and probable spy Robert Kelway, in Stella's flat:

> He heard the telephone before she did, being one of those people who receive the vibration just before the ring; he had jerked his head in the direction of the dividing door before she was aware of the telephone in there in her bedroom. The same possibility made them exchange a glance – as though already there were complicity. She stood where she was, head down, while the telephone continued its double-ringing – to which Harrison, for his part, listened closely as though trying to familiarise himself with a code. (pp. 43–4)

Harrison is unnerving because of his uncanny prescience about the telephone ringing. And he is unnerving too because of his secret agent/lover's understanding that everything about a telephone, even the fact of its ringing, is a form of 'code' to be deciphered. Indeed, because of his presence in the flat, even the phone's ringing is 'double'. Harrison is attentive, as Bowen is, to the ways in which telephones can be answered. Bowen is precise about picking up the telephone handset, devoting a whole paragraph to the action:

> She made a sweeping turn and went through to the other room, contemptuously leaving the door open behind her. Behind the mirror the curtains were still undrawn; there was an ashy glimmer of window – she went round the foot of the bed to sit at the pillow end, her back to the scene she had left behind. In the dark she took up the receiver with the unfumbling sureness of one who habitually answers a telephone at any, even the deepest, hour of the night. Her hand would have reached its mark before her eyes opened; before her brain stirred her ear would be ready, so that the first word she heard, even the first she spoke, would be misted over by some unfinished dream. This mechanical reflex of hers to a mechanical thing suggested to Harrison, standing there aware in the other room, the first idea he had had of poetry – her life. Enflamed by the picture he could not see, he could but think, 'So *that's* what it can be like!' Meanwhile, feet planted apart in the lamplit drawing-room, he looked about him like a German in Paris. (*HD*, p. 44)

The suggestiveness of this description of someone witnessing someone else answering a telephone heightens our expectations for the call. Everything here seems cryptic, seems to await interpretation and to require an ingenious and sophisticated effort of decoding – it seems to ask for a lover-like hermeneutics of suspicion, or a secret agent's refined attunement to the hidden, the telephonically decipherable. What is decoded and responded to is just Stella's act of answering the telephone. For Stella and Harrison, the significance of the call is heightened by the fact that both know it may be Stella's lover Robert Kelway, the German spy, who is calling. But the passage also suggests something about the poeticality of telephone usage as well as its latent or implicit eroticism. Stella's dreamily reflexive manipulation of the telephone's handset – a 'mechanical reflex . . . to a mechanical thing' – is itself productive of desire, enflaming even, and somehow evocative of the poetry of life.[20] It is as Stella answers the telephone – *because* she answers it and because of her embodied automaticity in answering it, we might say, because of the way that she is *like* a telephone in answering the telephone – that Harrison falls in love with her. It is not quite in the presence of Stella that Harrison's desire is awakened, but when she is in the dark and in another room, when she is almost telephonically or telepathically sensed, and indeed when she is herself distracted by a call from her lover. The voyeuristic, stalker-like secret agent – already obsessed with and already watching this woman from a distance – falls in love through, by and because of the telephone. Coming early in *The Heat of the Day*, this telephone-answering scene sets up an identification of espionage, treachery and sexual desire around which the plot revolves. The telephone is presented as the ideal site of desire and treachery, as a conflation of poetry, love, passion and the human with espionage, betrayal and the non-human, habitual or machinic.

In her later postwar novels, Bowen's focus on the telephone may be said to shift away from the device's plot-central role towards a looser and perhaps less emphatic concern with the gadget's fundamental eeriness. There is the question of the way that the telephone as object – as the 'dumb black instrument' (*TN*, p. 115), in all its solid, moulded, electrically wired, metallic, Bakelite materiality – is combined with an insistent and uncanny anthropomorphism.[21] In *The Little Girls* (1963), for example, Dinah gets ready for a 'protracted session' on Clare's telephone by taking the telephone handset onto her knee, 'where it took on the air of a favoured nurseling'.[22] When Dinah puts the telephone down after the call she gives it 'an affectionate look' after 'its brief good time' (*LG*, p. 150). In *Eva Trout*, when Eva is called to the phone, she 'raised a receiver already speaking' (*ET*, p. 191). In Bowen, the telephone is often an object that one looks at or faces with a certain disquiet or even fear. 'You know how a telephone makes you feel . . . quite in disgrace', Gerda declares to Lady Waters in *To the North* (*TN*, p. 90). And the telephone is something that one has to face up to: 'That a day of reckoning could come did not occur to me. It did when I faced up to the telephone', Iseult remarks at one point in *Eva Trout* (*ET*, p. 206). A little earlier, on learning that Jeremy has been 'stolen', Miss Applethwaite looks 'with abhorrence towards her telephone' at the thought of calling the police (p. 197, p. 199). When Mr Denge asks about a telephone in her rented house, the seemingly phone-phobic Eva reacts with horror: 'She flew into a panic. "I WON'T have one!"' she declares (p. 78).[23]

Bowen's telephones have lives and minds and even personalities of their own. In the middle of Clare's Mopsie Pye novelty-ware gift shop in *The Little Girls* there is a 'saturnine-looking telephone', a telephone that looks grave or gloomy or phlegmatic, as only an old-fashioned black telephone can do when it is not in use and placed among the jolly bric-a-brac of novelty goods (*LG*, 138). But telephones can be lively, lovely, too, particularly after 1959 when the General Post Office developed a range of coloured handsets: 'Sheikie', Dinah declares at one point, 'what a wonderful scarlet telephone! That's the one we had such a happy time on?' (p. 162). And telephones can be liked or (more often) disliked, as in *To the North*, when Emmeline tells Markie not to 'ring up' and longs to be with him in the country, 'inaccessible, green and quiet, where telephones were not' (*TN* p. 175). Uncle Bill in *The House in Paris* has a distinct dislike of the telephone in general (*HP*, p. 173), and in *The Heat of the Day*, the ringing of the telephone at Holme Dene is, for Mrs Kelway, 'demoniac' (*HD*, p. 264). It is possible to be aggressive towards the phone, even violent, as if to punish it, like Thomas in *The Death of the Heart*, who 'defiantly jab[s] a button of the house telephone' when he is unsettled by Portia (*DH*, p. 33). In the 1941 short story 'Summer Night', Justin Cavey looks 'crucified at having the talk torn' when the telephone interrupts a conversation: 'Beastly', he says, taking it personally, to Robinson, his host, when Robinson returns from the call, 'you've a beastly telephone' (*CS*, p. 587).

As well as being unsettling, beastly even, Bowen's telephones have a marked relationship with death. As Bowen comments in the Preface to Cynthia Asquith's *The Second Ghost Book* (1952), 'telephones, motors, planes and radio wave-lengths' allow ghosts new modes of 'self-expression'.[24] The idea of speaking to the dead on the telephone occurs, for example, in a remarkable moment from Bowen's final and most outlandish novel, *Eva Trout* (1969). Eva speaks to her former teacher Iseult Smith on the telephone after she returns from her years of exile in the United States. On finishing the call, however, Eva starts to wonder if the person she has just spoken to is Iseult after all: 'Had this *been* Miss Smith, or was she dead and somebody impersonating her?' (*ET*, p. 192). Something about the voice, she thinks to herself in a somewhat inevitable pun, 'had not rung true' (p. 193): '[T]he voice's inflections, even, had been, if not quite parodied exaggerated, over-stretched, harshened; more than once a hollow ring had been given them' (p. 193). But then in the realisation of this hollow ring, the other possibility strikes Eva – not that it had been an imposter on the telephone but that it had been the dead Miss Smith, that the imposture being played on her had in fact involved 'a deceased person purporting to be a living one'. Miss Smith, she decides, had 'given an impression of dissolution': 'Not that she necessarily was in her coffin', Eva reasonably adds, but in a way that also allows for the unreasonable, outlandish suggestion that Miss Smith may indeed have been phoning from her coffin (p. 193).

Eva also wonders about the instrument of communication itself, and about whether it might be this very instrument that produces the ghost-effect. She goes on to ask one of the novel's central question: how can one know a person?

> Or had it all been a trick played by the wire? Alone with a voice, shut up with it, you are fooled by what can be it distortedness. Eva's could be an over-excitable ear, so long-lasting having been its desuetude. Might the ear not seem to have registered what it had not? Anyhow, what a slippery fish is identity; and what *is* it, besides a slippery fish? If Miss Smith had not rung up Eva, nobody else had: 'X' could be counted out. What *is* a person? Is it true there is not more than one of each? (p. 193)

It is the relationship between the ear and the voice on the one hand, and the 'wire' and the whole electromagnetic apparatus on the other that is at stake here, the relationship between the bodily or organic and the mechanical, prosthetic organ-like telephone-object. As Avital Ronnell suggests in *The Telephone Book*, the telephone confronts us with new uncertainties and aporias in literature and in philosophical thinking, in epistemology and the theory of mind, in our conception of other people and ourselves, and in our conception of the body and its relationship with technology. In the context of a telephone conversation, it is, after all, not just the philosophical sceptic that might ask questions about the very existence of the person to whom one is talking. As Marshall McLuhan argues, the telephone produces or allows for 'a kind of extra-sensory perception'.[25] It has the potential to disengage the speaker, McLuhan and Bruce Powers remark, from his or her identity: the telephone can make of one a 'phone poltergeist'.[26] Bowen's novels and stories are ever alert to the strangeness of what haunts, to what is both there and not there – like the ghost and like the voice over the telephone, or like the 'ghostly click from the telephone' that a character, the imperturbable adolescent Bennet, hears in the 1941 story 'In the Square' (*CS*, p. 615).[27] Bowen's sense of the disconcerting, ghostly, phantasmagorical, even threatening nature of telephones is marked by her use of a conventional but morbid metaphor in both *Friends and Relations* and *The Death of the Heart*: in *Friends and Relations*, Laurel is summoned to the 'strait little telephone box like a coffin upright' in the semi-public space of her London club (*FR*, p. 118), and at the end of *The Death of the Heart* the hotel telephone booth that Major Brutt uses to call the Quaynes is an 'upright telephone coffin' (*DH*, p. 298).

The ghostliness of the telephone involves the way that it marks an absence even as it evokes presence. In *Friends and Relations* one of the twelve telephone moments that punctuate the novel's culminating crisis engages directly with this question. As he wanders the streets of London in the morning after almost absconding with his sister-in-law Janet, a 'scarlet telephone-box' makes Edward 'contract' as he almost incoherently registers its presence: 'Telephone? He looked through the scarlet lattice: empty: the directory dangled. Telephone?' Prompted to call his wife, he wonders what other men would say in such a call. But there is no other man and there is nothing to say on the telephone. Instead, he thinks about a different speech act – about what he might say to justify not calling his wife. 'I could not come back to you', he would say in an imagined but impossible, logically recursive statement: 'If I could have told you I could not, I could have come' (*FR*, p. 149). Both the telephone call, which cannot logically happen, and the hypothetical explanation for why he did not make it (which seems to presuppose both that the relationship has ended and that it has not) explore, in different ways, the logic of telephoning. There is a sense in which these are telephone-specific statements, statements that cannot have been uttered or indeed thought before the famous and much mythologised inaugural telephone call from Alexander Graham Bell to his assistant Thomas Watson on 10 March 1876 ('Mr. Watson – come here – I want to see you!') – a call that can be figured as the archetype of all telephone calls, the quintessence of the telephone call, in demanding a presence that both is and is not already achieved via the telephone connection.[28] Bowen is thinking through the specific techno-logic of the telephone in this scene. 'If I could have told you [on the telephone that] I could not [come back to you]', Edward imagines saying, 'I could have come [back to you].' In other words, it is logically if not affectively impossible to telephone his wife to say that he cannot come back because had he been able to do so then he *could* have come back and therefore would not have needed to make the call. The episode indicates that Edward is tormented, in effect, by the ethics of telephoning, by the new moral responsibility that the very fact of telephone technology places on the individual. The passage recognises that the telephone imposes a permanent but undecidable responsibility on a person to communicate with those who are absent, just because it is possible to do so (even when such a call may not be possible emotionally or logically). Thus Edward pauses at the corner of the road to examine his own 'cruelty' in not using the telephone box that he has just walked past (*FR*, p. 149), and then tries to 'dismiss' Laurel's 'nearness to him in the 'spaceless present' that the telephone produces, to dismiss from his thoughts the 'agonising tension between them now of the silent telephone-wire' (p. 150).

It is, then, through the telephone that electromagnetism transmits the embodied human – its flesh, skin, bone, muscle, cochlea, Eustachian tube, tympanum, hair, lungs, vocal chords, teeth, tongue, lips, glottis, trachea, uvula, larynx. It is as a supplement to the ear and voice, as a prosthetic ear and a prosthetic voice that the telephone works its affective and ethical apparent magic – as embodied and not, and 'as near as any human invention to being an extension of the human body'.[29] This disturbing, strangely intimate otherness of telephone communication is addressed again and again in Bowen's writing, but I want to suggest that her fiction does more than simply register the strangeness, the eeriness of the telephone. The telephone is, in effect, something like the ideal Bowen object. Bowen's fascination with inanimate objects – with furniture, rooms, clothing and other 'things' – has been well documented in recent critical work. But what characterises the telephone specifically is the way that it supplements and dissolves the subjectivity of the person. As such, it brings to a head questions of personal identity, communication and personal responsibility that are fundamental to and pervasive in Bowen's work. The problem of personal identity haunts all of Bowen's fiction and includes the possibility that there is no such thing, or that identity is loose, unhinged or uncertain. But the question is exacerbated, emphasised by and concentrated in the telephone call. One never knows, never can fully know, know with full certainty who, if anyone, is on the other end of the line.[30] In Bowen, just as the telephone may be said to disconnect people by connecting them at a distance, it is also a machine that both assists communication and compromises, restricts, even denies it. Bowen picks up on and relays the inherent resistance to communication that the telephone embodies but that is in fact already part of communication in general. While messages do get through on the line in Bowen, more often than not they are compromised, misunderstood, half-heard or just misinterpreted. Most often they falter or fail. And this is because the telephone in Bowen is the epitome and essence of verbal communication, because it defines and exaggerates communication in general, concentrates it, and because communication is so often compromised, difficult, obscure in Bowen's writing. Bowen is tremendous in her telephoning and also paralysed by it, just as she was valued by her friends for her conversational dexterity and grace while at the same time suffering from a stammer – and just as her syntax can be both formal, precise, clear and disjunctive, awkward and opaque.[31] 'Style', as St Quentin remarks in *The Death of the Heart*, 'is the thing that is always a bit phony', even if, as he concedes, 'you cannot write without style' (*DH*, p. 11). If style is phony, it perhaps goes without saying, so is the telephone – which is perhaps why the telephone call constitutes an ideal version of speech and more generally of conversation in Bowen. But the telephone call might also be seen as an ideal version of literature itself precisely in producing a sense of immediacy, of presence, of unmediatedness that is indelibly marked by absence. Literature itself is phony, and Bowen's telephones communicate to us the fact that communication is what her writing produces, calls for and evokes, but also resists, displaces and dissolves, in an eerie or phony modernist prosthesis of presence and verbal exchange.

Notes

1. Victoria Glendinning, *Elizabeth Bowen: Portrait of a Writer* (London: Orion Books, 1993), p. 211.
2. Victoria Glendinning (ed.), *Love's Civil War: Elizabeth Bowen and Charles Ritchie, Letters and Diaries from the Affair of a Lifetime* (London: Simon & Schuster, 2008), p. 203.
3. On Bowen's ambivalence towards the telephone, see her comment in an unpublished piece probably written in 1950 on the need to create a 'rather rigid . . . workshop atmosphere' in order to write: 'At my home in Ireland, deep in the country, or in London, if I don't answer the telephone, this can be contrived' ('Material for the BROADSHEET, from Elizabeth Bowen', uncorrected fair copy typescript at the Harry Ransom Center, University of Texas at Austin (HRC Box 1.5), p. 2). See also a letter from V. S. Pritchett to Bowen of 8 July 1947, sympathising with her distrust of the telephone: 'I rang up yesterday but I gather you, like myself, hide from the telephone. It is quite impossible to write with one of those instruments in the room. Screeching and impudent demons, I hate them and so I write to you instead' (HRC Box 11.7).
4. On the importance of letters in Bowen's novels, see Neil Corcoran, *Elizabeth Bowen: The Enforced Return* (Oxford: Clarendon, 2004), pp. 1–3. While significantly less prominent in Bowen's short stories, telephones are also important in the plotting of 'Look at All Those Roses', 'Summer Night' and 'In the Square'; and telephones and telephone conversations are mentioned in several others, including 'Foothold', 'The Disinherited', 'A Love Story', 'No. 16', 'Oh, Madam', 'The Inherited Clock', 'The Demon Lover', 'The Happy Autumn Fields',

'Pink May' and 'The Dolt's Tale' (*The Collected Stories of Elizabeth Bowen* (London: Penguin, 1983); hereafter cited parenthetically as *CS*); and 'Just Imagine', 'Brigands', 'So Much Depends', 'The Claimant', 'Happiness', 'The Bazaar', 'Miss Jolley Has No Plans for the Future', 'Story Scene', 'Flowers Will Do', 'The Last Bus', 'Fairies at the Christening' and 'Women in Love' (*The Bazaar and Other Stories*, ed. Allan Hepburn (Edinburgh: Edinburgh University Press, 2008)).

5. See Lis Christensen on the telephone as a 'metaphor of non-communication' (*Elizabeth Bowen: The Later Fiction* (Copenhagen: Museum Tusculanum Press, 2001), pp. 68–9; and see Maud Ellmann on Bowen's fascination with 'the gadgetry of modernity' (*Elizabeth Bowen: The Shadow Across the Page* (Edinburgh: Edinburgh University Press, 2003), p. 5).

6. On the absence of telephones in Bowen's Irish Big Houses (Mount Morris and Montefort), see Christensen, *The Later Fiction*, p. 68. There is one striking mention of the telephone in *The Hotel*: a hotel guest describes the telephone double-blind when one is alone at home in England in the winter: 'As winter comes on with those long evenings one begins to feel hardly human,' she remarks: 'If the telephone bell rings, to hear a voice and then be cut off simply unsettles one; and if it doesn't ring the whole evening, one begins to worry and imagine things about one's friends' (*The Hotel* (London: Penguin, 1987), p. 53; hereafter cited parenthetically as *H*). For the inhabitants of Danielstown in *The Last September*, the nearest telephone is six miles away and using it 'made excessive demands upon the sympathy of the post-mistress'. Marda Norton's inability to understand this marks her out as 'very modern' or as if 'she had come from America' (Elizabeth Bowen, *The Last September* (Harmondsworth: Penguin, 1982), p. 78). The novel does, however, feature another piece of modernist consumer technology, the gramophone (see Susanne S. Cammack, 'The Death of a Gramophone in Elizabeth Bowen's *The Last September*', *Journal of Modern Literature*, 40.2 (2017): 132–46). The absence of a telephone in Montefort is noted in *A World of Love* (Elizabeth Bowen, *A World of Love* (Harmondsworth: Penguin, 1983), p. 55; hereafter cited parenthetically as *WL*). In *The Heat of the Day*, we learn that 'There never had been a telephone at Mount Morris – assurance of being utterly out of reach added annullingness to [Stella's] deep sleep that night' (Elizabeth Bowen, *The Heat of the Day* (Harmondsworth: Penguin, 1979), p. 168; hereafter cited parenthetically as *HD*). Bowen writes to William Plomer from Bowen's Court on 30 October 1939 that 'we now have the telephone' – although, as she later records, the connection tended to be unreliable: 'I have a telephone, but the service is subject to inexhaustible "Acts of God",' she remarks in a 1958 essay, 'Bowen's Court' (in *People, Places, Things: Essays by Elizabeth Bowen*, ed. Allan Hepburn (Edinburgh: Edinburgh University Press, 2008), p. 3, p. 142).

7. See John Brooks's comment that 'It was in the 1920s that the telephone, reflecting its new place in real life, became almost all-pervasive in [US] popular literature', especially in drama, as a 'necessary and ever-present artifact in human intercourse', and that 1930, when the telephone was 'all but ubiquitous ... but had not yet been so long enough to be taken entirely for granted', was the 'high-water mark of telephone literature' (*Telephone: The First Hundred Years* (New York: Harper & Row, 1976), pp. 173–5). On the slightly later spread of telephones in the United Kingdom and on what we might call the telephone culture in the 1930s, see David Trotter, 'e-Modernism: Telephony in British Fiction, 1925–1940,' *Critical Quarterly*, 51.1 (2009): 1–32 (pp. 11–18).
8. Elizabeth Bowen, *Friends and Relations* (Harmondsworth: Penguin, 1982), p. 28. Hereafter cited parenthetically as *FR*.
9. A log of the calls would run as follows: Laurel to the telephone exchange (*FR*, p. 140); Laurel to Janet's hotel (ibid.); Anna's suggestion that Laurel should call Elfrida (p. 141); Anna's illicit call to Lewis and her and Laurel's conversation with him (pp. 142–3); Laurel's lie to the servants to explain his absence that Edward had been called on the telephone to be told urgently to go to work (p. 142); Lewis's suggestion that Anna or Laurel should phone Batts (p. 142) or that Laurel might phone Edward's office (p. 143); Theodora's call to Janet's hotel (p. 144, p. 145); Theodora's unanswered calls to Lewis (p. 145); Edward's thought of calling Laurel from a public phone box (p. 149); Rodney's call to Laurel confirming that Janet has returned safely to Batts (p. 151); the call home that Edward fails to make from Elfrida's phone when he sleeps at her house (p. 152).
10. Ellmann, *The Shadow Across the Page*, p. 98.
11. Elizabeth Bowen, *To the North* (London: Penguin, 1987), p. 29; hereafter cited parenthetically as *TN*. On telephones in *To the North* and especially on Cecilia's usage, see also Trotter, 'e-Modernism', pp. 10–11. There are more than thirty references to telephones or to telephone conversations in *To the North*: see pages 27, 28, 29, 30, 32, 87, 90, 91, 107, 109, 114–15, 121, 131, 132, 133, 134, 140, 154, 155, 156, 175, 193, 195, 197–8, 205, 212, 214–16, 217, 225, 235, 247.
12. Compare Bowen's immediately postwar essay on 'Opening up the House', in which she talks about finding, among other eerie traces of a former life, 'ghostly indentations of someone's doodling' on the 'left-behind telephone pad' (in Hepburn, *People, Places, Things*, p. 133).
13. Elizabeth Bowen, *The House in Paris* (London: Penguin, 1976), p. 237, pp. 238–9; hereafter cited parenthetically as *HP*. In addition to their significance in terms of plot, telephones have a striking affective power in *The House in Paris*: just before Max calls Karen from Paris, the telephone 'held her eye' and she 'saw it was going to speak' (p. 132). Later, the telephone signifies and exacerbates the lover's insecurity: 'this

is the worst of love, this unmeant mystification . . . "No, alas, I can't tonight," on the telephone' (p. 238).
14. Elizabeth Bowen, *The Death of the Heart* (Harmondsworth: Penguin, 1979), p. 28; hereafter cited parenthetically as *DH*.
15. Telephones and telephone calls frequently appear in *The Death of the Heart*, sometimes incidentally and fleetingly, sometimes more fully and with precise attention to questions of conversational and other propriety: see pages 28, 72, 87, 110, 111, 113, 116, 118, 121, 153, 171, 229, 234, 246, 257, 264, 266, 271, 272, 273, 283, 298, 300–1, 302, 303, 305, 307, 313.
16. Avital Ronnell, *The Telephone Book: Technology, Schizophrenia, Electric Speech* (Lincoln: University of Nebraska Press, 1991), p. 9. In *Eva Trout* (1968), there is a modern version of the home telephone, the intercom, in the house that Eva rents, a device whose 'purposes seem uncertain'; and Constantine, the rather creepy businessman, also uses an intercom in his office (Elizabeth Bowen, *Eva Trout, or Changing Scenes* (Harmondsworth: Penguin, 1982), p. 118, p. 218; hereafter cited parenthetically as *ET*).
17. Compare Matchett's disapproving comment on Thomas's overuse of the telephone and her sense that that is why his office has a total of three telephone lines (*DH*, p. 234).
18. Bowen, 'How They Live in Ireland: Conquest by Cheque-Book' (in Hepburn, *People, Places, Things*, p. 182).
19. Adam Piette, *Imagination at War: British Fiction and Poetry 1939–1945* (London: Papermac, 1995), p. 172; on Bowen's reports on Irish neutrality during the Second World War, see Corcoran, *The Enforced Return*, p. 186; Claire Wills, *That Neutral Island: A History of Ireland During the Second World War* (London: Faber & Faber, 2007), pp. 116–17; and Eibhear Walshe, *Elizabeth Bowen's Selected Irish Writings* (Cork: Cork University Press, 2011), pp. 11–13. See Ellman, *The Shadow Across the Page*, pp. 167–8 on the importance of the telephone in *The Heat of the Day*.
20. Although she does not refer to this scene, Melba Cuddy-Keane suggests that the novel's engagement with the machinic body in what she calls 'bodily cognition' is evident from the start: *The Heat of the Day* opens with a scene in which Harrison himself is mechanically punching his own fist into his other palm in an instance of 'cryptic behaviour' (p. 9) that involves what Bowen calls 'emotional thought' (p. 14) ('Narration, Navigation, and Non-Conscious Thought: Neuroscientific and Literary Approaches to the Thinking Body', *University of Toronto Quarterly*, 79.2 (2010): 680–701 (p. 683)).
21. Compare Ellmann on Bowen's 'addiction to personification' (*The Shadow Across the Page*, p. 6) and her comment that things in Bowen stand 'as monuments to lack and loss' (p. 8). See also Elizabeth C. Inglesby,

'"Expressive Objects": Elizabeth Bowen's Narrative Materialises', *Modern Fiction Studies*, 53.2 (2007): 306–33.
22. Elizabeth Bowen, *The Little Girls* (Harmondsworth: Penguin, 1982), p. 148; hereafter cited parenthetically as *LG*.
23. Eva even almost disappears into, is almost locked away in the telephone at another point: 'Along the bed she lay like a long log: the receiver was by her on the pillow, and her face was so locked away in it, in either passion or obstinacy, that only the jawline could be seen' (*ET*, p. 256).
24. Elizabeth Bowen, *Afterthought: Pieces About Writing* (London: Longmans, 1962), p. 101. Speaking to the dead on the telephone is a recurrent trope ever since the instrument's invention in the 1870s but is particularly prevalent in modernism: see, for example, Leopold Bloom's idea of placing telephones inside coffins to prevent the living being buried by mistake (James Joyce, *Ulysses*, ed. Jeri Johnson (Oxford: Oxford University Press, 1998), p. 107), an idea that had been more fully played out in an 1898 short story by the German writer Walter Rathenau, 'Die Resurrection Co' (cited in Sara Danius, *The Senses of Modernism: Technology, Perception, and Aesthetics* (Ithaca: Cornell University Press, 2002), p. 181; see also pp. 12–17); see also Max Brod's poem, 'Telephon' (1910) (cited in Ronell, *The Telephone Book*, p. 440). On the association of the telephone with death in Bowen, see Ellmann, *The Shadow Across the Page*, p. 168, p. 221; and Pamela Thurschwell, *Literature, Technology and Magical Thinking, 1880–1920* (Cambridge: Cambridge University Press, 2001), p. 23, on the association of the telephone with speaking to the dead in the late nineteenth and early twentieth centuries.
25. Marshall McLuhan, *Understanding Media: The Extensions of Man* (London: Routledge & Kegan Paul, 1964), p. 265.
26. Marshall McLuhan and Bruce Powers, 'Ma Bell Minus the Nantucket Gam: Or the Impact of High-Speed Data Transmission', *Journal of Communication*, 31.3 (1981): 191–9 (p. 195); see also Donald F. Theall, 'McLuan, Telematics, and the Toronto School of Communication', in *Marshall McLuhan: Critical Evaluations in Cultural Theory*, ed. Gary Genosko (Abingdon: Routledge, 2005), p. 236.
27. On the prevalence of ghosts in Bowen's fiction, see Derek Hand, 'Ghosts from Our Future: Bowen and the Unfinished Business of Living', in *Elizabeth Bowen*, ed. Eibhear Walshe (Dublin: Irish Academic Press, 2009), pp. 65–6 and *passim*; on the specific relation of ghosts to new technologies, including the telephone, see Sinead Moody, 'Bowen and the Modern Ghost', in Walshe, *Elizabeth Bowen*, pp. 77–94.
28. See Robert V. Bruce, *Bell: Alexander Graham Bell and the Conquest of Solitude* (London: Victor Gollancz, 1973), p. 181.
29. Brooks, *Telephone*, pp. 7–8.

30. 'What voice do you expect to hear on the telephone?', Mr Anapoupolis brutally asks Eva Trout in Bowen's final novel, as if existentially, as she awaits a call from the guardians, or vendors, of the little boy that she is set on acquiring and adopting (*ET*, p. 139). See also Ronnell, *The Telephone Book*, p. 9: the telephone 'destabilises the identity of self and other, subject and thing'.
31. See, for example, David Cecil, 'Chronicler of the Heart: The British Writer, Elizabeth Bowen', *Vogue*, 122 (1 November 1953), p. 19: 'Much of the time [Bowen] listens . . . When she does speak, her words come in little gusts and gushes of impressionistic, half-finished phrase that follow, rather than lead the trend of the conversation.' On Bowen's voice and her stammer, see Allan Hepburn's 'Introduction' to *Listening In: Broadcasts, Speeches, and Interviews by Elizabeth Bowen* (Edinburgh: Edinburgh University Press, 2010), pp. 3–9. There is considerable empirical work on the telephone behaviour of stutterers, most seeming to confirm the perhaps self-evident notion that telephoning is problematic for the speech-impaired, even while, as Ronnell points out, the invention of the telephone was an offshoot of research into the alleviation of difficulties experienced by the hearing and speech impaired (*The Telephone Book*, pp. 88, 282–3, 327–8).

Notes on Contributors

Andrew Bennett is Professor of English at the University of Bristol. With Nicholas Royle, he is the author of *Elizabeth Bowen and the Dissolution of the Novel: Still Lives* (Macmillan, 1995). His other publications include *Suicide Century: Literature and Suicide from James Joyce to David Foster Wallace* (Cambridge University Press, 2018), *Ignorance: Literature and Agnoiology* (Manchester University Press, 2009), *An Introduction to Literature, Criticism and Theory*, with Nicholas Royle (5th edn, Routledge, 2016), *Wordsworth Writing* (Cambridge University Press, 2007), *The Author* (Routledge, 2005), *Katherine Mansfield* (Northcote House, 2004), *Romantic Poets and the Culture of Posterity* (Cambridge University Press, 1999) and *Keats, Narrative and Audience: The Posthumous Life of Writing* (Cambridge University Press, 1994).

Aimee Gasston received her PhD from Birkbeck, University of London, researching modernist short fiction and modes of reading in the light of other everyday practices. She has published articles on modernism and snacks, cannibalism and phenomenology and co-convenes the Modernist Magazines Research Seminar at the Institute of English Studies. In 2013, she was winner of the Fourth International Katherine Mansfield Essay Prize with a piece on the theme of (post)colonialism.

Jessica Gildersleeve is Associate Professor of English Literature at the University of Southern Queensland. She is the author of *Elizabeth Bowen and the Writing of Trauma: The Ethics of Survival* (Rodopi, 2014), *Christos Tsiolkas: The Utopian Vision* (Cambria, 2017), and *Don't Look Now* (Auteur, 2017) and editor of *Memory and the Wars on Terror: Australian and British Perspectives* (with Richard Gehrmann, Palgrave Macmillan, 2017).

renée c. hoogland is Professor of English at Wayne State University in Detroit. She is the author of three books: *A Violent Embrace: Art and*

Aesthetics after Representation (2014); *Lesbian Configurations* (1997); and *Elizabeth Bowen: A Reputation in Writing* (1994). She served as the editor of *Criticism: A Quarterly for Literature and the Arts* for six years, and edited the first volume of *Macmillan Interdisciplinary Handbooks on Gender: Sources, Perspectives, and Methodologies* (2016) – a ten-volume series for which she also acts as Senior Editor in Chief.

Laurie Johnson is Professor of English and Cultural Studies at the University of Southern Queensland. His publications include *Shakespeare's Lost Playhouse: Eleven Days at Newington Butts* (Routledge, 2018), *The Tain of Hamlet* (Cambridge Scholars, 2013), *The Wolf Man's Burden* (Cornell University Press, 2001), two edited collections – *Embodied Cognition and Shakespeare's Theatre: The Early Modern Body-Mind* (edited with John Sutton and Lyn Tribble, Routledge, 2014), *Rapt in Secret Studies: Emerging Shakespeares* (with Darryl Chalk, Cambridge Scholars, 2010) – and articles and book chapters on Cultural theory, early modern studies, ethics, psychoanalysis, Shakespeare studies and related fields.

Jasmin Kelaita received her PhD in English Literature from the University of New South Wales, researching transnational modernisms.

Ulrika Maude is Professor of Modern and Twentieth-Century Literature at the University of Bristol, where she is also Director of the Centre for Health, Humanities and Science. She is the author of *Beckett, Technology and the Body* (Cambridge University Press, 2009) and the forthcoming *Samuel Beckett and Medicine* (Cambridge University Press), and co-editor of a number of volumes, including *Beckett and Phenomenology* (Continuum, 2009), *The Cambridge Companion to the Body in Literature* (Cambridge University Press, 2015) and *The Bloomsbury Companion to Modernist Literature* (Bloomsbury Academic, 2018). She is a member of the editorial board of the *Journal of Beckett Studies*.

Emma Short is a Research and Teaching Associate in the School of English at Newcastle University. Her previous publications include *The Female Figure in Contemporary Historical Fiction*, co-edited with Katherine Cooper, and an essay on Elizabeth Bowen in *Women in Transit Through Literary Liminal Spaces* (Palgrave, 2013). She has articles forthcoming in *Feminist Theory*, *Journeys: The International Journal of Travel Writing* and *First World War Studies*. She is currently working on a monograph, *The Hotel: A Cultural History,*

1850–1950, as well as on her next research project, which considers Gertrude Bell's literary heritage and the making of the modern Middle East.

Patricia Juliana Smith is Associate Professor of English at Hofstra University in New York. She is the author of *Lesbian Panic: Homoeroticism in Modern British Women's Fictions* (1997) and editor of *En Travesti, Women, Gender Subversion, Opera* (with Corinne E. Blackmer, 1995), *The Queer Sixties* (1999) and *Catholic Figures, Queer Narratives* (with Lowell Gallagher and Frederick S. Roden, 2007). Her book in progress is *Britannia Waives the Rules: The Permissive Society and the Afterlife of Modernism in 1960s British Literature and Culture*.

Damian Tarnopolsky is the Barbara Moon/Ars Medica Fellow at Massey College in Toronto. His research focuses on style in the later modernist novel, and he has taught literature and creative writing at the University of Toronto and Humber College. His most recent book is the novel *Goya's Dog*, which was published by Penguin Canada and nominated for the Commonwealth Writers' Prize and the Amazon.ca First Novel Award.

Keri Walsh is Assistant Professor in the English Department at Fordham University in New York. She is the editor of *The Letters of Sylvia Beach* (Columbia University Press, 2010) and James Joyce's *Dubliners* (Broadview Press, 2014). She recently contributed to the British Film Institute's 'Film Stars' series with a short book on Mickey Rourke (2014).

Index

References to Bowen's works are followed by date of publication; references to other works are listed beneath author's names.

References to notes are indicated by n.

Abraham, Nicolas, 130
absence, 118–19, 121
adolescence, 6, 62–5, 66–71, 72–3, 75
Adorno, Theodor, 114–15, 120
aesthetics, 49–50, 51, 63–4, 65, 66, 74–5
  and objects, 71, 72
  and Surrealism, 28, 30, 39
agoraphobia, 91, 92–3
Alpers, Antony, 101
Ann Lee's (1926), 16
Apter, Emily, 147, 148
Aragon, Louis, 28, 38
Aristotle, 81, 82
art, 30
Asquith, Cynthia, *The Second Ghost Book*, 189
assemblages, 72–3, 74, 75
Austen, Jane, 29
Austin, Allan E., 5, 9

Backus, Margot Gayle, 36
Ball, Benjamin, 91
Barnes, Djuna, 29
Barthes, Roland, 4, 13, 48–50

Baudrillard, Jean, 10, 12
Beard, George Miller, 92
Beckett, Samuel, 17, 29, 130
  Happy Days, 83
  and nothing, 114–15, 124n4, 126n20
  Trilogy, 83
Bell, Vanessa, 98
belongings, 6
Bennett, Andrew, 4, 6, 54, 70, 89, 97, 148–9, 159
Bennett, Jane, 73
Bergson, Henri, 81
Besnault-Levita, Anne, 133
Blitz, the, 30, 39–40, 91, 140, 141
  and houses, 139
  and nothing, 118–20
  and recesses, 129–31, 132
Bloomsbury set, 97, 98;
  see also Woolf, Virginia
Böhme, Harmut, *Fetishism and Culture: A Different Theory of Modernity*, 146
'Books that Grow Up With One' (1949), 56

Bowen, Elizabeth, 1–7, 65–6, 73–5
 and adolescence, 62–5, 66–7, 69–71, 72–3
 and childhood, 32–3
 and fashion, 16–19
 and habit, 79–81, 83–91, 93
 and Ireland, 98–9
 and Mansfield, 96–7, 99–100
 and reading, 48–9, 50, 51–8
 and realism, 127–9
 and short stories, 14–16
 and spaces, 101–10, 165–6
 and style, 9–14, 20–2
 and Surrealism, 29–32, 33–43
 and telephones, 182, 186, 187, 191, 192–3
 and women, 145–8
Bowen's Court (1942), 139–40
Bradley, Fiona, 33–4
'Breakfast' (1923), 1
Breton, André, 28, 29, 31, 36, 38
 and childhood, 32, 33
 'Discourse on the Paucity of Reality', 40, 42
 Nadja (Breton), 34, 35
Briganti, Chiara, 174
Brown, Spencer Curtis, 149

'Candles in the Window' (1958), 17
'Careless Talk' (1941), 134
Cat Jumps, The (1934), 31–2, 36–7
character, 135–9
Charcot, Jean-Martin, 92
Chessman, Harriet S., 53–4, 56
childhood, 32–3, 64; *see also* adolescence
Christensen, Lis, 136, 149
Christie, Agatha, 14

cinema, 14
claustrophobia, 91, 92–3, 108
clothing, 14, 15–19
Coates, John, 179
colonialism, 96, 97, 98
'Coming to London' (1956), 101
communication, 6; *see also* telephones
Connor, Steven, 17
consumerism, 145, 146, 157
'Contessina, The' (1924), 12–13, 102
convulsive beauty, 34–6
Corcoran, Neil, 4, 29–30, 54, 57, 122, 128–9, 130, 131, 162n12
Craig, Patricia, 73, 74
Crevel, René, 29
crypt, 130
Cunningham, Valentine, 31, 36

'Daffodils' (1923), 16
Dali, Salvador, 30, 31, 32, 38, 40–2
Davies, Hugh Sykes, *Petron*, 31
death, 1, 119
Death of the Heart, The (1938), 33, 53, 71, 100, 132
 and claustrophobia, 108–9
 and habit, 79
 and negatives, 117–18, 120, 123
 and telephones, 185–6, 189, 190–1, 193
Deleuze, Gilles, 71–2, 81
'Demon Lover, The' (1941), 137, 138
Demon Lover, The (1945), 21, 88
Derdiger, Paula, 139
Dickens, Charles, 128

discomfort, 90–1
Dollimore, Jonathan, 88
'Dolt's Tale, The' (1944), 140
domestic spaces *see* home
doorways, 107–8
Dumont, Leon, 82

Early Stories (1951), 99
'Easter Egg Party, The' (1941), 20
'Ecstasy of the Eye' (1968), 88–9
Edensor, Louise, 101
Eliot, T. S., 5
  and objects, 149
  'The Waste Land', 1
Ellmann, Maud, 3–4, 12, 29, 65–6, 70, 88, 101, 127, 128, 130–1, 149, 165, 183
Eluard, Paul, 29
'Emergency in the Gothic Wing' (1954), 11
Encounters (1923), 80, 99
Ensee, James, 93
Erikson, Erik, 68
Ernst, Max, 38
eroticism, 145, 146
Eva Trout, or Changing Scenes (1968), 43, 57, 73–5, 128, 130
  and home, 166–73
  and homelessness, 178–80
  and telephones, 188, 189–90, 196n16
'Evil That Men Do, The' (1923), 17–18

fashion, 9–10, 12, 13, 14, 15–19
'Fear of Pleasure, The' (1951), 51–2
feelings, 62–4, 76n4, 77n17

femme-enfant, 33–4
fetishism, 145–8, 149–52, 154–61
'Firelight in the Flat' (1934), 37
Flaubert, Gustave, 128
'Foothold' (1929), 20
Fraustino, Daniel V., 128
Freud, Sigmund, 51, 52, 68, 88, 130, 146
Friends and Relations (1931), 89, 100, 102, 183, 190, 191–2
Frost, Laura, 50–1, 57–8
furniture, 167–8, 171

Gan, Wendy, 106
Gascoyne, David, *A Short Survey of Surrealism*, 31
Gasston, Aimee, 4
gender, 67–8; *see also* women
George, Daniel, 90
ghost stories, 137–9, 140
ghosts, 37, 85–6, 189, 190–1
Gildersleeve, Jessica, 4, 129–31, 137, 176, 178
Glamour (magazine), 18
Glendinning, Victoria, 11, 73, 182
Gothic, 3, 28, 30, 36
Greene, Graham, 15
Guadet, Julien, 92
Guattari, Félix, 71–2

habit, 79–91, 93
Haggard, Rider, *She*, 54, 134
hallucination, 39–40
Hand, Derek, 139
'Hand in Glove' (1952), 16
'Happy Autumn Fields, The' (1944), 30, 41–3, 54–5
hats, 18

Haule, James M., 128
Heat of the Day, The (1949), 43, 52–3, 91, 141–2
  and habit, 86–8, 89, 90
  and negatives, 115–16, 117, 118, 120, 122–3
  and telephones, 186–8, 189, 194n6
Hebdige, Dick, 11
Hegel, Friedrich, 81
Hepburn, Allan, 14–15, 99
'Her Table Spread' (1930), 34
heterosexuality, 67–8
home, 6, 99, 139–40, 166–73; *see also* houses
homelessness, 166, 167–8, 171, 173–9
hoogland, renée c., 3, 5–6, 131, 132, 178
Hotel, The (1927), 5, 69–70, 89–90, 135
  and spaces, 100, 102
  and telephones, 182, 194n6
hotel rooms, 173–4, 175, 176–8
House in Paris, The (1935), 5, 33, 35–6, 139
  and negatives, 115, 116, 117, 118, 120, 123
  and spaces, 104, 107–8
  and telephones, 184–5, 189, 195n13
housekeeping, 167–8
houses, 139–40, 165–6
'How to Be Yourself – But Not Eccentric' (1958), 20, 21
Hughes, Robert, 34–5
Huxley, Aldous, 'Pleasures', 52

'I Died of Love' (1926), 16
'Idea of Home, The' (1953), 166

identity, 6–7, 19–21, 192
'In the Square' (1941), 190
in-between, 100–1, 102–4
Inglesby, Elizabeth C., 135, 136, 165
inter-objectivity, 129, 139–42
International Surrealist Exhibition (1936), 30–1
Ireland, 28, 29, 43, 80, 84–6
  and Bowen, 96, 97, 98
'Ivy Gripped the Steps' (1945), 137–8

James, Henry, 29, 128
James, William, *The Principles of Psychology*, 82–3, 87, 90
Johnson, Laurie, 6
Joyce, James
  'The Dead', 32
  Finnegans Wake, 28–9
  Ulysses, 13, 28
'Just Imagine. . .' (1926), 16

Kant, Immanuel, 81
Keown, Edwina, 101
Kiberd, Declan, 28
Kristeva, Julia, 68–9, 71

Laird, Heather, 3
Lassner, Phyllis, 10, 41, 128, 129, 139–40
'Last Night in the Old Home' (1934), 35, 37
Last September, The (1929), 5, 53, 66, 70, 100
  and habit, 80, 85
  and home, 139
  and nothing, 114
  and telephones, 182–3, 194n6
  and uncanny, 109

Lee, Hermione, 13, 14, 15, 29, 66, 73, 74, 98, 162n12, 178
Levi-Strauss, Claude, 155
literary allusions, 128–9
Little Girls, The (1963), 55–6, 130–1, 135, 136, 148–61, 188–9
'London, 1940' (1940), 91
Look at All Those Roses (1941), 36
Lukács, Georg, 19

McCallum, E. L., *Object Lessons: How to Do Things with Fetishism*, 146–7, 148, 161
Macdonell, A. G., 10
McLuhan, Marshall, 190
Magot, Céline, 134
Magritte, René, 41
Maher, Ashley, 165
'Making Arrangements' (1925), 14
'Man of the Family, The' (1934), 37
Man Ray, *Le Violin d'Ingres*, 31
Mansfield, Katherine, 6, 13, 15, 96–101, 106–8, 109–10
  'At the Bay', 103–4
  'Father and the Girls', 104
  'The Garden-Party', 107
  'The Little Governess', 105, 107
  'Marriage a la Mode', 102
  'Prelude', 102, 108
Marcus, Sharon, 174
Maude, Ulrika, 6
Merleau-Ponty, Maurice, 81, 87, 89, 93
Mezei, Kathy, 174
Middleton, Colin, 30, 31

Miller, J. Hillis, 50
Miller, Lee, 30, 39
modernism, 1, 2, 5, 118–19, 121
  and Ireland, 28, 29
  and Mansfield, 97–8
  and reading, 50–2
  and telephones, 197n24
modernity, 168–9
Mooney, Sinéad, 138
Moore, Thomas, 28
Moran, Patricia, 176
Moran, Patrick W., 135
'Mulberry Tree, The' (1934), 148
Muldoon, Paul, 29, 32
Mulvey, Laura, 149
'Mysterious Kôr' (1944), 29–30, 39–40, 43, 54, 134–5

narrative, 6, 132–4, 135–9, 140–1, 178–9
nationhood, 98–9
'Needlecase, The' (1934), 11
negatives, 113–14, 115–22, 123n1, 131
neuroses, 127
Night and Day (journal), 32
'No. 16' (1939), 37–9
nothing, 6, 113–23

objects, 6, 87–8, 130–1
  and fetishism, 145–6, 147–52, 154–61
obnoxiousness, 66–7, 69, 73, 75
'Oh! Madam. . .' (1941), 133–4, 136
Oppenheim, Meret, 30
Osborn, Susan, 49, 114, 121
'Out of a Book' (1946), 54, 56, 63, 71

Phillips, Adam, 92, 121
phobia, 90–3
Piaget, Jean, 151–2, 153
Pictures and Conversations (1974), 54, 62, 100
pleasure, 50–8
Plock, Vike Martina, 13–14
Plomer, William, 30
Poirier, Richard, 50
positives, 113–14, 115–16, 120, 121–2
postmodernism, 1, 2
Powers, Bruce, 190
Proust, Marcel, 81, 83

queerness, 6, 64

Ravaisson, Félix, 90
 Of Habit, 81–2
Read, Herbert, 32
reading, 48–51, 52–8, 64–5, 71
realism, 127–9, 130, 135
recesses, 129–30, 132–42
Rhys, Jean, 6
 Good Morning, Midnight, 167, 173–8
Ricoeur, Paul, 81
Ritcher, Eva, *The ABC of Millinery, The*, 18
Ritchie, Charles, 20, 182
Rodney, Stella, 116
Ronnell, Avital, *The Telephone Book*, 190
Royle, Nicholas, 4, 54, 70, 148–9, 159

Savitt, Sarah, 128
Schiaparelli, Elsa, 10, 18–19
Second World War, 132–5; *see also* Blitz, the
sensationalism, 64

Seventh Continent, The (film), 88
sex, 37–9, 67–8
Shakespeare, William, *The Tempest*, 129
Shaviro, Stephen, 75
Shiach, Morag, 52
shock, 36–7
'Shoes: An International Episode' (1929), 16
Short, Emma, 6
short stories, 9, 10, 11, 14–16, 19, 102
Smith, Angela, 101
Smith, Patricia Juliana, 6, 172
Snaith, Anna, 97–8
'So Much Depends' (1951), 16–17
something, 6, 113–16, 118–20, 121–3
Soupault, Philippe, 28, 38
spaces, 96–7, 99–110, 165–6
 and domestic, 166–73
spatial phobia, 90–3
spies, 186–7
Stein, Gertrude, 29
Stevens, Julie Anne, 127, 128
'Storm, The' (1926), 102
style, 9–11
'Summer Night' (1941), 21, 39, 40–1, 136–7, 189
Summers-Bremner, Eluned, 58
'Sunday Afternoon' (1941), 129
Surrealism, 28–32, 33–43, 140
suspension, 103
Swift, Jonathan, 28

Tanning, Dorothea, 30, 41
Tarnopolsky, Damian, 6
'Tears, Idle Tears' (1941), 35
telephones, 6, 89, 182–93, 195n7

text, 48–58
Thomas, Dylan, 31
thought, 1, 2, 4–6
time-lapse technique, 139–40
To the North (1932), 5, 83–4, 91–3
  and spaces, 104–6, 107
  and telephones, 183–4, 185, 188, 189
'Tommy Crans, The' (1934), 15, 32–3, 34, 36
Torok, Maria, 130
Toynbee, Phillip, 14
transition, 103–4, 106–7, 109–10
Turkle, Sherry, 155

uncanny, 103, 109–10
understanding, 121–2
'Unwelcome Idea' (1941), 132–3, 136, 140
unwords, 116–17, 119

Vogue (magazine), 18

Walsh, Keri, 4, 140
war, 21–2, 39–40, 54–5, 88; *see also* Second World War

Wells-Lassagne, Shannon, 55–6, 98
Welty, Eudora, 9
Williams, Raymond, 76n4
women, 2, 29, 33–4
  and adolescence, 63, 66, 69
  and fetishism, 145, 146–8
  and nationhood, 98–9
  and reading, 52–7
  and Rhys, 177
  and Surrealism, 37–8
  and transition, 106–7, 109–10
Woolf, Virginia, 4, 13, 14, 15, 29
  and Bowen, 98
  'How Should One Read a Book?', 50
  and nostalgia, 121
  and realism, 127
World of Love, A (1955), 43, 80, 85–6, 130, 182–3, 194n6
writing, 56–7, 64–5

Yeats, W. B., 28
Young, Iris Marion, 167, 168, 170, 171, 173